The Riverside Press, Cambridge, Mass., U. S. A.
Electrotyped and Printed by H. O. Houghton & Company.

CONTENTS.

		Page
I.	Introductory	1
II.	Hereditary Traits	7
III.	Girlhood at Cambridge	20
IV.	Country Life at Groton	43
V.	Finding a Friend	62
VI.	School-Teaching in Boston and Providence	75
VII.	Suburban Life at Jamaica Plain	94
VIII.	Conversations in Boston	109
IX.	A Literary Club and its Organ	130
X.	The Dial	154
XI.	Brook Farm	173
XII.	Books Published	187
XIII.	Business Life in New York	205
XIV.	European Travel	220
XV.	Marriage and Motherhood	232
XVI.	Letters between Husband and Wife	248
XVII.	Closing Scenes	266
XVIII.	Literary Traits	281
XIX.	Personal Traits	299
	Bibliographical Appendix	315
	Index	319

MARGARET FULLER OSSOLI.

I.

INTRODUCTORY.

IT has long been my desire to write a new memoir of Margaret Fuller Ossoli, a person whose career is more interesting, as it seems to me, than that of any other American of her sex; a woman whose aims were high and whose services great; one whose intellect was uncommon, whose activity incessant, whose life varied, and whose death dramatic. Thirty years having passed since the publication of her "Memoirs," it has seemed possible that a biography might now be written almost wholly from new or unused material, thus affording a positive addition to what was before known of her, and not a mere restatement of what was already before the public. In this aspect, at least, the effort has been successful, nearly every citation in the book being from manuscript sources; and the study of these materials having in all respects controlled the delineation here given of her life. Recognizing the great value of the portrait-ure already drawn of her character by the authors of the "Memoirs," and the excellence of Mrs. Howe's more condensed biography, I have sometimes ventured to vary from their estimate, and to rely on my own.

It so happened that Margaret Fuller was associated with me, not closely but definitely, by various personal ties. She was born and bred in the same town, though more than thirteen years older; she was the friend of my older sisters, and I was the playmate of her younger brothers; her only sister was afterwards closely connected with me by marriage, and came for especial reasons, with her children, peculiarly under my charge; and, though this was after Margaret Fuller's death, it yet contributed with all the other circumstances to make the Fuller family seem like kindred of my own. It moreover happened that Margaret Fuller had upon me, through her writings, a more immediate intellectual influence than any one except Emerson, and possibly Parker. All this guarantees that warm feeling of personal interest, without which no memoir can be well written, while there was yet too little of intimacy to give place for the glamour of affection. This biography may therefore serve as an intermediate step between the original "Memoirs" — which gave the estimate offered by personal friendship — and that remoter verdict which will be the judgment of an impartial posterity.

The sources on which I have chiefly relied are

(1) the five bulky volumes in possession of the Fuller family, into which a great variety of written material was transcribed by Rev. A. B. Fuller, after the publication of the " Memoirs," — and to which I have referred always as the " Fuller MSS."; (2) Margaret Fuller's letters to Mr. Emerson, kindly lent me by Mr. Emerson's executors; (3) her letters to Dr. F. H. Hedge, lent me by himself; (4) those to the Hon. A. G. Greene, of Providence, R. I., sent me by his daughter, Mrs. S. C. Eastman, of Concord, N. H.; (5) those to the Hon. George T. Davis, shown to me by his son, James C. Davis, Esq.; (6) many letters and papers of different periods, sent to me from London by the Rev. W. H. Channing; (7) Margaret Fuller's diary of 1844, lent by Mrs. R. B. Storer, of Cambridge; (8) her traveling diary in England and Scotland, which I own; (9) several volumes of Mr. A. Bronson Alcott's MS. diary; (10) a translation of her letters to her husband in Italy, the version being made by the late Miss Elizabeth Hoar, and lent me by her sister, Mrs. R. B. Storer. To this I may add a store of reminiscences from Margaret Fuller's old Cambridge friends. In the cases where I have used the same written material with the editors of the " Memoirs," the selections employed have been wholly different. A few printed books, issued since the publication of the " Memoirs," have given some aid, especially Horace Greeley's " Recollections of a Busy Life," Weiss's " Life of Theodore Parker,"

and the "Carlyle-Emerson Correspondence;" but the main reliance has necessarily been placed on material not hitherto made public; and to all the friends who have helped me to this I am profoundly grateful.

If my view of Margaret Fuller differs a little from that of previous biographers, it is due to the study of these original sources. With every disposition to defer to the authors of the "Memoirs," all of whom have been in one way or another my friends and teachers, I am compelled in some cases to go with what seems the preponderance of written evidence against their view. Margaret Fuller was indeed, as one of them has lately said to me, many women in one, and there is room for a difference of opinion even in assigning a keynote to her life. In their analysis, these biographers seem to me to have given an inevitable prominence to her desire for self-culture, perhaps because it was on this side that she encountered them; but I think that any one who will patiently study her in her own unreserved moments will now admit that what she always most desired was not merely self-culture, but a career of mingled thought and action, such as she finally found. She who, at the age of thirteen, met young scholars returned from Europe with enthusiastic vindications of American society against their attacks; she who, a few years after, read with delight all Jefferson's correspondence, was not framed by nature for a mystic, a dreamer, or a book-worm. She longed, as she herself said, to be a Pericles rather than an Anaxagoras; and she occupied her time with omnivorous study, with writing, with talking, with mysticism, while waiting for her career. In view of all this, I cannot resist the opinion that the prevalent tone of the "Memoirs" leaves her a little too much in the clouds, and gives us too little of that vigorous executive side which was always prominent in her aspirations for herself, and which was visible to all after she reached Italy.

I am the more led to say this because it is essential to the plan of the present series that I should dwell chiefly on her literary life, while knowing that this life was only preliminary, and that she would not have wished to be judged by it after she had once entered on the life of action. The following pages will, I hope, be a more adequate record than has before been given of what she did for our dawning literature; but they yet leave room for a book by some other hand that shall fully delineate the Margaret Fuller Ossoli who stood by the side of Mazzini in Italy, and whose hands the young patriots clasped in the hospital crying, "Viva l'Italia" as they died. At the very moment when Lowell was satirizing her in his "Fable for Critics," she was leading such a life as no American woman had led in this century before. During our own civil war many women afterwards led it, and found out for themselves what it was; but by that time Margaret Fuller Ossoli had passed away. Still, as I said,

I must now make that part of her record secondary and dwell chiefly on its intellectual side;
only keeping before my readers the fact that the
best part of intellect is action, and that this was
always her especial creed.

II.

HEREDITARY TRAITS.

"WE are never better understood," says Margaret Fuller in her fragment of autobiographical romance, "than when we speak of 'a Roman virtue,' 'a Roman outline.'" She goes on : "There is somewhat indefinite, somewhat yet unfulfilled in the thought of Greece, of Spain, of modern Italy ; but ROME, it stands by itself a clear Word. The power of will, the dignity of a fixed purpose, is what it utters. Every Roman was an emperor." Tried by this standard, she herself may be said to have had a Roman parentage. An element of strength went through all her ancestry.

And the quality which was their drawback — too much of self-assertion — was essentially Roman also. "It never shocks us," the autobiography continues, "that the Roman is self-conscious. One wants no universal truth from him, no philosophy, no creation, but only his life, his Roman life, felt in every pulse, realized in every gesture. The universal heaven takes in the Roman only to make us feel his individuality the more. The Will, the Resolve of Man ; it has been expressed, fully expressed."

There is no evidence that Margaret Fuller herself had ever thought of any such analogy as I find between the type thus strongly indicated and the race from which she sprung; but in my own mind it is clear and gave the key to her life. Let us go back to her ancestry and trace this fine thread of New England vigor — which was a Roman vigor, touched by Christianity — running through it all.

Thomas Fuller, entitled "Lieutenant" in the probate proceedings on his will, came from England to America in 1638, and left this record of his spiritual experiences.

> "In thirty-eight I set my foot
> On this New England shore;
> My thoughts were then to stay one year,
> And here remain no more.

> "But, by the preaching of God's word
> By famous Shepard he,
> In what a woful state I was,
> I then began to see.

> "Christ cast his garments over me,
> And all my sins did cover:
> More precious to my soul was he
> Than dearest friend or lover.

> "His pardoning mercy to my soul
> All thought did far surmount;
> The measure of his love to me
> Was quite beyond account. . . .

> "I said, My mountain does stand strong,
> And doubtless 't will forever;
> But soon God turned his face away,
> And joy from me did sever.

> " Sometimes I am on mountains high,
>   Sometimes in valleys low : —
>   The state that man 's in here below,
>   Doth ofttimes ebb and flow. . . .
>
> " But surely God will save my soul !
>   And, though you trouble have,
>   My children dear, who fear the Lord,
>   Your souls at death he 'll save."

The author of these lines was detained in America, it seems, by the preaching of Rev. Mr. Shepard, of Cambridge, known in the obituaries of that period as " the holy, heavenly, sweet-affecting and soul-ravishing Mr. Shepard." Thus guided and influenced, Lieutenant Fuller bought lands in Middleton, then a part of Salem, Mass., — lands a portion of which is still in the possession of some of his descendants. He built a house there, but afterwards removed to Woburn, where he died. His son Jacob and his grandson Jacob succeeded him at Middleton, and a great-grandson, Timothy, was also born there in 1739, of whom more must be said.

Timothy Fuller graduated at Harvard College in 1760, and his name, with that date, might long be seen upon the corner-stone of the building called Stoughton. He became a clergyman, was settled in Princeton, Mass., and differed from most of his parishioners in regarding the impending American Revolution as premature. He therefore preached a sermon to the " minute-men," choosing for his text the passage, " Let not him that girdeth on the harness boast himself as he that putteth

it off." But the minute-men found it more satisfactory to gird on the harness and put off the minister ; so the Rev. Timothy Fuller was dismissed
from his parish by an ecclesiastical council in
1776. He preached elsewhere ; sued the town of
Princeton in vain for his salary ; had even to pay
the costs, for which contingency he had carefully
kept money ; but finally came back to the town as
a farmer, his large farm embracing the Wachusett
Mountain. He evidently regained the full confidence of his rebellious parishioners, for he represented Princeton in the state convention which
accepted the Constitution of the United States.
Independent as ever, he voted steadily against
that instrument, and has left on record his reasons, all based on the fact that the Constitution
recognized human slavery. In this attitude he no
doubt found support from his wife, whose father,
the Rev. Abraham Williams, had emancipated his
own slaves by will ; had required his children to
give bonds for their support in old age, if needed ;
and had deprived any child so delinquent of all
share in his estate, substituting in that case " a
new Bible of the cheapest sort, hoping that, by
the blessing of Heaven, it may teach them to do
justice and love mercy." Thus fortified on his
wife's side, also, in Roman virtue and anti-slavery
principles, the Rev. Timothy Fuller died in 1805,
five years before the birth of his most eminent
grandchild, Margaret.

He left five daughters and five sons, all these

last being lawyers, — a monotony of occupation more common in those days than now. These sons were men of marked character, possessing many admirable and some unpleasing qualities, and these in sufficient uniformity to cause their being liked and disliked — especially the latter — in a body. Horace Mann, who was a person of rather vehement preferences, and who, as a lawyer, knew the brothers well, once said to me that if Margaret Fuller was unpopular, it was not from any prejudice against her as a woman, but because she probably combined "the disagreeableness of forty Fullers." It was not true, for she had fortunately one of the sweetest mothers who ever lived, and her nature was thus tempered on the "spindle-side;" but the remark showed the traditions of the paternal race. Several of the Fuller brothers I can distinctly remember, and, to one thus recalling them, it is not difficult to comprehend just where Horace Mann's dislike came in, although to some of the brotherhood he doubtless did injustice. They were in general men of great energy, pushing, successful, of immense and varied information, of great self-esteem, and without a particle of tact. My mother used to tell a characteristic story of Abraham Fuller, who was a frequent visitor at her house in Cambridge, and whom every Cantabrigian of that period must remember. Coming in and finding my mother darning her children's stockings, he watched her a little while, and then said, abruptly, " You do not know how to darn stockings; let me show you." He being an old bachelor, and she the mother of ten children, the remark seemed the very climax of impudence; but he took the needle from her, and taught her, as she always maintained, more about darning stockings than she had ever known in her life before. This combination of unexpected knowledge and amazing frankness in its proclamation shows what a critic like Horace Mann, himself not wanting in self-assertion, might have found to suggest antagonism in "forty Fullers."

Of a family thus gifted and thus opinionated, Timothy Fuller, Margaret Fuller's father, was the oldest, the most successful, and the most assured. He was born July 11, 1778, and received his father's name; graduated at Harvard College, with the second honors of his class, in 1801; was at different times a member of various branches of the state government of Massachusetts; and was a representative in Congress from 1817 to 1825. He was in politics a Jeffersonian Democrat, was chairman of the House committee on naval affairs, and was a warm supporter of John Quincy Adams for the presidency. Many references to him may be found in Mr. Adams's voluminous diary. Inheriting anti-slavery principles on both sides, he warmly opposed the Missouri Compromise, and his speeches on this and other subjects found their way into print. He worked hard in his profession, kept up his classical reading, and was making preparations to write a history of the United

States, when he died suddenly of Asiatic cholera, October 1, 1835.

I have carefully read some of his published addresses : a Fourth-of-July oration at Watertown in 1809, and one at Lexington in 1814; also an address before the American Peace Society in 1826. In all these there are the characteristics to be found in a thousand similar speeches of that period, together with some not so common. They are fervent, patriotic, florid; but there is also a certain exceptional flavor arising from the fact that, unlike nine tenths of those who made such addresses in New England, the speaker was a Republican — or, as men were beginning to say, a Democrat — and not a Federalist. He does not appear in these addresses as a bitter partisan ; he is as ready to praise Washington and Adams as Jefferson and Madison ; but he never mentions Hamilton and Jay, and seems by implication to condemn the policy of the one, and the treaty with which the name of the other is still identified. Nor does he take sides with Napoleon Bonaparte, as the Federalists charged the Democrats with doing, while he condemns, in a really striking and felicitous passage, the selfish motives of the Allied Powers in crushing him : —

" At length the mighty warrior is prostrate; his proud trophies, the spoils of so many vanquished princes, are leveled with the dust. Napoleon is no more ! No more, did I say ? The blaze of that portentous meteor shall gleam resplendent through all future time !

"The proud banner of England, in close contact with her imperial coadjutors, waves in triumph over the French metropolis. The destinies of the vast empire of France and the partition of Europe await the nod of those same princes, who so lately trembled in their capitals. The 'disinterested and magnanimous allies,' the 'deliverers of the world,' seem very *affectionate* to the world they have delivered. Their 'labor of love' is only begun. One takes Poland under his gracious protection, another is pleased to take Norway, a third Italy; and modest England resigns to each his favorite portion of prostrate Europe, and only claims, as a small gratuity, the rest of the world! France pays fifteen hundred millions of francs for the acquisition of her ancient dynasty. Oh, how would the heart of every American rejoice; how should we at this moment hymn praises to Heaven, if the generous prince who once espoused our cause in distress, now filled his rightful throne! But it may not be, — 'The son of St. Louis is ascended to heaven.' " [1]

True to the anti-slavery traditions of his father and grandfather, Timothy Fuller pointed out, as early as 1809, that the Constitution manifested "a temporary indulgence to a system which it nevertheless reprehends in the Southern States," — yet he found in this concession a masterpiece of skill, although, as has been said, his own father had voted against the instrument on this very ground. He was faithful in denouncing, three years before the war of 1812, those English outrages in the way of search and impressment for

[1] *Address,* July 4, 1814, p. 20.

which the Federalists mistakenly apologized ; and
if he was so hopeful as to assert, without qualifi-
cation, "None but just wars can ever be waged
by a free country," we can pardon something to
republican zeal.   Like other Americans in that
day, he found a hero in Bolivar ; and he held up
Napoleon Bonaparte with some vigor as a warn-
ing to that popular leader : —

"Should Bolivar, so much admired, so much ap-
plauded, so often dignified by a comparison with the
highest name in the annals of patriotism, degenerate at
last into a vulgar hero, a military usurper, the betrayer
of his country ; great indeed will be his degradation,
loud the execrations of mankind, deep and eternal the
odium of posterity.   Let him beware of the temptation,
lest he share the fate of *him*, who so lately seemed to
hold the destinies of EUROPE in his hand.   The career
of military power glared upon the eye, and bewildered
the senses, but was followed by swift retribution upon
the usurper.   He, who might forever have been honored
as the champion of freedom, is consigned to the faithful
historian to record in blood his deeds of injustice, usur-
pation and oppression.   Let *him* then, who still soars
in the meridian of success, warned by the fate of law-
less ambition, take counsel from the GREAT and GOOD
FAYETTE, crowned with the benedictions of a grateful
nation ; let him learn wisdom from his own imputed
prototype, and become unequivocally, irrevocably, glo-
riously, the benefactor of nations, 'THE WASHINGTON
OF THE SOUTH.' "[1]

But that Timothy Fuller was capable of doing

[1] *Oration on Peace*, p. 19.

some justice to opponents is evident in the tribute which he pays, as a lawyer, to the integrity of the British admiralty courts even in time of war. When we consider how hard it was for the disciples of Jefferson to admit that anything good could come out of England, we are justified, I think, in attributing to Timothy Fuller a certain candor as well as independence of mind, in writing thus: —

"During the late wars in Europe, in which Great Britain so largely participated, and when her cruisers arrested the progress of our neutral commerce, the appeals to her justice were first made through her Courts of Admiralty ; and it is due to those courts to admit that those appeals were seldom made in vain, until the *Executive* power interposed, and required their obedience to unjust and arbitrary rules, and orders of the King in Council, unknown to the codes of international law. The interference was open, and avowed, under the odious and infamous plea of retaliation upon the enemy. The obstacle was too great to be overcome by the integrity of the judge; yet the rectitude of his principles has not been questioned.

"This and other examples prove that it is not difficult to constitute a tribunal of learned, intelligent, and upright men, selected upon fair principles of reciprocal and equal rights for the adjustment of controversies between nations." [1]

Such was the father of Margaret Fuller, a man of some narrowness and undue self-assertion, very

[1] *Peace Address*, p. 24.

likely ; but conscientious, vigorous, well-informed, and public-spirited. His daughter Margaret always recognized, after all his mistakes, her great intellectual obligations to him ; and his accurate habits of mind were always mentioned by her with admiration. " Your father " she wrote to her brother Richard, many years later, " had very great power of attention ; I have never seen any person who excelled him in that ; "[1] and she essayed to carry into her ideal realms the same laborious and careful habits which he had brought to bear in law and statesmanship. Meanwhile she derived from her mother a different, and, in some ways, a more elevating influence. Mrs. Fuller long outlived both daughter and husband, and I remember her very well. She must have been one of the sweetest and most self-effacing wives ever ruled by a strong-willed spouse. Her maiden name was Margaret Crane, and she was the daughter of Major Peter Crane, of Canton, Mass. Of what good Puritan stock she also came may be seen not alone in the sturdy militia-title which her father bore, but in the following picture, recalling some of Heine's or Erckmann-Chatrian's peasant sketches, of her old mother — the maternal grandmother of Margaret Fuller. The grand-daughter gives this description of the good lady, as she appeared in later life : —

" Mother writes that my dear old grandmother is dead. I am sorry you never saw her. She was a

[1] Fuller MSS. ii. p. 691.

2

picture of primitive piety as she sat, holding the 'Saints'
Rest' in her hand, with her bowed, trembling figure
and her emphatic nods, and her bright, sweet blue eyes.
They were bright to the last, though she was ninety.
I went to see her just before I came back here. It is a
great loss to mother, who felt a large place warmed in
her heart by the fond and grateful love of this aged
parent." [1]

Margaret Fuller's mother was married May 28,
1809; and came to dwell, with her husband, in
Cambridge. She had in youth great personal
beauty, the inheritance of which has conspicuously come down, here and there, to her descendants. This consisted especially in a peculiar richness of complexion, which time had spared even
to the period when I knew her. She was tall,
slender, dignified in bearing, but awkward rather
than graceful in movement, and with an especial
sweetness of expression in her face. Her manner
is excellently described in a phrase applied by
Bettina Brentano to her friend Günderode: "She
was timid-friendly." During her husband's public life she was much in Washington society; but
withdrew, as years went on, into a sort of double
domesticity, dividing her life between her children and her flowers. Of each she had a large
family, and, when she removed from one residence
to another, the garden was transplanted like the
nursery. She had eight different homes during
her married life; but there were families and gen-

[1] MS. (W. H. C.)

erations of plants which went with her from place to place, adhering to her fortunes, in the words of her son, " like the tenantry of a feudal lord." One family of lilies was thus perpetuated for a quarter of a century, and was bequeathed to her children. She wrote once to her daughter, " One must have grown up with flowers and found joy and sweetness in them, amidst disagreeable occupations, to take delight in them as I do. They have long had power to bring me into harmony with the Creator, and to soothe almost any irritation." In accordance with this, the mother seems to have naturally suggested to the daughter some flower-like symbol. Margaret Fuller writes to her brother, " We cannot be sufficiently grateful for our mother — so fair a blossom of the white amaranth — truly to us a mother in this, that we can venerate her piety. Our relations to her have known no jar. Nothing vulgar has sullied them; and in this respect life has been truly domesticated." When we remember that she of whom this was written was no feudal lady, " flower-like and delicate " like Browning's Duchess ; but a faithful and laborious New England matron, able and willing to perform for her large household the humblest services, we can see the value of this tribute, and the treasure of this inheritance.

Such were the father and mother, such the ancestry, of Margaret Fuller. We shall see, as we go on, the traces of their inherited qualities pervading her life.

III.

GIRLHOOD AT CAMBRIDGE.

(1810–1833.)

SARAH MARGARET, the oldest of the eight children of Timothy and Margaret (Crane) Fuller,
was born May 23, 1810, in that part of Cambridge
still known as Cambridgeport. There are attractive situations in that suburb, but Cherry Street
can scarcely be classed among them, and the
tide of business and the pressure of a tenement-
house population have closed in upon it since then.
The dwelling of Timothy Fuller still stands at the
corner of Eaton Street, and is easily recognized
by the three elms in front, two of which, at
least, were planted by him in the year when
Margaret was born. The garden, in which she
and her mother delighted, has long since vanished ; but the house still retains a certain dignity, though now divided into three separate tenements, numbered respectively 27, 29, and 31
Cherry Street, and occupied by a rather migra-
tory class of tenants. The pillared doorway, and
the carved wreaths above it, give still an old-fashioned grace to the somewhat dilapidated birthplace of Margaret Fuller.

In the fragment of an autobiographical romance, given in her " Memoirs," there is a graphic sketch of this early home; and the following briefer one, hitherto unpublished, occurs in a journal of travel kept, many years after, for her brother Richard : —.

"I feel satisfied, as I thought I should, with reading these bolder lines in the manuscript of Nature. Merely gentle and winning scenes are not enough for me; I wish my lot had been cast amid the sources of the streams, where the voice of the hidden torrent is heard by night; where the eagle soars, and the thunder resounds in long peals from side to side; where the grasp of a more powerful emotion has rent asunder the rocks, and the long purple shadows fall like a broad wing upon the valley. All places, like all persons, I know, have beauty which may be discovered by a thoughtful and observing mind; but only in some scenes and with some people can I expand, and feel myself at home. I feel this all the more for having passed my childhood in such a place as Cambridgeport. There I had nothing except the little flower-garden behind the house, and the elms before the door. I used to long and pine for beautiful places such as I read of. There was not one walk for me except over the bridge; I liked that very much, the river, and the city glittering in sunset, and the lovely undulating line all round, and the light smokes seen in some weather." [1]

Her father, from her early childhood, took charge of her education, and devoted to it much time. She began to study Latin at the age of six, and was carried on, from that period, by an intel-

[1] Fuller MSS. ii. 711-3.

lectual forcing process. It was the custom of the
time. Rev. Dr. Hedge, afterwards her intimate
intellectual companion, assures me that there was
nothing peculiar, for that period, in Mr. Fuller's
method, except that it was applied to a girl.
Cambridge boys, if the sons of college-bred men,
were brought up in much the same way. Dr.
Hedge himself was fitted for college at eleven,
and had read half the body of Latin literature before that time. What made the matter worse in
her case was not the mere fact that she was a girl,
though that doubtless created a need of such
watchful care as only a mother can give. There
was the serious additional evil that all her lessons
must be recited after her father came back from
his office, and therefore at irregular hours, often
extending late into the evening. High pressure
is bad enough for an imaginative and excitable
child, but high pressure by candle-light is ruin-
ous; yet that was the life she lived. The fragment of autobiographical romance in which she
vividly describes the horrors of this method must
not, as her brother Arthur has suggested, be taken
too literally; but frequent references in her later
journals show her deep sense of the wrong she
suffered in mind and body by the mistaken system applied in her early youth. Writing in her
diary, many years afterwards, of some improve-
ments in physical training, especially as to tight-
lacing, she says: —

" If we had only been as well brought up in these

respects! It is not mother's fault that she was ignorant of every physical law, young, untaught country girl as she was; but I can't help mourning, sometimes, that my bodily life should have been so destroyed by the ignorance of *both* my parents." [1]

At thirteen, Margaret Fuller was so precocious in mind and appearance as to take her place in society with much older girls; she went to parties of young people, and gave such entertainments for herself. Having been a pupil at the school, then celebrated, of Dr. Park, in Boston, she once attempted to mingle her two sets of friends — Boston and Cambridge — at a party given in her own house. The attempt was disastrous; she had little natural tact, and her endeavors to pay, as was proper, the chief attention to the stranger guests brought upon her the general indignation of her little world in Cambridge. Partly in consequence of this untoward state of things, and in order to change the scene, she was sent as a pupil to the school of the Misses Prescott, in Groton. There she had a curious episode of personal experience, recorded in her "Summer on the Lakes" as having occurred to a certain fabled "Mariana;" and she received from her teachers a guidance so kind and tender as to make her grateful for it during all her life. She returned from this school in the spring of 1825, being then just fifteen.

At this time she lived, as always, a busy life, — rose before five in summer, walked an hour, prac

[1] MS. Diary, 1844

ticed an hour on the piano, breakfasted at seven,
read Sismondi's "European Literature" in French
till eight, then Brown's "Philosophy" till half
past nine, then went to school for Greek at twelve,
then practiced again till dinner. After the early
dinner she read two hours in Italian, then walked
or rode ; and in the evening played, sang, and retired at eleven to write in her diary. This, be it
observed, was at the very season when girls of
fifteen or sixteen are, in these days, on their
way to the seashore or the mountains. The school
where she recited Greek was a private institution
of high character in Cambridgeport, known famil-
iarly as the "C. P. P. G. S.," or "Cambridge
Port Private Grammar School," a sort of academy, kept at that time by Mr. Perkins, a graduate of Yale College. It was so excellent that it
drew many pupils from what was then called Old
Cambridge, — now Harvard Square, — then quite
distinct from "the Port," and not especially disposed to go to it for instruction. Dr. Oliver
Wendell Holmes was one of Margaret Fuller's
fellow pupils, as were John Holmes, his younger
brother, and Richard Henry Dana. From those
who were her associates in this school, it is possible to obtain a very distinct impression of her
as she then appeared.

She came to school for these Greek recitations
only, and was wont to walk in with that peculiar
carriage of the head and those half-shut eyelids
which have been so often described ; and which

were so far from producing antagonism among the younger girls that they rather caused an amusing sense of envy and emulation. "We thought," said one among them to me, "that if we could only come into school that way, we could know as much Greek as she did." Other traits of hers these youthful observers also noted with admiration. There was then a social library in one of the village shops ; to this she would go, wearing a hooded cloak ; she would take off the cloak, fill the hood with books, swing it over her shoulders, books and all, and so carry it home. "We all wished," said my informant, "that our mothers would let us have hooded cloaks, that we might carry our books in the same way." Yet it does not seem to have been their impression that she neglected her home duties for the sake of knowledge ; such was her conceded ability that she was supposed equal to doing everything at once. It was currently reported that she could rock the cradle, read a book, eat an apple, and knit a stocking, all at the same time ; and here also the indefatigable imitation of her young admirers toiled after her in vain. How she impressed the boys, meanwhile, may be gathered from Dr. Holmes's amusing description of the awe with which he regarded the opening sentence of one of her school compositions : "It is a trite remark."[1] Alas ! he did not know the meaning of the word "trite."

A lady, who at a later period knew Margaret

[1] *Atlantic Monthly*, xxiii. 117.

Fuller well, writes me a characteristic reminiscence of the first glimpse of her; at a time when she came as an unexpected guest to my informant's house, on the occasion of a little party of younger children. She entered, a tall girl of fifteen, plain, but with " a peculiar swaying grace in her motion." She happened to carry in her hand a large handkerchief, such as it was the fashion of those days to use; and with this handkerchief for a *bâton* she at once assumed direction of the children ; waving her sign of office by one corner as she guided them in new games, to the great amusement of the mother and elder sisters, who found themselves relieved of all trouble in the entertainment. " I was greatly drawn to her," says my informant, then a girl of eleven or twelve. Children are keen critics of one another, and this testimony from a juvenile hostess proves the essential *bonhomie* and cordiality of the stranger guest. And whenever, from this time on, she assumed the part of leadership in a mixed company, it is to be observed that the attitude was always accepted as natural and agreeable by those present ; it was only the absent who criticised.

There seems to be no foundation for the view suggested recently, that Mr. Fuller was moved, in his efforts to give his daughter a high education, by a baffled social ambition. In the first place, there was very little room for any such thing ; the Cambridge society was very simple, as it still remains ; and Mr. Fuller's standing, being that of

a lawyer and congressman, was as good as anybody's. There was a prejudice against him politically, no doubt, he being a Democrat when the
ruling classes in Massachusetts were Federalists;
but his social position was unimpaired. Neither
he nor his wife had the attribute of personal elegance or grace; but he evidently took pains to fill
the prominent place to which he was justly entitled; and an entertainment given by him to John
Quincy Adams, the President, in 1826, was one of
the most elaborate affairs of the kind that had occurred in Cambridge since the ante-revolutionary
days of the Lechmeres and Vassalls. He was then
residing in a fine old mansion, built by Chief
Justice Dana, on what is still called Dana Hill, —
a house destroyed by fire in 1839, — and his guests
were invited from far and near to a dinner and a
ball. Few Cambridge hosts would then have attempted so much as this; but had Mr. Fuller's
social prominence been far less than it was, he
would have been the very last person to find out
the deficiency. Had he lived next door to an imperial palace, he would have thought that it was
he who did the favor by mingling with his neighbors. As to his daughter, he took pride in her
precocious abilities, and enjoyed her companionship in his favorite studies; that tells the whole
story. Stimulating, even flattering, his companionship might be; but tender, wise, considerate,
it could not be. On that side — and it was with
her the important side — she cast herself against

an iron wall. Her early diaries were burned by herself long after, and it is only by glimpses in her later papers that we can reconstruct this girlish life. Looking back, at the age of thirty, she writes in a fragment of journal: —

"When I recollect how deep the anguish, how deeper still the want, with which I walked alone in hours of childish passion and called for a Father, after saying the word a hundred times, till it was stifled by sobs, how great seems the duty that name imposes." [1]

Under ordinary circumstances, the mother's influence comes in to fill this void. Unfortunately Mr. Fuller for many years deemed it his mission to be both father and mother; and his sweet wife, absorbed in her younger children, insensibly yielded. His authority over his daughter did not stop with the world of books. Many a man feels bound vigorously to superintend the intellectual education of his little maiden, and then leaves all else — dress, society, correspondence — to the domain of the mother. Not so with Mr. Fuller. It is the testimony of those who then knew the family well that his wife surrendered all these departments also to his sway. He was to control the daughter's whole existence. Jean Paul says that the mother puts the commas and the semicolons into the child's life, but the father the colons and the periods. In the Fuller household the whole punctuation was masculine. Had Margaret an invitation, her father decided whether it should

[1] MS.

be accepted, and suggested what she should wear; did she receive company at home, he made out the list; and when the evening came, he and his daughter received them: the mother only casually appearing, a shy and dignified figure in the background. At a later period, after his death, Margaret Fuller and her mother became all-in-all to each other, but at this early period the tie between them, though affectionate, was not intimate; for almost all purposes of direction and guidance she was her father's child.

Margaret Fuller's personal appearance at this early period has been described by several of her biographers; but one hears very different accounts of it from different quarters, the least flattering being those given by her own sex. The inexorable memory of a certain venerable Cambridge lady recalls her graphically as she appeared at the ball given by her father to President Adams; a young girl of sixteen with a very plain face, half-shut eyes, and hair curled all over her head; she was laced so tightly, my informant declares, by reason of stoutness, that she had to hold her arms back as if they were pinioned; she was dressed in a badly-cut, low-necked pink silk, with white muslin over it; and she danced quadrilles very awkwardly, being withal so near-sighted that she could hardly see her partner. On the other hand, it is maintained that she had in childhood something of her mother's peculiar beauty of complexion, this being, however, spoiled at twelve years old

by a tendency of blood to the head, which the
tight-lacing must have assisted. It is also said
that her eyes would have been good had they not
been injured by near-sightedness, and that her peculiar smile had only a passing effect of supercil-
iousness, and was really kind and truthful. She
had what her school-mate Dr. O. W. Holmes described as " a long and flexile neck, arching and
undulating in strange, sinuous movements, which
one who loved her would compare to a swan, and
one who loved her not to those of the ophidian
who tempted our common mother." [1]   Her hands
were smooth and white, and she made such prominent use of them that she was charged by her
critics — as was also charged upon Madame de
Staël in respect to her arms — with making the
most of her only point of beauty.

The total effect was undoubtedly that of personal plainness ; and the consciousness of this fact
was no doubt made more vivid to her by the traditions and remains of her mother's beauty, and by
the fact that this quality was transmitted in even
an enhanced form to her own younger sister Ellen,
whom she reared and educated. Ellen Fuller,
afterwards the wife of Ellery Channing, the poet,
was in person and character one of the most attractive of women. She had a Madonna face, a
broad brow, exquisite coloring, and the most noble
and ingenuous expression, mingled, in her sister
Margaret's phrase, with " the look of an appeal-

[1] *Atlantic Monthly*, xxiii. 116.

ing child." I knew her intimately, her husband
being my near relative, and our households being
for various reasons closely brought together; and
have always considered her one of the most admirable women I have ever had the good fortune
to meet. She not only had an active and cultivated mind, and a strength of character that sur-
mounted some of life's severest trials, but she was
as singularly gifted in the sphere of home and social life as was her sister in that of literature.
She instantly drew to her all strangers by her
face, while her elder sister had no such advantage;
and though it is certain that no shade of jealousy
ever came between these high-minded persons, it
was not in human nature that Margaret Fuller
should not have felt her own conscious want of
attractions to be enhanced by the contrast.

As a tribute to this fair sister, and also to the
deep feeling which Margaret Fuller at last learned
to cherish toward her father, I copy the following
reminiscence from a diary kept by her many years
later: —

"I remembered our walking in the garden avenue,
between the tall white lilies and Ellen's apple-tree; she
was a lovely child then, and happy, but my heart ached,
and I lived in just the way I do now. Father said, seeing me at a distance, 'Incedo regina,' etc. Poor Juno!
Father admired me, and, though he caused me so much
suffering, had a true sense at times of what is tragic for
me. The other day, when C—— was cutting a lock of
my hair for one who so little knows how to value it, I

thought of my finding it in Father's desk, with all these
other little tokens. It was a touching sight. Father, if
you hear me, know that your daughter thinks of you
with the respect and relenting tenderness you deserve.
Time has removed all obstructions to a clear view of
what you were. I am glad you were withdrawn from a
world which had grown so bitter to you; but I wish we
might reach you with our gentle thoughts." [1]

Cambridge, Massachusetts, which is now a city
of 52,000 inhabitants, had, at the time of Margaret Fuller's birth, but 2,323. When she was
twenty years old it had 6,072, divided between
three detached villages; and was in many respects
a very pleasant place in which to be born and
bred. It was, no doubt, in the current phrase of
to-day, " provincial ; " in other words, it was not
one of the two or three great capitals of the civilized world; but there are few places in any country which bring together a larger proportion of
cultivated and agreeable families than must then
have been found in this quiet academic suburb.
One could not quite venture to say of it as Stuart
Newton, the painter, said of Boston, during a brilliant London career about that period, " I meet in
London occasionally such society as I met in Boston all the time ; " but it needs only to mention
some of the men who made Cambridge what it
was, between 1810 and 1830, to show that my
claim for the little town is not too high. Judge

[1] MS. Diary, 1844. Mr. Fuller's reference was to Virgil's de
scription of Juno, "Ast ego quæ divum incedo regina."

Story, whose reputation is still very wide, was then the head of the law school, and in the zenith of his fame; the all-accomplished Edward Everett was Greek professor; English was taught by Edward T. Channing, who certainly trained more and better authors than any teacher yet known in America; George Ticknor was organizing the department of modern languages; George Bancroft was a tutor. The town in which these men lived and taught may have been provincial in population, but it was intellectually metropolitan; where McGregor sits, there is the head of the table. Moreover, by a happy chance, the revolutions of Europe were sending to this country, about that time, many highly cultivated Germans and Italians, of whom Harvard College had its full share. Charles Follen taught German; Charles Beck, Latin; Pietro Bachi, Italian; Friedrich Gräter gave drawing lessons. England, too, contributed to the American Cambridge the most delightful of botanists and ornithologists, — his books being still classics, — Thomas Nuttall. He organized the Botanic Garden of the college, and initiated the modern tendency toward the scientific side of education. From some of these men Margaret Fuller had direct instruction; but she was, at any rate, formed in a society which was itself formed by their presence.

And, since young people are trained quite as much by each other as by their elders, it was fortunate that Margaret Fuller found among the

3

young men who were her contemporaries some
companions well worth having. She went into
society, as has been seen, very early — far too
early. The class with which she may be said to
have danced through college — to adopt Howells's
phrase — was that of 1829, which has been made,
by the wit and poetry of Holmes, the most eminent class that ever left Harvard. With Holmes
she was not especially intimate, though they had
been school-mates; but with two of the most
conspicuous members of the class — William
Henry Channing and James Freeman Clarke —
she formed a life-long friendship, and they became
her biographers. Another of these biographers —
the Rev. Frederick Henry Hedge, her townsman
— knew her also at this period, though he had
already left college and had previously been absent from Cambridge for some years, at a German gymnasium. Still another associate, also of
the class of 1829, was her kinsman, George T.
Davis, afterwards well known as a member of
Congress from the Greenfield (Mass.) district, —
a man of the world and of brilliant gifts.

But after all, the most important part of a
woman's training is that which she obtains from
her own sex; and since Margaret Fuller's mother
was one of the self-effacing sort, it was fortunate
for the young girl that, by a natural reaction, she
sought feminine influences outside of her own
home. She was one of those maidens who form
passionate attachments to older women; and there

was fortunately in Cambridge at that time a group of highly cultivated ladies, most of whom belonged to the college circle, and who in turn won her ardent loyalty. My elder sister can well remember this studious, self-conscious, overgrown girl as sitting at my mother's feet, covering her hands with kisses and treasuring her every word. It was the same at another time with my aunt, Miss Ann G. Storrow, a person of great wit and mental brilliancy; the same with Mrs. J. W. Webster, a most winning and lovely woman, born at the Azores and bearing a tropic softness and sweetness in her manners. Most of these ladies were too much absorbed in their own duties to give more than a passing solicitude to this rather odd and sometimes inconvenient adorer; but she fortunately encountered one friend who resolutely took her in hand.

This lady was the wife of the Harvard professor of astronomy; a woman of uncommon character and cultivation, who had lived much in Europe, and who, with no children of her own, did many good services for the children of her friends. She was Mrs. Eliza Farrar, or, as she always preferred to call herself on her title-pages, Mrs. John Farrar. Having myself resided for some time beneath this lady's roof, I can certify to her strong and well-balanced nature, and her resolute zeal in moulding the manners as well as morals of the young. She was one of our first and best writers for children; her " Young Lady's Friend " was almost

the pioneer manual of its kind; and her "Recollections of Seventy Years" is an admirable record
of a well-spent life. She was the friend of Miss
Martineau and others of the ablest English women
of her time; she readily saw the remarkable intellect of Margaret Fuller, and also perceived the
defects of her training. She undertook to mould
her externally, to make her less abrupt, less self-
asserting, more *comme il faut* in ideas, manners,
and even costume. She had her constantly at
her own house, reformed her hairdresser, and in-
structed her dressmaker; took her to make calls,
took her on journeys. Mrs. Farrar had, moreover,
often with her a young kinswoman who furnished
outwardly and inwardly a charming model, Miss
Anna Barker, of New Orleans, now Mrs. S. G.
Ward. This lady, whose gifts and graces have
since won affectionate admiration in two conti-
nents, was soon a warm friend of Margaret Fuller; who had already another friend of similar
attractions in Miss Harriet Fay, now Mrs. W. H.
Greenough, then living in the very next house at
Cambridgeport and for a time her inseparable
companion. Dr. Holmes has once or twice referred to this last fair maiden in his writings as
"the golden blonde," and describes vividly in his
"Cinders from the Ashes" the manner in which
she won the hearts of all the school-boys.[1] One
of her especial attractions was a head covered
with sunny curls, the free gift of nature; and it

[1] *Atlantic Monthly*, xxiii. 116.

was believed by penetrating — that is, feminine — observers that the less facile ringlets for which Margaret Fuller's hair was kept in unsightly curl-papers all the morning were due to a hopeless emulation of her lovely friend. It was, in short, Madame de Staël and Madame Récamier in a school-room. At any rate, it is very probable that the early intimacy with these beautiful and attractive maidens had much to do with creating in Margaret Fuller that strong admiration for personal charms — amounting almost to envy, but never to ungenerous jealousy — which marked her life-time.

How ardent and how deep were her emotions towards these early friends can best be seen from this passage, which appears without date in her diary : —

"I loved —— for a time with as much passion as I was then strong enough to feel. Her face was always gleaming before me, her voice was echoing in my ear, all poetic thoughts clustered round the dear image. This love was for me a key which unlocked many a treasure which I still possess; it was the carbuncle (emblematic gem!) which cast light into many of the darkest corners of human nature. She loved me, too, though not so much, because her nature was 'less high, less grave, less large, less deep;' but she loved more tenderly, less passionately. She loved me, for I well remember her suffering when she first could feel my faults, and knew one part of the exquisite veil rent away." [1]

[1] Fuller MSS. i. 445.

Margaret Fuller's precocity and her taste for hard study naturally created for her the reputation, among those who did not know her, of a grave young pedant. Nothing could be wider of the mark; she was full of sentiment, began to write poetry at fifteen, and produced some verses at seventeen which her brother has preserved in print; verses mourning, as is the wont of early youth, over the flight of years and life's freshness already vanished.

STANZAS.

WRITTEN AT THE AGE OF SEVENTEEN.

I.

"Come, breath of dawn! and o'er my temples play;
　　Rouse to the draught of life the wearied sense;
Fly, sleep! with thy sad phantoms, far away;
　　Let the glad light scare those pale troublous shadows hence!

II.

"I rise, and leaning from my casement high,
　　Feel from the morning twilight a delight;
Once more youth's portion, hope, lights up my eye,
　　And for a moment I forget the sorrows of the night.

III.

"O glorious morn! how great is yet thy power!
　　Yet how unlike to that which once I knew,
When, plumed with glittering thoughts, my soul would soar,
　　And pleasures visited my heart like daily dew!

IV.

"Gone is life's primal freshness all too soon;
　　For me the dream is vanished ere my time;
I feel the heat and weariness of noon,
　　And long in night's cool shadows to recline." [1]

[1] *Life Without and Within*, p. 370.

When these moods passed by, she was the gayest
of companions, overflowing with wit, humor, anecdote, and only too ready sarcasm. This can best
be seen in one of her letters to the correspondent
with whom she was at her gayest, a brilliant and
attractive woman long since dead, the wife of
the Rev. D. H. Barlow, of Lynn, Mass., and the
mother of General F. C. Barlow. To her Margaret Fuller writes thus, with girlish exuberance,
at the age of twenty; fully recognizing, as the
closing words show, the ordeal of criticism through
which she often had to make her way : —

"CAMBRIDGE, *November* 19, 1830.

. . . "Many things have happened since I echoed
your farewell laugh. Elizabeth [Randall] and I have
been fully occupied. She has cried a great deal, painted
a good deal, and played the harp most of all. I have
neither fertilized the earth with my tears, edified its inhabitants by my delicacy of constitution, nor wakened its
echoes to my harmony; yet some things have I achieved
in my own soft feminine style. I hate glare, thou
knowest, and have hitherto successfully screened my
virtues therefrom. I have made several garments fitted
for the wear of American youth; I have written six
letters, and received a correspondent number; I have
read one book, — a piece of poetry entitled, 'Two Agonies,' by M. A. Browne, (pretty caption, is it not?) — and
J. J. Knapp's trial; I have given advice twenty times, —
I have taken it once; I have gained two friends and recovered two; I have felt admiration four times, honor
once, and disgust twice; I have been a journey, and

showed my penetration in discovering the beauties of
Nature through a thick and never-lifted shroud of rain ;
I have turned two new leaves in the book of human nature ; I have got a new pink bag (beautiful !). I have
imposed on the world, time and again, by describing your
Lynn life as the perfection of human felicity, and adorn-
ing my visit there with all sorts of impossible adventures, — thus at once exhibiting my own rich invention
and the credulous ignorance of my auditors (light and
dark, you know, dear, give life to a picture) ; I have
had tears for others' woes, and patience for my own, —
in short, to climax this journal of many-colored deeds
and chances, so well have I played my part, that in the
self-same night I was styled by two several persons, 'a
sprightly young lady,' and 'a Syren !!' Oh rapturous
sound ! I have reached the goal of my ambition. Earth
has nothing fairer or brighter to offer. '*Intelligency*'
was nothing to it. A 'supercilious,' 'satirical,' 'affected,' 'pedantic,' 'Syren'!!!! Can the *olla podrida*
of human nature present a compound of more varied
ingredients, or higher gusto ?" [1] . . .

At the beginning of 1833 she wrote as follows in
her diary, looking forward to an uneventful year.
She was at this time living in what was then a
picturesque old house, now shorn of part of its
amplitude and of its superb row of great linden
trees, — the Brattle House on Brattle Street,
Cambridge. The great buildings of the University Press now cover the ground once laid out in
formal old - fashioned gardens, with fish ponds,
bridges, and spring-houses, every inch of which

[1] Fuller MSS. i. 1.

was once familiar to me as I played there with the younger Fullers, little dreaming that I should ever be the biographer of the staid elder sister who sat, book in hand, beneath the doorway, or perhaps wrote at the window this passage in her diary, by way of forecast of the immediate future : —

"I have settled the occupations of the coming six months. Some duties come first, — to parents, brothers, and sisters, — but these will not consume above one sixth of the time : the family is so small now, mother will have little need of my sewing : we shall probably see very little company. The visits required of me by civility will be few. When the Farrars return, I hope to see them frequently, and E. Woodward I may possibly know, if she comes. But I shall not, of free-will, look out of doors for a moment's pleasure. I shall have no one to stay here for any time except E. I love her, and she is never in the way. All hopes of traveling I have dismissed. All youthful hopes, of every kind, I have pushed from my thoughts. I will not, if I can help it, lose an hour in castle-building and repining, — too much of that already. I have now a pursuit of immediate importance : to the German language and literature I will give my undivided attention. I have made rapid progress for one quite unassisted. I have always hitherto been too constantly distracted by childish feelings to acquire anything properly, but have snatched a little here and there to feed my restless fancy therewith. Please God now to keep my mind composed, that I may store it with all that may be hereafter conducive to the best good of others. Oh, keep me steady in an honorable ambition; favored by this calm, this obscurity of life, I might learn everything, did not feeling lavish away my strength. Let it be no longer thus. Teach me to think justly and act firmly. Stifle in my breast those feelings which, pouring forth so aimlessly, did indeed water but the desert, and offend the sun's clear eye by producing weeds of rank luxuriance. Thou art my only Friend! Thou hast not seen fit to interpose one feeling, understanding breast between me and a rude, woful world. Vouchsafe then thy protection, that I may hold on in courage of soul!" [1]

Before midsummer it had been decided that the family should remove to Groton, and we find her writing from that village, July 4, 1833.

---

[1] Fuller MSS. i. 409. She was reading Shelley at this time, and in his early poem *On Death* occur the lines : —

> " O man, hold thee on in courage of soul
> Through the stormy shades of thy worldly way."

IV.

COUNTRY LIFE AT GROTON.

(1833–1836.)

In removing with her family to Groton, a village nearly forty miles from Boston, and then rather difficult of access, — for this was long before the building of the Fitchburg Railroad, — Margaret Fuller felt a natural depression. If even the Boston of those days afforded but a limited supply of books and intellectual companionship, what would Groton offer? She gave up Cambridge with its youthful society on one side, Boston with its books on the other; and this for a young woman of twenty-three, overflowing with energy and ambition, was quite a trial. She saw in advance what it would be, and she found what she expected. But her letters are enough to show that her mind was still actively employed; and that a life more wholly rural gave a new and strong development to her love of out-door nature.

She wrote to Dr. Hedge from Groton, July 4, 1833:—

"I highly enjoy being surrounded with new and beautiful natural objects. My eyes and my soul were

so weary of Cambridge scenery, my heart would not
give access to a summer feeling there. The evenings
lately have been those of Paradise, and I have been
very happy in them. The people here are much more
agreeable than in most country towns; there is no vul-
garity of manners, but little of feeling, and I hear no
gossip." [1]

Again she writes to him that she keeps "Uhland's poems for some still and lovely afternoon,"
and there is henceforth a blending of natural objects with literature and art in all she writes.

Cordial letters from her friends also removed
the natural dread of dropping out from her old
circle, and finding herself not missed. In the
same note to Dr. Hedge she wrote thus: —

"Your letter was very grateful to me, and I confess I
had not expected such a token of remembrance. Since
I came here I have had much reason to believe that
there exists more warmth of feeling in the little world
wherein I have been living than I had supposed. I
expected that my place would immediately be filled
by some person "about my age and height." I have not
found it so. My former intimates sigh at least, if they
do not pine, for my society."

In Groton she read profusely, borrowing her
books chiefly from Dr. Hedge, then, as always, a
fountain of knowledge in the way of German.
It was a period, we must remember, when the
mere perusal of German books was considered

[1] MS.

dangerous; and even Mrs. Farrar records in her " Recollections " the pious but extraordinary suspicion that Harriet Martineau's final materialism was due to her early study of Kant. Margaret Fuller wrote at twenty-three, " I have with me those works of Goethe which I have not read and am now perusing, ' Kunst und Alterthum' and ' Campagne in Frankreich.' I still prefer reading Goethe to anybody, and, as I proceed, find more and more to learn." [1]

She read also at this time Uhland, Novalis, Tieck, and some volumes of Richter. She dipped a good deal into theology and read Eichhorn and Jahn in the original. She was considering what were then called " the evidences of Christianity," and wrote to Dr. Hedge that she had doubted the providence of God, but not the immortality of the soul. During the few years following she studied architecture, being moved to it by what she had read in Goethe; she also read Herschel's " Astronomy," recommended to her by Professor Farrar; read in Schiller, Heine, Alfieri, Bacon, Madame de Staël, Wordsworth, and Southey; with " Sartor Resartus " and some of Carlyle's shorter essays; besides a good deal of European and American history, including all Jefferson's letters. Mr. Emerson says justly that her reading at Groton was at a rate like Gibbon's.

All this continuous study was not the easy amusement of a young lady of leisure; but it was

[1] MS. letter to Dr. Hedge, July 4, 1833.

accomplished under such difficulties and preoccu-
pations that every book might almost be said to
have cost her a drop of life-blood. " Teaching
little Fullers," as she called it, occupied much
of her time; she had the sewing of four children
also on her hands; her mother was often ill, her
grandmother always; often they had no domestic; and she sometimes had pupils not of her own
family. Three evenings in the week and odd
hours during the day were all that this omnivorous student could command for herself. She
worked herself ill at last, desperately ill; her life
was saved with difficulty; and her father spoke
to her, as she came back to life, such words of
praise as his reticent lips had never before uttered. From this time the relation between her
and her father grew tenderer, and that with her
mother more intimate.

The earliest specimen of Margaret Fuller's
composition, so far as I have seen, is a single
school exercise, corrected by her father and preserved by her for the sake of those corrections.
It is upon the Latin motto, " Possunt quia posse
videntur," and it certainly has the vigor of the
Roman temperament that she loved. It was
written probably between the ages of twelve and
sixteen, and her father's few corrections are all
in the direction of terseness and strength. The
position she takes is that while men can, up to a
certain point, do what they will to do, they are
yet so liable to be overruled by the pressure of

events that the only thing surely moulded by their efforts is their own character. This she thus illustrates : —

" Leonidas saved his country by a strong exertion of will, inspired by the most generous sentiment. Brutus nerved his soul to break those ties most sacred to one like him — and failed. Resolved, united hearts, freed America. The strongest exertion, the most generous concentration of will, for a similar purpose, left Poland in blood and chains at the feet of a tyrant." [1]

Her conclusion is that, although all outward results may fail, " it is not in the power of circumstance to prevent the earnest will from shaping round itself the character of a great, a wise, or a good man." It was strong meat, surely, for a young girl to be feeding on such thoughts as these ; such is not the diet on which mere sentimentalists and dreamers are reared.

It is a striking fact in the development of her mind, that when we next find her writing something to please her father, she is still harping on Brutus. The first composition ever published by her, so far as I know, was in the " Daily Advertiser," in 1834. She had wished during the previous autumn to print her translation of Goethe's " Tasso," but had failed ; and this newspaper communication was called forth by something written by George Bancroft. In a letter to Dr. Hedge (March 6, 1835), she thus describes the occurrence : —

[1] Fuller MSS. ii. 249.

"Your *ci-devant* tutor, Mr. Bancroft, has been deliv-
ering a curious (as we say in Groton) address at Deer-
field. If I thought you would care for it I would send
you the account in Cousin George's paper. My father
requested me to write a little piece in answer to Mr.
B.'s attack on Brutus in the 'North American Review,'
which he published in the ' Daily Advertiser ' some time
since. It was responded to (I flatter myself by some
big-wig) from Salem. He detected some ignorance in
me ; nevertheless, as he remarked that I wrote with
' ability,' and seemed to *consider me* as an elderly gentleman, *I considered* the affair as highly flattering, and
beg you will keep it in mind and furnish it for my
memoirs as such after I am dead." [1]

Mr. Bancroft's paper on " Slavery in Rome "
appeared in the " North American Review " for
October, 1834,[2] and contained a very low estimate of Brutus. For some reason, although this
number of the review was then considered important enough to be elaborately criticised in several
successive issues of the "Advertiser," yet the indignation of Mr. Fuller and his daughter was
not brought to bear until nearly two months had
passed. On November 27, however, — Miss Fuller being then twenty-four, — there appeared in
the leading Boston journal a communication in
small print, signed " J." and filling nearly a column. It handled Mr. Bancroft firmly though respectfully, but disputed his view in regard to Brutus, and showed a good deal of care in consulting

[1] MS.   [2] xxxix. 413.

original authorities. Plutarch was largely quoted,
in an English version, and Velleius Paterculus in
the original Latin, — one extract filling five lines.
Upon these grounds the writer defends Brutus
successively from the charges of sycophancy, time-
serving, cruelty, and avarice; and modestly adds:
" I doubt not an infinity of similar authorities
might be quoted by one of more extensive reading and accurate memory." The conclusion is the
only part that can be called ambitious in tone, but
it is written with a wholly generous fervor, and
without conceit : —

" The hearts of the dead are now tranquillized. . . .
But the faith of the young bleeds, and young ambition
droops when the shades of the just are summoned back
from the Elysium to which their appropriate judges had
consigned them, and appear before some revolutionary
tribunal of modern date. Let us not be too hasty in
questioning what is established, and tearing to pieces the
archives of the past. There are other sorts of skepti-
cism, and not less desolating in their tendencies, than
that of religion. That keen observer, Dr. Spurzheim,
warned the people of this country that their great danger lay in want of reverence. Those most distinguished
among us for talent and culture should rather check
than encourage this delay." [1]

For one who was to help in organizing, six
years later, the most formidable party of literary
iconoclasts yet brought together in America, this
was beginning pretty well. The protest closes

[1] *Boston Daily Advertiser,* November 27, 1834.

with courteous expressions toward "the accomplished gentleman said to be the author of the article in question;" and the only thing about the whole communication that suggests a woman's pen is the delicate adroitness with which she turns against Mr. Bancroft, in closing, two lines from one of his own juvenile effusions : —

> "Was it for this that Brutus left a name
> Bright with the beams of freedom's holiest flame ?"

A few days later, Mr. Bancroft found a defender, as Miss Fuller indicates, in a correspondent signing "H.," and giving Salem as his residence. He in turn is courteous and complimentary, — probably not being at all aware that it is a young woman of twenty-four to whom he is replying, — and says of the first communication that it is written "with ability and candor, but I think without fully investigating the subject." Nevertheless, as he can only cite Gibbon and Middleton's Cicero, while she had brought up Plutarch and Velleius Paterculus, the heavier ordnance was certainly with the defender of Brutus. But it was quite a triumph to be gravely answered; and the father and daughter in that quiet Groton farm-house must have taken great delight in cutting out for preservation those two momentous extracts from the "Daily Advertiser."

It often happens that young people, when banished from society to what seems solitude, find compensation in being anew introduced to parents, brothers, and sisters. This was eminently true of

Margaret Fuller. To be sure, her brother Eugene, who was her nearest companion, was now absent. " Eugene and I," she writes in a later diary, " were near of an age, and loved to wander out together, over the streams and through the woods, walking and talking or oftener silent." [1] Eugene Fuller was not the most intellectual of her brothers, but the most winning and attractive ; he had graduated at Harvard in 1834, and was at this time private tutor at the plantation of my uncle, Colonel Samuel Storrow, at Farley, Culpeper County, Virginia. This explains an allusion in the following letter, written by Margaret Fuller to her father during a temporary visit in Cambridge, — which I give to show how cordial a tie really united them, in spite of her criticisms. The " dearest " and " most affectionate " mean a good deal.

"BOSTON, *June* 2, 1835.

" DEAREST FATHER, — I was very glad to receive your letter although 't was but brief. You have of late omitted to write to me when I was absent, and I have felt as if you thought of me less than I wished you should.

"I have been passing ten days at Cambridge, with Mrs. Farrar, and indeed they were most happy. Everybody so kind, the country so beautiful, and my own spirits so light. We made little excursions almost every day. Last Thursday I rode twenty-two miles on horseback without any fatigue. Mrs. F. had a most agreeable party the day before I came away. But of

[1] MS. Diary, 1844.

all these things, Ellen will give you the particulars, if you are interested to hear them. The Higginsons say that Eugene's pupils love him extremely, and that Colonel Storrow, too, seems much pleased with him. I think we ought to feel satisfied that he should secure so much love and esteem after five or six months' close scrutiny. W. H. is still very good, and as well-disposed as ever. They seem much pleased with him at Avon-Place. He passed yesterday with us, — being excused from the store, as it was Marsylvia's wedding-day. I believe it is the first amusement he has allowed himself since he left us. I saw a good deal of your former ward, Thornton Davis, while in Cambridge, but prefer giving you the account *viva voce.*

"And now I have something to tell you which I hope, oh, I HOPE will give you as much pleasure as it does me. Mr. and Mrs. Farrar propose taking me, with several other delightful persons, to Trenton Falls this summer. The plan is to set out about the 20th of July, go on to New York, then up the North River to West Point, — pass a day there ; then to Catskill, — pass a day there ; then on to Trenton, and devote a week to that beautiful scenery. I said I had scarcely a doubt of your consent, as you had said several times last winter you should like to have me take a pleasant journey this summer. Oh, I cannot describe the positive ecstasy with which I think of this journey ! to see the North River at last, and in such society ! Oh, do sympathize with me ! do feel about it as I do ! The positive expenses of the journey we have computed at forty-seven dollars ; I shall want ten more for spending-money, — but you will not think of the money, will you? I would rather you would take two hundred

dollars from my portion, than feel even the least unwilling. Will you not write to me immediately, and
say you love me, and are very glad I am to be so
happy ? ? ?

"It was very unkind in Mr. Robinson to have Mr.
Emerson [preach] during my absence. I think I shall
join Richard and Arthur in attending Mr. Kittredge's
[church]. I must write a few words to mother, so adieu,
from   Your most affectionate daughter, M." [1]

Fathers are fortunately so constituted as rarely
to refuse appeals like this, and Margaret Fuller
had her journey. It was her first experience of
a pleasure which then, perhaps, had a greater zest
than now, as being rarer, and involving more adventure. She went to Newport, then dear to her
as the summer home of the Rev. Dr. Channing,
— to New York, and to Trenton Falls, accounted
one of the glories of America in the simple days
when the wonders of Colorado and the Yosemite
Valley were unknown. In the autumn she met
Miss Harriet Martineau at the house of Professor
Farrar, and a new delight opened before her vision. It was proposed that she should make a voyage to England with the Farrars; and under the
guidance of her kind friends, long resident in
England, she hoped to meet the larger intellectual circle of which she had dreamed. But suddenly a blow fell which crushed this hope and
brought the profoundest emotions. Her father
was taken ill of cholera, September 30, 1835, and

[1] Fuller MSS. i. 153.

died October 1. His widow used to tell the story, to the end of her days, how Margaret brought the younger children together around the lifeless form of her father, and, kneeling, pledged herself to God that if she had ever been ungrateful or un-filial to her father, she would atone for it by fidelity to her brothers and sisters. This vow she surely kept.

She wrote thus to her friend Mrs. Barlow, after her father's death : —

"GROTON, *February* 1, 1836.

. . . "I returned into life to bear a sorrow of which you know the heaviness. But my hard-won faith has not deserted me, and I have so far preserved a serenity which might seem heartlessness to a common observer. It was indeed sad when I went back, in some sort, into the world, and felt myself fatherless. Yet I gave no sign, and hope to preserve more or less fortitude." [1]

Her father had made no will ; his property was sorely involved, and she has told her keen regret at that absence of business education which left her unable to take direct charge of the family affairs. They were placed finally under the care of her uncle Abraham, the narrowest and most arbitrary of all the paternal race. The estate was probably well managed, as it finally yielded two thousand dollars to each of the children ; but this success was bought at a great cost of dicta-torial domineering on the part of the bachelor uncle. — the same man who gave my mother les-

[1] Fuller MSS. i. 21.

sons in darning stockings, — and there is extant
much correspondence which throws light on this.
Margaret Fuller fought like a lioness for the
proper education of her younger brothers and sisters, and especially for Ellen, whom the uncle
would evidently have brought up in old-fashioned
feminine ignorance, rather than let a dollar be
spent upon her schooling. The elder sister insisted
that she should be sent to a suitable school, offering, if necessary, to sacrifice her own share of the
family income, or even of the estate itself, for this
purpose. Every New England farm-house has
been the scene of some touching tale of sisterly
devotion, but nowhere more genuine than in that
old homestead at Groton.

And, with other hopes, the dream of Europe
must go. Her family begged her to take in advance her share of the family property and carry
out her purpose ; but she made, early in 1836,
what she called " the last great sacrifice," and decided to remain. Feeling no immediate strength,
as she records, to carry out her literary plans, she
planned to help her mother by teaching. " Circumstances have decided," she wrote, " that I
must not go to Europe, and shut upon me the
door, as I think, forever, to the scenes I could
have loved. Let me now try to forget myself and
act for others' sakes." [1]

Her mind recovered its tone, and deeper experience gave her profounder sympathy. During

[1] *Memoirs*, i. 161.

her last summer in Groton she wrote this letter to her friend Samuel G. Ward, showing at once how external nature had made her a student and observer of itself, and how penetrating and imaginative were her powers of mind. I know of no more delicate analysis of one of the most recondite and elusive aspects of nature.

"GROTON, *20th April,* 1836.

"You have probably just received a packet from me, (oh! what wild work makes a female pen!) yet I feel tempted to scribble to you, my fellow votary, on the subject of this morning's devotions to our common shrine.

"I strolled languidly far and far over the dull-brown fields, and not an attempt at a life-like tint could I see. Some tawny evergreens and oaks, with their last year's leaves lingering, 'like unloved guests,' in vain attempted to give animation to the landscape. The sweetest southwest wind was blowing, but it did not make the heavens very blue, and was not enough for me, who wanted something to look at, and had not vital energy enough to be made happy through the pores of my skin. I was returning homeward quite comfortless and ill-paid for my time and trouble, when I suddenly came upon just what I wanted. It was a little shallow pool of the clearest amber. The afore-mentioned southwest was at work to some purpose, breaking it into exquisite wavelets, which flashed a myriad of diamonds up at each instant.

"Why is it that the sight of water stirs and fills the mind so much more than that of any other thing in nature? — why? Is it that here we see the most *subtle force* combined with the most *winning gentleness,* or the most *impetuous force* with the most *irresistible subtlety?*

" I used to love, at Trenton, to go to that place where the water seemed collecting its energies so quietly, glid-ing on so stealthily, you could scarcely believe it was firmly resolved to display such vehemence in one more moment of time and rood of space.

" I love the force of water much, but its subtlety is magic in its effects. Perfectly do I comprehend what I have heard of gazers on a river-side being tempted to drown themselves by sight of the water, and all those tales of mermaid enchantments which embody this feel-ing. This morning I felt a sort of timidity about stand-ing quite at that point to which the undulatory motions (of all earthly things most lovely) seemed to tend. I felt that, unless I had an arm of flesh and blood to cling to, I should be too much seduced from humanity.

" These undulations I have seen compared in poesy to the heaving of the bosom, and they do create a sim-ilar feeling, — at least, I, when I see this in the human frame, am tempted to draw near with a vague, instinct-ive anticipation (as far as ever I could analyze the emo-tion) that a heart will leap forth, and I be able to take it in my hand.

" I dislike the comparison, as I always do illustrating so-called inanimate nature by man or any shape of an-imal life. Byron's comparisons of a mountain splendor to the ' light of a dark eye in woman,' the cataract to a tiger's leap, etc., displease my taste. Why, again ? I am not sure whether it is because man seems more than nature, or whether less, and that the whole is injured in illustrating it by a part, or whether it is that one hates to be forced back upon personalities when one is getting calmed by meditations on the elemental manifestations. Yet, though these comparisons displease my taste, they

throw a light on the sympathies between the human
mind and nature. I feel as if I should some time attain
a precise notion of the meaning of Nature's most beautiful display, the *undulatory motion.*" [1]

Margaret Fuller made great sacrifices for her
own household while living in Groton; and showed
a self-devotion that undoubtedly told severely on
her health. She not only had the courage to do
this, but the courage to let it be known by those
for whom it was done, when it was best that they
should know it. Feminine self-sacrifice is a very
common fruit on every soil, and certainly on that
of New England; but it often spoils its object by
leading to selfishness and then dying unrevealed,
— all from a mistaken sense of duty. To make
this devotion, by revealing it, a means of elevating
the person for whom it is made, — this is a far
rarer thing, and requires absolute frankness and a
wholly generous heart. To stimulate the brother
to do the work which the sister for his sake left
undone is to extract the very finest aroma of gratitude. He to whom the following letter was addressed — the Rev. Arthur Fuller — did not adopt
that literary career to which his sister would fain
have led him; but his was a life of unwearied
labor and great practical usefulness; and when,
after the resignation of his army chaplaincy, he
took a musket from the hands of a wounded soldier, saying, "I must do something for my country," and went forward to his death at the battle

[1] MS.

of Fredericksburg, he showed that his sister's influence had not been exerted in vain.

"You express gratitude for what I have taught you. It is in your power to repay me a hundred-fold, by making every exertion now to improve. I did not teach you as I would; yet I think the confinement and care I took of you children, at a time when my mind was so excited by many painful feelings, have had a very bad effect upon my health. I do not say this to pain you, or to make you more grateful to me (for, probably, if I had been aware at the time what I was doing, I might not have sacrificed myself so); but I say it that you may feel it your duty to fill my place, and do what I may never be permitted to do. Three precious years, at the best period of my life, I gave all my best hours to you children; let me not see you idle away time, which I have always valued so much; let me not find you unworthy of the love I felt for you. Those three years would have enabled me to make great attainments, which now I never may. Do you make them in my stead, that I may not remember that time with sadness."[1]

In another letter to her younger brother, Richard, four years later, she thus sums up their life at Groton, and pictures the position of the household after the father's death.

"Father's removal there was ill-judged, at least as regarded himself, your mother, and myself. The younger ones were not violently rent from all their former life and cast on toils for which they were unprepared. There your mother's health was injured and mine de-

[1] Fuller MSS. i. 623.

stroyed; there your father died, but not till the cares of
a narrowed income, and collision with his elder sons,
which would not have ended there, had so embittered
his life and made him so over anxious, that I have
never regretted that he did not stay longer to watch the
turning of the tide : for his life up to 1830 had been
one of well-earned prosperity, which, after that time,
was rapidly ebbing from him, and I do not think ad-
versity would have done him good; he could not recon-
cile himself to it; his feeling was that after thirty years'
labor and self-denial he was entitled to peace, and he
would not have had it.

"You were too young to feel how trying are the
disorders of a house which has lost its head, the miserable perplexities which were in our affairs, the wounds
your mother underwent in that time of deep dejection
from the unfeeling and insolent conduct of many who
had been kept in check by respect for your father, her
loneliness and sense of unfitness for the new and heavy
burden of care. It will be many years yet before you
can appreciate the conflicts of my mind, as I doubted
whether to give up all which my heart desired for a
path for which I had no skill, and no call, except that
some one must tread it, and none else was ready. The
Peterborough hills and the Wachusetts are associated
in my mind with many hours of anguish, as great, I
think, as I am capable of feeling. I used to look at
them, towering to the sky, and feel that I, too, from my
birth had longed to rise, but I felt crushed to earth; yet
again a nobler spirit said *that* could never be ; the good
knight may come forth scarred and maimed from the
unequal contest, shorn of his strength and unsightly to
the careless eye, but the same fire burns within and

deeper than ever, and he may be conquered, but *never subdued.*

"But if these beautiful hills, and wide, rich fields saw this sad lore well learned, they also saw some precious lessons given too, of faith, of fortitude, of self-command, and of less selfish love. There, too, in solitude, heart and mind acquired more power of concentration, and discerned the beauty of a stricter method. There the heart was awakened to sympathize with the ignorant, to pity the vulgar, and hope for the seemingly worthless ; for a need was felt of realizing the only reality, the divine soul of this visible creation, which cannot err and will not sleep, which cannot permit evil to be permanent or its aim of beauty to be eventually frustrated in the smallest particular." [1]

Before these last letters were written, she had left Groton, for a time, and had entered on the life of a teacher, first in Boston and then in Providence.

[1] Fuller MSS. ii. 721.

V.

FINDING A FRIEND.

THE personal influence of Ralph Waldo Emerson was so marked, during Miss Fuller's early career, that a separate chapter may well be devoted to delineating it. The first trace of him that I have found among her voluminous papers is this from one of her lively and girlish letters to Mrs. Barlow, dated October 6, 1834. She describes an interview with the Rev. Dr. Dewey, who was, with herself, a guest at Mrs. Farrar's in Cambridge, and adds: —

" He spoke with admiration of the Rev. W. Emerson, that only clergyman of all possible clergymen who eludes my acquaintance. But *n'importe!* I keep his image bright in my mind." [1]

Again, she writes to another correspondent about the same time: —

" I cannot care much for *preached* elevation of sentiment unless I have seen it borne out by some *proof*, as in case of Mr. Emerson. It is so easy for a cultivated mind to excite itself with that tone !" [2]

More than a month later she writes to the Rev. F. H. Hedge, from Groton (November 30, 1834).

[1] Fuller MSS. i. 17.   [2] Fuller MSS. iii. 281.

"With regard to Mr. Emerson, I had two reasons, if they may deserve to be so called, for wishing him to see my 'Tasso' [translated from Goethe]. It gratified me that a mind which had affected mine so powerfully should be dwelling on something of mine, even though 't were only some new dress for the thoughts of another. And I thought he might express something which would be useful to me. I should like very much his correction as well as yours, if it be not too much trouble." [1]

This clearly shows how powerfully Emerson was already influencing other minds while he was still a clergyman, and had not printed a word that is now included in his writings.

Before this, according to Mr. Emerson's own statement, he had heard Margaret Fuller praised by Dr. Hedge; and he thinks, but is not quite sure, that he first met her at Mrs. Farrar's in 1835.[2] In July, 1836, she visited him in Concord. He has left a record, in one of the most graphic passages contributed by him to her "Memoirs," of impressions received from her at this first visit. I am glad to be able to place beside this a companion picture of her, during a subsequent visit — in a letter written by that gifted and high-minded woman, Elizabeth Hoar, of Concord, sister of the judge and the senator of that family, and one of the most intimate personal friends of Mr. Emerson. Miss Hoar had been betrothed to Charles Emerson at the time of his early death, and lived all her subsequent life in the close vicinity of his

[1] MS.   [2] *Memoirs,* i. 201.

more eminent brother, to whom she was as a younger sister. Being a constant visitor at his house, she was at times brought closely in contact with Margaret Fuller, of whom she thus records her judgment in a letter addressed to her friend, Miss H. L. Chappell, of Southington, Conn.

" CONCORD, *April* 3, 1839.

" MY DEAR HANNAH, — Both your letters found me at Mr. Emerson's, but I waited until I came home, to answer them. Miss Fuller has been there for a week past, and I have not yet learned the art of self-regulation so far as to be able to do anything when she is near. I see so few people who are anything but pictures or furniture, to me, that the stimulus of such a person is great and overpowering for the time. And indeed, if I saw all the people whom I think of as desirable, and if I *could* help myself, I do not think I should abate any of my interest in her. Her wit, her insight into characters, — such that she seems to read them aloud to you as if they were printed books, her wide range of thought and cultivation, — the rapidity with which she appropriates all knowledge, joined with habits of severe mental discipline (so rare in women, and in literary men not technically ' men of science') ; her passionate love of all beauty, her sympathy with all noble effort; then her energy of character and the regal manner in which she takes possession of society wherever she is, and creates her own circumstances ; all these things keep me full of admiration — not astonished, but pleased admiration — and, as genius does always (*vide* R. W. E. on ' Genius'), inspire me with new life, new confidence in my own power, new desires to fulfill 'the possible' in myself. You would, perhaps, have an impression of levity, of want of tenderness, from her *superficial* manner. The mean hindrances of life, the mistakes, the tedium, which eat into your soul, and will take no form to you but the tragic, she takes up with her defying wit and sets them down in comic groups and they cease to be 'respectabilities.' You feel at first as if this included ridicule or disregard of the sufferings they bring to you; but not so. Her heart is helpfully sympathizing with all striving souls. And she has overcome so much extreme physical and mental pain, and such disappointments of external fortune, that she has a right to play as she will with these arrows of fate. She is a high-minded and generous servant of Duty, and a Christian (not a *traditional* Christian, not made one by *authority*) in her idea of life. But this is all catalogue; you cannot write down Genius, and I write it more because I am thinking about her than from any hope of doing her justice. Only her presence can give you the meaning of the name Margaret Fuller, and this not once or twice, but as various occasions bring out the many sides. And her power of bringing out Mr. Emerson has doubled my enjoyment of that blessing to be in one house and room with him." [1]

In a fragment of diary, without date, all too short, preserved among the Fuller papers, we have a glimpse at these Concord interviews; but not at the very outset; rather, after time had mellowed the companionship and made it less exciting, but more wholly unconscious. In describ-

[1] MS.

ing a long walk by Walden Pond, Margaret Fuller says of Mr. Emerson, " He is a much better companion than formerly, — for once he would talk obstinately through the walk, but now we can be silent and see things together." [1]

In another place she gives this striking glimpse of his personal appearance: "It was raining hard and quite cold — he had on his blue cloak, falling in large straight folds ; in that he looks as if he had come to his immortality as a statue." [2]

Elsewhere she describes him as reading to her passages of his poetry, and quotes some lines which I am unable to identify, while others appear in the appendix to the edition just published : —

" Waldo and I have good meetings, though we stop at all our old places. But my expectations are moderate now ; it is his beautiful presence that I prize, far more than our intercourse. He has been reading me his new poems and the others. At the end he asked me how I liked the ' little subjective twinkle all through.' He has indeed set off the picture lively.

> ' Lonely he sat, the men were strange,
>   The women all forbidden.'

And,

> ' Merge me in the brute universe
>   Or lift to some diviner dream.'

And,

> ' His loves were sharp, sharp pains.'

And,

> ' Content with gods or fools to live.'

> ' In the resolves of [fate ?] I acquiesce.'

> ' Gentle Saadi, mind thy rhyme.'

[1] Fuller MSS. iii. 165.   [2] Fuller MSS. iii. 183.

" And that he will no more plague himself with the mysteries of another sphere from his." [1]

Her visits to Concord not only established intimacy with Mr. Emerson, but with all the members of his family. She writes to her mother, during her first visit, " The baby here is beautiful. . . . I play with him a good deal and he comes so *natural* after Dante and other poems." [2] The cordial gayety of all her interchange of messages in her letters to the Concord household shows clearly the friendliness of her relations with all. " Good love to Mrs. Emerson: I hope the baby has not grown too large for me to hold." Then in another letter, " What does Waldo say? and what has Ellen learnt?" and again, "Say to little Waldo that I have thought since I came away of a hundred witty things I forgot to say to him, and he must want to see me again." In her diary she has much to say of this remarkable child, who will always have an interest for all lovers of poetry as having occasioned Emerson's " Threnody."

It has been my privilege to examine a long series of unpublished letters that passed thenceforward from Margaret Fuller to Emerson. Franker and truer letters never went from woman to man; they were written under all circumstances and from all places; in one case from his own library, while he was away. How much Mr. Emerson valued them is plain from the fact that in some cases where a letter is missing there is substituted

[1] Fuller MSS. iii. 175, 176.   [2] Fuller MSS. i. 83.

a copy in his handwriting. All are indorsed by
him in his systematic way, with date and theme,
and at first with the name "Miss S. M. Fuller;"
then the more familiar "Margaret Fuller" takes
its place. She in turn, beginning with remote
and reverential phrases, grows gradually more intimate. In the first letter I have seen (September, 1836), she writes meekly from Boston, "My
dear friend, — I may venture to say so, since you
have subscribed yourself my friend," — but in a
year or two it becomes "Dear Waldo," at least.
In this first letter there is a phrase which shows
the honest beginning of their friendship: "While
I was with you," she says, "you very justly corrected me for using too strong expressions on
some subject. But there is no exaggeration in
saying — I must be allowed to say — that I *de-
test* Mr. Robinson at this time," — he being her
Groton pastor who had twice invited Mr. Emerson
to preach there while she was away from home.
In this same letter she speaks of "Nature," then
just published, which he had sent her, and which
she and Miss Anna Barker had also mutually presented to each other. To "show Anna to Mr.
Emerson" was just then one of her strong desires.

Soon the borrowing of books becomes a constant theme. On April 11, 1837, she returns him
Goethe's letters to Merck and the first two volumes of those to Zelter, and writes, "I look to Concord as my Lethe and Eunoë after this purgatory
of distracting petty tasks. I am sure you will

purify and strengthen me to enter the Paradise of
thought once more." In addressing Mrs. Emerson she sends " dear love to the sainted Lidian,"
— who becomes simply Lidian in later messages.
" Mrs. Emerson does not love me," she says in
one place, " more than I love her."

On May 30, 1837, she returns to Emerson, Coleridge's "Literary Remains," which she has " ran-
sacked pretty thoroughly," and " The Friend,"
with which she " should never have done ; " also
a volume of Goethe and one of Scougal, and she
asks him on the outside of the note what these
two worthies will be likely to say to one another
" as they journey side by side." She begs to
keep for summer two volumes of Milton, two of
Degerando, the seventh and eighth of Goethe's
"Nachgelassene Werke," besides one volume of
Jonson and one of Plutarch's " Morals." She
also subscribes for two copies of Carlyle's " Miscellanies." Later she writes (November 25, 1839)
to ask him " What is the ' Harleyan (*sic*) Miscel-
lany ' ? — an account of a library ? " and says, " I
thought to send Tennyson next time, but I cannot part with him, it must be for next pacquet
(*sic*). I have been reading Milnes ; he is rich in
fine thoughts but not in fine poetry."

One of the best passages in these letters of Margaret Fuller, a passage that has in it a flavor of
Browning's imaginative wealth, is a little sketch
by her of the melancholy position of a queen who
has borne no heir to the throne. It is only by

way of prelude to a playful condolence with **Mr.**
Emerson, followed by a very frank criticism : —

" November, 1843.

. . . " I always thought the saddest position in the
world must be that of some regal dame to whom husband, court, kingdom, world look in vain for an heir!
She is only supposed to eat, breathe, move, think, nay!
love, for this ; the book of her life is only perused for the
sake of its appendix. Meanwhile, she, perhaps, persists
in living on, as if her life by itself were of any consequence, is the mother of no prince, or has even the impertinence to incumber the kingdom with a parcel of
princesses, girls who must be ' weel-tochered ' to make
them of any value.

" But what is this pathos compared to that perceptible in the situation of a Jove, under the masculine obligations of all-sufficingness, who rubs his forehead in
vain to induce the Minerva-bearing headache! Alas!
his brain remains tranquil, his fancy daughterless !
Nature keeps on feeding him and putting him to sleep
as if she thought the oak was of consequence, whether
it bear the mistletoe or not!

" Heaven help thee, my Druid! if this blessed, brood-
ing, rainy day do not. It is a fine day for composition,
were it not in Concord. But I trow the fates which
gave this place Concord, took away the animating influences of Discord. Life here slumbers and steals on
like the river. A very good place for a sage, but not
for the lyrist or the orator.

" Gentle river,
Stealing on so slowly ever,
From reeds that grow thy bank along
Easy would flow the pastoral song.

> " But the shell
> Which may be strong for lyric swell
> Or trumpet spire for oratory,
> Seek these mid the tritons hoary,
> Where an incalculable wave
> Wrecks the war-ship tall and brave,
> Rushes up a mile-long strand,
> Hails the stars and spurns the land,
> Pushes back the noblest river
> Seeking in vain its love forever,
> There mightst thou find a shell
> Fit to be strung for strains of Delphian swell." [1]

Margaret Fuller's verses are not commonly quite worth preserving, though no one could think so ill of them as did she herself. But these which I have just quoted have in them some of those "lyric glimpses" that Emerson praised in her; the "incalculable wave" and "mile-long strand" are terse and poetic; and the suggestion that Emerson may have lost, as well as gained, by a life-long residence among scenes so soothing, — this is something of value, and perhaps no one else ventured to speak so frankly to the great leader of thought as did this feminine disciple. Nor can I remember to have seen elsewhere so much as a hint that the world might have been the better had some great combination of events wrenched him for a time from that ideal chimney-corner in Concord. Here one may easily differ from her; nevertheless, her suggestion is worth preserving.

At any rate, this was the tone and temper of her intercourse with the closest and most eminent

[1] MS.

of her friends.   Many other friendships she had, which are commemorated in the pages of her published " Memoirs," and which, indeed, produced the book.   Moreover, she had half a dozen friendships with women for every one she maintained with men, and yet made it a matter of conscience to keep all these intimacies apart from one another. She writes once to Emerson (July 5, 1840) : " Do not think, because persons are intimate with me, that they know this or any of my other friends' secrets : I know how to keep relations." [1]   What was her ideal of such a tie may be seen from this passage, written to one of those nearest to her in sympathy, and dissenting both from his and from Emerson's definitions of friendship : —

"July, 1841.

" The more I think of it, the more deeply do I feel the imperfection of your view of friendship, which is the same Waldo E. takes in that letter on Charles's death.   It is very noble, but not enough for our manifold nature.   Our friends should be our incentives to Right, but not only our guiding, but our prophetic stars. To love by right is much, to love by faith is more ; both are the entire love, without which heart, mind, and soul cannot be alike satisfied.   We love and ought to love one another not merely for the absolute worth of each, but on account of a mutual fitness of temporary character.   We are not merely one another's priests or gods, but ministering angels, exercising in the part the same function as the Great Soul in the whole, of seeing the perfect through the imperfect, nay, making it come

[1] MS.

there. Why am I to love any friend the less for any
obstruction in his life? Is not the very time for me to
love most tenderly when I must see his life in despite
of seeming; when he *shows it me* I can only admire : I
do not *give* myself. I am *taken captive.* How shall I
express my meaning? Perhaps I can do so from the
tales of chivalry, where I find what corresponds far
more thoroughly with my nature than in these stoical
statements. The friend of Amadis expects to hear prod-
igies of valor of the absent preux [chevalier]; but if
he be mutilated in one of his first battles, shall he be
mistrusted by the brother of his soul more than if he
had been tested in a hundred? If Britomart finds Ar-
tegall bound in the enchanter's spell, can she doubt,
therefore, him whom she has seen in the magic glass?
A Britomart does battle in his cause, and frees him from
the evil power; a dame of less nobleness sits and watches
the enchanted sleep, weeping night and day, or spurs
away on her white palfrey to find some one more help-
ful than herself. But they are always faithful through
the dark hours to the bright. The Douglas motto,
'Tender and true,' seems to me the worthiest of the
strongest breast. To borrow again from your Spenser,
I am entirely suited with the fate of the three brothers,
Diamond and the rest. I could not die while there was
yet life in my brother's breast. I would return from
the shades and nerve him with twofold life for the fight.
I could do it, for our hearts beat with one blood. Do you
not see the truth and happiness of this waiting tenderness? The verse,

> ' Have I a lover
>   Who is noble and free,
> I would he were nobler
>   Than to love me.'

does not quite come home to me, though *this* does, —

> ' I could not love thee, sweet,[1] so much,
> Loved I not honor more.' . . .

"Do not, I implore you, whether from pride or affection, wish to exile me from the dark hour. The manly mind might love best in the triumphant hour; but the woman could no more stay from the foot of the cross than from the transfiguration." [2]

[1] Thus in the MS.   [2] MS. (W. H. C.)

VI.

SCHOOL-TEACHING IN BOSTON AND PROVIDENCE.

(1837–1838.)

FOR a young American woman who wishes to support herself and educate her younger brothers and sisters, the natural refuge is still the desk of a school-teacher. In Margaret Fuller's time this was even more true than now. After her father's death she must seek a shorter path to self-support than was to be found in those alluring ways of literature and philosophy which she would have much preferred. An opening offered itself in the school of Mr. A. B. Alcott, in Boston, where Miss Elizabeth P. Peabody had been previously employed. Mr. Alcott's unpublished diary gives the successive steps in the negotiation and enables me to present the beginning and the end together.

" 1836, August 2d. Emerson called this morning and took me to Concord to pass the day. At his house I met Margaret Fuller (I had seen her once before this), and had some conversation with her about taking Miss Peabody's place in my school."

" December 17th. I have seen M. F., who, besides giving instruction in the languages, will report 'the Conversations on the Gospels' as they proceed."

"1837, January 8th. I resume the Conversations, which have been suspended since last July. Subject, 'The Sermon on the Mount,' for a beginning. Miss F. reports them; if she succeeds in seizing their form and spirit, we may add a third to the two published volumes."

"1837, 12th January. This evening with M. F. Clearly a person given to the boldest speculations, and of liberal and varied acquirements. Not wanting in imaginary power, she strikes me as having the rarest good sense and discretion: — qualities so essential to success in any sphere, and especially to a woman ambitious of literary distinction, and relying solely on native work. She adopts the spiritual philosophy, and has the subtlest perceptions of its necessities and bearings."

"February 8th. Miss F. succeeds, after some trial, in reporting the Conversations."

"March 17th. An agreeable hour with M. F., in whose sympathy and insight I find great content. She takes large and generous views of things, and her dispositions are singularly catholic and liberal. She has great skill in discourse, too: few converse with the like freedom and elegance. I am pleased to learn of the interest taken in her behalf by persons here in our city whose favor is a passport to success. To her has been given with the gift of intellect that of prudence, and when these are united in one person, success must follow in their train."

"April. Miss Fuller left town this week for Groton, where she intends passing a few weeks, for recruiting her health to enter the Green Street School at Providence. Here, during the last winter, she has been engaged in teaching the French, German, and Italian languages to private classes, also Latin and French in my school." [1]

Her connection with Mr. Alcott's school, like the school itself, was destined to be short-lived. Mr. Alcott's characteristic methods of dealing with children through minute questioning, joined with some peculiar theories as to punishment, called out an amount of indignation which, at this distance of time, appears almost incredible. The little volume called " Record of a School," followed by the two volumes called " Conversations on the Gospels," roused this wrath to the highest point. The books and the school were bitterly denounced by the " Daily Advertiser " and " Courier," the latter seriously urging that Mr. Alcott should be prosecuted for blasphemy, as Abner Kneeland had lately been. To this Mr. R. W. Emerson wrote an indignant reply, asserting that Mr. Alcott's only offense lay in his efforts to "make children think," and that his experiment was one in which all the friends of education were interested. The editor of the " Courier, " Mr. J. T. Buckingham, rejoined by quoting the opinion of a Harvard professsor that " one third of Mr. Alcott's book was absurd, one third was blasphemous, and one third was obscene." [2]

Such was the hornet's nest into which Margaret Fuller had unwarily plunged herself by following the very mildest-mannered saint who ever tried

[1] MS. by Mr. Alcott.
[2] *Biographical Sketch of A. B. Alcott*, p. 15.

his hand at the spiritual training of children.
With what discrimination she viewed the whole
affair — how well she saw defects on the practical
side as well as moral excellence, is shown clearly
in this letter, addressed to one of her most cultivated friends.

"BOSTON, *6th April,* 1837.

. . . " Why is it that I hear you are writing a piece
to ' cut up ' Mr. Alcott. I do not believe you are going
to cut up Mr. Alcott. There are plenty of fish in the
net created solely for markets, etc. ; — no need to try
your knife on a dolphin like him. I should be charmed
if I thought you were writing a long, beautiful, wise-like
article, showing the elevated air, and at the same time
the practical defects of his system. You would do a
great service to him as well as to the public, and I know
no one so well qualified as yourself to act as a mediator
between the two, and set both sides of the question in
a proper light. But the phrase ' cutting up ' alarms
me. If you were here I am sure that you would feel
as I do, and that your wit would never lend its patronage to the ugly blinking owls, who are now hooting
from their snug tenements, overgrown rather with net-
tles than with ivy, at this star of purest ray serene.
But you are not here, more 's the pity, and perhaps do
not know exactly what you are doing ; do write to me
and reassure me." [1]

But whether the newspapers were right or
wrong, their criticisms killed the school. Mr. Alcott's receipts, which during the previous year
had been $1,395, sank to $549 during the year

[1] MS.

after the attack ; the forty pupils dwindled to ten, and in April, 1837, the school furniture and apparatus were sold, and the assistant necessarily discharged. The school itself lingered for two years more, until fresh wrath was kindled by the admission of a colored child ; there was another withdrawal of pupils, leaving Mr. Alcott with nobody to teach but his own three daughters, the colored child, and one undismayed white pupil. "I earn little or nothing in this miserable school," he writes in his unpublished diary, April 23, 1839, "nor am I laboring towards any prospective good in it." During the same month (April 11), in a summary of his small income — for a period not stated — he credits the parents of his pupils with thirty dollars.[1] The school closed finally in June or July, 1839, and left its projector free to adopt his favorite conversational methods of urging his thought, — methods with which he has been identified for forty years. This is not the place to discuss the merits or demerits of his theories of teaching, but the final close of his experiment certainly did him no discredit ; he went down with his flag still flying.

The school in which Margaret Fuller was to teach at Providence was the Green Street Academy, founded by Colonel Hiram Fuller, a gentleman in no way her relative. He was a person of some force of character and a good deal of ambition, who perhaps showed both qualities in inviting

---

[1] Alcott's MS. Diary, vol. xii.

Miss Fuller to be his assistant. She wrote of him
to Miss Peabody : "Mr. Fuller is as unlike as
possible to Mr. Alcott. He has neither his poetic
beauty nor his practical defects." [1] His offer to
her, as stated in Mr. Alcott's diary, was a liberal
one for those days, and I am assured by Miss Jacobs, who followed Miss Fuller in the school, that
the thousand dollars were undoubtedly paid, though
Horace Greeley, in his " Recollections," states the
contrary. Mr. Fuller taught the school for a few
years only, then went to New York and became
connected with the New York "Mirror," edited
by N. P. Willis and George P. Morris. This he
abandoned after a time, " being tired," as he said,
" of supporting two poets," and was afterwards
editor of the London " Cosmopolitan." In addition to his bold choice of an assistant, he invoked
the rising *prestige* of Ralph Waldo Emerson, inviting him to give an address at the dedication
of the Academy (Saturday, June 10, 1837), and
suggesting to him, he being still in the ministry,
to bring sermons and preach in the two Unitarian
churches.

Margaret Fuller was ill for a time after reach-
ing Providence, and wrote to Mr. Emerson in June,
1837 : "Concord, dear Concord, haven of repose,
where headache, vertigo, other sins that flesh is heir
to, cannot long continue." After this came a period of unusual health, during which she wrote in
great exhilaration to her friends. To Miss Pea-

[1] MS.

body, for instance (July 8, 1837), she exulted in
the "glow of returning health," and then gave
this account of the school : —

"As to the school, . . . I believe I do very well
there. I am in it four hours every morning, five days
in the week ; thus you see I can have much time, notwithstanding many casual interruptions. All Saturday
and Sunday to myself. I rise so early that I often get
an hour and a half before breakfast, besides two or three
hours in the afternoon on school days. This is quite
enough for health, and the time is good time, for the
school rarely tires me at all. I feel so perfectly equal
to all I do there, without any effort ; my pupils, although miserably prepared, are very docile, their hearts
are right, and I already perceive that I am producing
some effect on their heads. My plan grows quietly and
easily in my mind ; this experience here will be useful
to me, if not to Providence, for I am bringing my opinions to the test, and thus far have reason to be satis ·
fied." [1]

Her mode of life in Providence, during this
period, she described in letters to her younger
brother. She lived methodically, as she usually
did ; almost always rose at five, — it was in summer, — and sometimes at half-past four ; it took
her till six to dress ; she studied till half-past seven,
the breakfast hour; school lasted from half-past
eight to half-past twelve ; she got home at one,
dined at half-past one ; lay down till three ; then
wrote or studied till tea-time, probably at six ; in
the evening, walked or made calls till ten; this

[1] MS.

was her day.[1] Her task as to mere instruction
was not difficult, and her letters everywhere show
her to have had that natural love of children so
essential to the teacher. She never leaves a house
but some gay message, sent back to the youngest
members, shows unerringly that they, at least,
cannot have complained of her as haughty or supercilious.

A lady who was, when a child, a housemate of
Margaret Fuller while in Providence, has lately
told me an anecdote which thoroughly illustrates
the noble and truthful way in which she habitually dealt with children. My informant, who was
then a little girl, says that there were beautiful
books and other curiosities upon Miss Fuller's
table, and that the children in the house were allowed to see them sometimes, on condition that
they would not touch them. One day, in Miss
Fuller's absence, a young visitor came, and insist-
ing on taking down a microscope, despite the little
girl's remonstrances, dropped and broke it. My
informant was found in an agony of tears amidst
the wreck ; all her protestations of innocence were
unheeded, and she was shut up as a prisoner, not
merely for disobedience, but for falsehood. No
one would even listen to her story, the circum-
stantial evidence seemed so overwhelming. Miss
Fuller returned, and was told the incident ; she
came instantly to the room and took the weeping
child upon her knee. " Now, my dear little girl,"

[1] Fuller MSS. i. 619.

she said, "tell me all about it, only remember that
you must be careful, for I shall believe every word
you say." Thus encouraged, the innocent tale
was told ; investigation followed, and complete
acquittal. My informant, herself to this day an
eminently successful teacher, told me that she then
learned the life-long lesson of treating children
with a noble confidence.

It is impossible for a teacher to write about
teaching without disclosing her own theories and
revealing her own experience. The year after
Margaret Fuller left Providence, we find her
writing to her brother Arthur, then teaching a
district school in Massachusetts ; and never had
young teacher a better counselor. She tells him,
for instance (December 20, 1840), —

> "The most important rule is, in all relations with our
> fellow-creatures, never forget that if they are imperfect
> persons they are immortal souls ; and treat them as you
> would wish to be treated by the light of that thought."

> "Beware of over-great pleasure in being popular or
> even beloved. As far as an amiable disposition and
> powers of entertainment make you so, it is a happiness,
> but if there is one grain of plausibility, it is a poison."

This last maxim seems to me simply admirable ; and she has an equally good passage in
which she warns him against flattery, which, as
she keenly points out, is even more injurious to
children than to grown people. She adds : —

> "For to the child, the parent or teacher is the repre-
> sentative of justice, and as that [*i. e.*, the justice] of life

is severe, an education which in any way excites vanity is the very worst preparation for that general and crowded school." [1]

It would be easy to transcribe many more of these admirable aphorisms, which prove as clearly as if one had seen her in school, that she who wrote them had rare gifts for the work of education. With all this, I do not suppose that Margaret Fuller was a perfect teacher; her health was variable, and her heart was set on something else; she did not accept this as her life-work. The teacher who followed her has told me that she was worshiped by the girls as in her earlier school-days, but was sometimes too sarcastic for the boys; and yet they certainly gave every evidence of attachment when she left them. Outside the school, too, her personal qualities or her exceptional attainments brought on her some of those criticisms from which educated men are not exempt, and which are quite sure to visit highly-educated women. One lady said to her successor, Miss Jacobs, soon after her arrival at the school: " Miss Fuller says she *thinks* in German ; do you believe it ? " It was a discourteous question to a new-comer, who would naturally wish to keep clear of the feuds and the claims of her predecessor; but fortunately Miss Jacobs had ready tact, if Miss Fuller had not. " Oh, yes ! " she said, " I do not doubt it; I myself dream in Cherokee; " which left her assailant discomfited.

[2] Fuller MSS. i. 643–645.

James Freeman Clarke has lately said in a sermon that he once went to see Margaret Fuller when she had been teaching in Providence for a year or two. She showed him two packages of letters which she had received from her pupils. "These letters," said she, "if you should read them, would show you the work I have been doing for my scholars. The first package contains the letters which they usually write to me after they have been in the school two or three months. They say, 'O Miss Fuller, we did not know, till we came to you, how ignorant we were. We seem to know nothing at all, and not to be able to learn anything. We might as well stop, and give up. We are sure we shall never be able to study to any purpose.' This package of letters," said their teacher, "I have labeled, *Under conviction.*"

"This other package," she continued, "holds the letters they write some time afterward. In these they say, 'We owe you ever so much for showing us how we can become something better. We are still very stupid, but we now feel as if we were in the right way, and were making some progress. Pray help us to do more and better. You have given us courage, and taught us how to go forward!' This package," said she, "I label, *Obtained a hope.*"

She went for occasional brief visits from Providence to Boston, and it may be well to insert a passage from one of her letters to Mr. Emerson, in which she gives a glimpse of the gay world of that city forty-seven years ago. The picture of Daniel Webster and Theodore Parker moving among the *jeunesse dorée* in a ball-room seems like one of the far-fetched improbabilities of an historical novel. The " Gigman " allusion is to Carlyle's afterwards hackneyed phrase about the respectability that keeps a gig. It is possible that the entertainment may have occurred just before her actual removal to Providence.

. . . " Last night I took my boldest peep into the 'Gigman' world of Boston. I have not been to a large party before, and only seen said world in half-boots ; so I thought, as it was an occasion in which I felt real interest, to wit, a fête given by Mrs. Thorndike for my beautiful Susan, I would look at it for once in satin slippers. Dr. Channing meant to go, but was too weary when the hour came. I spent the early part of the evening in reading bits of Dante with him, and talking about the material sublime till half-past nine, when I went with Mrs. C. and graceful Mary. It was very pretty to look at. So many fair maidens dressed as if they had stepped out of their grandmothers' picture frames, and youths with their long locks, suitable to represent pages if not nobles. Signor Figaro was there also in propriâ [personâ] *là et là.* And Daniel the Great, not, however, when I saw him, engaged in an operation peculiarly favorable to his style of beauty, to wit, eating oysters. Theodore Parker was there, and introduced to me. I had some pleasant talk with him, but before I could get to Spinoza, somebody seized on me and carried me off to quite another S, — to supper.

On the whole, it all pleased my eye ; my fashionable fellow-creatures were very civil to me, and I went home,
glad to have looked at this slide in the magic lantern
also." [1]

Writing from Providence, August 14, 1837, she
lays plans for her summer vacation, which is to
begin with unmerciful tardiness on August 19.
For her three weeks' vacation she plans to visit,
with her friend Caroline Sturgis, that delicious
land of lotus-eating, Artichoke Mills, on the Merrimack, " there to be silent and enjoy daily wood-
walks or boat excursions with her," — or else to
go to Concord. As to Providence, she writes : —

" I fear I have not much to tell that will amuse you.
With books and pens I have, maugre my best efforts,
been able to do miserably little. If I cannot be differently situated, I *must* leave Providence at the end of
another term. My time here has been full of petty an-
noyances, but I regret none of them, they have so en-
larged my practical knowledge. I now begin really to
feel myself a citizen of the world. My plan lies clearer
before my mind, and I have examined almost all my
materials, but beyond this I have done nothing. I shall,
however, have so soon an opportunity to tell you all
that I will not now take time and paper. I attended
last week, somewhat to the horror of Mr. Fuller, the
Whig Caucus here, and heard Tristam Burges. It is
rather the best thing I have done." [2]

Jefferson's correspondence bearing fruit again !
With that impressed upon her, and her business-
like father in her mind, she shrank from a merely

[1] MS.   [2] MS.

intellectual life, while she yet felt its charms. Her residence in Providence had made her "a citizen of the world," and the "best thing she had done" there was to defy the disapproval of her employer and attend a caucus, — in those days a rare exploit for a woman. We see the same half-conscious impulse toward action manifested in one of her letters to her younger brothers, in which she describes with great fullness a visit to a French man-of-war, the Hercules, which had anchored in Narragansett Bay. She says, incidentally, "I thought I much should like to command such a vessel, despite all the hardships and privations of such a situation."[1] When she wrote, years after, the oft-quoted passage in "Woman in the Nineteenth Century," "Let them be sea-captains, if they will," it may have been with this reminiscence in her mind.

On March 1, 1838, she wrote to Mr. Emerson one of her most characteristic letters. I reproduce it from the manuscript, because it shows what Mr. Emerson was to her, — a saint in her oratory, — and because it puts what was often called, in her case, self-consciousness and vanity, in their clearest light. She was sometimes said to despise her fellow-creatures, and all that passed for contempt in her is frankly uttered here. Yet behind it, if I understand it rightly, is a profound and even self-torturing humility. Always dissatisfied with herself, she finds to her dismay that

---

[1] Fuller MSS. i. 635.

other people share the same condition, or worse.
" I see no divine person ; I myself am more divine
than any one I see. *I think that is enough to
say about them.*" To a lower depth, that is, she
can scarcely assign them than to say that they
seem to be accomplishing even less than she does.
The woman who wrote this was but twenty-seven,
poor, a martyr to ill-health, and with a desperate
hungering of the soul to do her appointed work
in the world, and make full use of the talents
confided to her. When we consider that she was
writing to her father-confessor, in absolute freedom and in an almost fantastic mood of depression, — with her supposed profession of teaching
crumbling beneath her feet, and nothing before
her but an intellectual career, which in a worldly
way was then no career ; her plans uncertain, her
aims thwarted, her destiny a conundrum, — what
man of intellectual pursuits, looking back on the
struggles of his own early years, can throw a stone
at Margaret Fuller ?

"Providence, 1*st March,* 1838.

" My dear Friend, — Many a Zelterian [1] epistle
have I mentally addressed to you, full of sprightly
scraps about the books I have read, the spectacles I
have seen, and the attempts at men and women with
whom I have come in contact. But I have not been
able to put them on paper ; for, even when I have attempted it, you have seemed so busy and noble, and I

[1] A phrase suggested by the correspondence between Goethe
and Zelter, which she had been reading.

so poor and dissipated, that I have not felt worthy to address you.

"At present I am not at all Zelterian in my mood, but very sombre and sullen. I have shut the door for a few days, and tried to do something; you have *really* been doing something. And that is why I write. I want to see you, and still more to hear you. I must kindle my torch again. Why have I not heard you this winter? I feel very humble just now, yet I have to say that being lives not who would have received from your lectures as much as I should. There are noble books, but one wants the breath of life sometimes. And I see no divine person. I myself am more divine than any I see. I think that is enough to say about them. I know Dr. Wayland now, but I shall not care for him. He would never understand me, and, if I met him, it must be by those means of suppression and accommodation which I at present hate to my heart's core. I hate everything that is reasonable just now, 'wise limitations' and all. I have behaved much too well for some time past; it has spoiled my peace. What grieves me, too, is to find or fear my theory a cheat. I cannot serve two masters, and I fear all the hope of being a worldling and a literary existence also must be resigned. Isolation is necessary to me, as to others. Yet I keep on 'fulfilling all my duties,' as the technical phrase is, except to myself. But why do I write thus to you who like nothing but what is good, that is, cheerfulness and fortitude? It is partly because yours is an image of my oratory,[1] and if I do not jest when I write to you, I must *pray*. And partly as a preliminary to asking you,

---

[1] "I suppose you will not know what this means, whether you come or no. Do not disappoint me."

unsympathizing, unhelpful, wise, good man that you
are, to do several things for me. I hear you are to deliver one of your lectures again in Boston. I would
have you do it while I am there. I shall come on
Wednesday next, and stay till the following Monday.
Perhaps you will come to see me, for, though I am
not as good as I was, yet, as I said before, I am better
than most persons *I* see, and, I dare say, better than
most persons *you* see. But perhaps you do not need to
see anybody, for you are acting, and nobly. If so, you
need not come yourself, but send me your two lectures
on ' Holiness' and ' Heroism.' Let me have these two
lectures, at any rate, to read while in Boston."

But her prediction was fulfilled ; if she followed
her literary longings she must leave Providence,
and so she did. Mr. Ripley had suggested to her
to write a life of Goethe, but it ended in a translation of Eckermann's "Conversations" with that
great man, prefaced by one of her "Dial" essays
on the subject and published in Ripley's series of
"Specimens of German Authors," probably without compensation. Her plans and purposes on
retiring from her school are best stated in a letter
to the Rev. W. H. Channing, not before published : —

"PROVIDENCE, 9th *December,* 1838.

"I am on the point of leaving Providence, and I do so
with unfeigned delight, not only because I am weary
and want rest, because my mind has so long been turned
outward and longs for concentration and leisure for
tranquil thought, but because I have here been always
in a false position and my energies been consequently

much repressed. To common observers I seem well placed here, but I know that it is not so, and that I have had more than average difficulties to encounter, some of them insurmountable. But from these difficulties I have learned so much that I cannot but suppose my experience is to be of further use.

"I do not wish to teach again at all. If I consult my own wishes I shall employ the remainder of my life in quite a different manner. But I foresee circumstances that may make it wrong for me to obey my wishes.

"Mother has sold her place at Groton, and as she is to leave it in April, I shall go home and stay three months at least. I dream of Elysian peace, of quiet growth, and other benefits no doubt well-known to your imagination. Then I hope to prevail on her to board with Ellen and me, and send the boys to school for some months. But after that we must find a sure foothold on the earth somewhere and plan anew a home.

"But this leaves me nearly a year for my own inventions. If at the end of that time it should seem necessary for the good of all concerned that I should teach again, I wish to do it, and by the success I have already attained, and by the confidence I now feel in my powers, both of arrangement of a whole and action on parts, feel myself justified in thinking I may do it to much greater pecuniary advantage and with much more extensive good results to others than I have yet done."

A plan suggested by Cincinnati friends for a school in that city came to nothing, and she left Providence for Boston in December, 1838. This was the end of her school-teaching, though she continued to take occasional private pupils in languages and other matters; for whom she was paid, as she wrote to her younger brother, at the rate of two dollars an hour, or, rather, half a dollar for quarter-hour lessons. That winter, however, as she tells him, she is too tired to take them at any price; she must rest; but she will give her younger sister lessons in German, and will teach Latin and composition to himself. This was her idea of resting, and thus she rested at Groton for the remainder of that winter.

VII.

SUBURBAN LIFE AT JAMAICA PLAIN.

(1838-1844.)

In looking forward to leaving the scene of her school-teaching, Margaret Fuller wrote thus to Mrs. Barlow in a moment of headache and nervous exhaustion : —

"November 8, 1838.

"I shall go home about Christmas and stay till April, and never set foot out of doors unless to take exercise ; and see no human face, divine or otherwise, out of my own family. But I am wearied out and I have gabbled and simpered and given my mind to the public view these two years back, till there seems to be no good left in me."[1]

She wrote to Mr. Emerson of the remaining months of that winter, "My sufferings last winter in Groton were almost constant, and I see the journal is very sickly in its tone. I have taken out some leaves. Now I am a perfect Phœnix compared with what I was then, and it all seems past to me."[2]

During this invalid winter, however, she made a brief visit to Boston, where she had three en-

[1] Fuller MSS. i. 22.   [2] MS. letter, November 25, 1839.

joyments, so characteristic as to be worth quoting : —

"7 *January*, 1839.

"Three things were specially noteworthy. First, a talk with Mr. Alcott, in which he appeared to me so great, that I am inclined to think he deserves your praise, and that he deceived neither you nor himself in saying that I had not yet seen him. Beside his usual attitude and closeness to the ideal, he showed range, grasp, power of illustration, and precision of statement such as I never saw in him before. I will begin him again and read by faith awhile.

"There was a book of studies from Salvator Rosa, from the Brimmer donation, at the Athenæum, which I looked over with great delight and got many thoughts for my journal. There was at last an interview with Mr. Allston. He is as beautiful as the town-criers have said, and deserves to be Mr. Dana's Olympus, Lares, and Penates, as he is. He got engaged upon his Art, and flamed up into a galaxy of Platonism. Yet what he said was not as beautiful as his smile of genius in saying it. Unfortunately, I was so fascinated, that I forgot to make myself interesting, and shall not dare to go and see him." [1]

Three months later the family left Groton forever, having taken a house at Jamaica Plain, then and perhaps now the most rural and attractive suburb of Boston. Here their dwelling was near a little stream, called Willow Brook, and there were rocks behind it covered with cardinal flowers. Margaret Fuller had with her two pu-

[1] MS.

pils from Providence; she was within easy reach
of friends, and could at the same time renew that
love of nature which Groton had first taught her,
and which city-life had only suspended. From
this time, many charming outdoor sketches appear among her papers. Inheriting a love of
flowers from her mother, she gave to them mean-
ings and mysticisms of her own. Of her later
" Dial " sketches, " The Magnolia of Lake Pontchartrain " grew, as she writes in one of her unpublished letters, out of the suggestion by some
one that its odor was so exquisite at that spot as
to be unlike any other magnolia; and the " Yucca
Filamentosa " came wholly from a description
given her by Dr. Eustis, in his garden at Brook-
line, of its flowering at full-moon. " If you like
it " (the sketch of the magnolia), — she says to
one of her correspondents, — "I will draw the soul
also from the Yucca and put it into words." [1]

Among her unpublished papers there are several similar flower-pieces; one upon the Passion
Flower, whose petals had just fallen from her
girdle, she says, while all her other flowers remained intact; and with which she connects a
striking delineation of human character, as em-
bodied in some person not now to be identified.
Again she has been hearing in some conversation
a description of the thorn called *Spina Christi*,
which still grows on the plains of Judæa, and this
leads her to a noble winter reverie: —

[1] MS. (W. H. C.)

" January 30, 1841.

" Recipe to prevent the cold of January from utterly destroying life.

"Beneath all pain inflicted by Nature, be not only serene, but more, let it avail thee in prayer. Put up at the moment of greatest suffering a prayer, not for thy own escape, but for the enfranchisement of some being dear to thee, and the sovereign spirit will accept thy ransom.

"My head is very sensitive, and as they described the *Spina Christi* I shuddered all over, and could have fainted only at the thought of its pressure on his head. Yet if he had experienced the sufferings of humanity and believed that by 'thy will be done' — a steady feeling in his breast during these hours of torture from an ungrateful race — he could free them from suffering and sin, I feel how he might have borne it. It seems to me I might be educated through suffering to the same purity.

"Does any man wound thee; not only forgive, but work into thy thought intelligence of the kind of pain, that thou mayst never inflict it on another spirit. When its work is done, it will never search thy whole nature again.

"Oh, love much, and be forgiven." [1]

It will be seen from another letter that she set an especial value on her flower sketches : —

"You often tell me what to do when you are gone; if you survive me, will you not collect my little flower-pieces, even the insignificant ones? I feel as if from mother I had received a connection with the flowers;

[1] MS. (W. H. C.)

7

she has the love, I the interpretation. My writings about them are no fancies, but whispers from themselves. I am deeply taught by the constant presence of any growing thing. This apple-tree before my window I shall mourn to leave. Seeing fruit trees in a garden is entirely another thing from having this one before my eyes constantly, so that I can't help seeing all that happens to it. But I shall write out the history of our acquaintance and give you a copy." [1]

Yet I must confess to liking her out - door sketches even better when they are more wholly descriptive and less imaginative, as with the following : —

"*September* 27 [1840 ?].

"Oh, it is the loveliest morning. After those days of glad light and calm, benign, roseate sunsets, how sweet the 'unutterable love' of such clouds as the west wind has brought; they keep sighing themselves away and letting us see, behind the tenderest blue, the sky of May. The utmost purity with such tenderness ! All the fragrance of farewell is breathing out of the earth. The flowers seem to have grown up express for the day. In the wood where I have been they all thronged the path ; it is a wood where none but me goes, and they can smile secure. I was looking at the clouds and thinking they could not choose but weep, — there was no other way to express such intense tenderness, — when down came such a sun-shower as you describe from Waldo's thoughts, the clouds only looking the sweeter and more sunlit all the time for being able to express themselves. All this music is playing upon me almost too fully ; I have scarcely

[1] MS. (W. H. C.)

force to bear it. Perhaps it will be well when cold winter comes and locks the instrument up. I am living like an angel, and I don't know how to get down. Yet they are waiting all around, leaning on the packs they expect me to lift; they look at me reverently, affectionately; they are patient, yet I see they are waiting." [1]

Then comes the following, in which she extracts quite as much from the wild asters as from yuccas and magnolias: —

" Tuesday [September, 1840 ?].

"I have just returned from a walk this golden autumn morning, with its cloudless sky and champagne air. I found some new wood walks, glades among black pines and hemlocks, openings to the distant hills, graceful in silvery veils. A very peculiar feeling these asters give me, gleaming on every side. They seem my true sisters. They look so refined, so saintly, so melancholy, so generous of their beauty, and the flowers look at me more like eyes than any other. These are good reasons for loving ye, sweet asters, but they do not go to the root of the matter. I feel a really yearning tenderness, a sense of relationship. But the golden-rod is one of the fairy, magical flowers; it grows not up to seek human love amid the light of day, but to mark to the discerning what wealth lies hid in the secret caves of earth. . . . The disgust at unworthy care, the aching sense of how far deeds are transcended by our lowest aspiration, pass away, and for a while I lean on the bosom of nature, and inhale new life with her breath. Could but love, like knowledge, be its own reward; could we look upon the objects of our affection and rejoice in their existence, purely for its own sake, as we do with the ferns

[1] MS. (W. H. C.)

and asters, — but that is contrary to the nature of love; though it be true in one sense, as Schiller says, that he only loves who loves without hope, yet in another it is true that love cannot exist without desire, though it be the desire of the moth for the star." [1]

Sometimes she records rambles with others, and we have here a visit to Mount Auburn, at the period when it still retained its rural beauty: —

"Saturday, ——.

" Ellery [Channing] and I had a good afternoon at Mount Auburn. He was wondering why men had expressed so little of any worth about death. I said I thought they attached too much importance to it. On this subject I always feel that I can speak with some certainty, having been on the verge of bodily dissolution. I felt at that time disengaged from the body, hovering and calm. And in moments of profound thought or feeling, or when, after violent pain in the head, my exhausted body loses power to hem me in, I have felt changes more important than then. I believe that the mere death of the body has no great importance except when it is in no sense accidental, that is, when the mind, by operations native to it, has gradually cast aside its covering, and is ready for a new one. But this is very seldom the case. Persons die generally, not as a natural thing, but from extraneous causes; then it must be a change only one degree more important than going to sleep; for what the mind wants to develop it, it must have, here or elsewhere. A death from love would be perfectly natural.

" Reasons why there are no good monuments? I must write upon this subject. March, 1840." [2]

---

[1] MS.   [2] Fuller MSS. i. 429.

She had fancies, as Mr. Emerson tells us, about days and precious stones and talismans; and in one of her letters I find these reveries about proper names: —

"It pleases that Raphael and Michael Angelo should have received the archangelic names; it seems inspiration in the parents. So that Swedenborg should bear the name of Emanuel, and Kant, too. The name of Beethoven's mother does not seem without meaning. In writing yesterday, I observed the names of Mary and Elizabeth meeting again in the two queens with some pleasure. William is the Conqueror. Perhaps it is from such association that I thought from earliest childhood I could never love one that bore another name; I am glad it was Shakespeare's. Shelley chose it for his child. It is linked with mine in ballad as if they belonged together, but the story is always tragic. In the Douglas tragedy, the beauty is more than the sorrow. In one of the later ones the connection is dismal."[1]

Again, after study of Goethe's "Farbenlehre" (Theory of Colors), she writes, with similar zest:

"*Sunday, February* 21, 1841.

"I have been reading, most of the day, the 'Farbenlehre.' The facts interest me only in their mystical significance. As of the colors demanding one another in the chromatic circle, each demanding its opposite, and the eye making the opposite of that it once possessed. And of nature only giving the tints pure in the inferior natures, subduing and breaking them as she ascends. Of the cochineal making mordants to fix its dye on the

[1] MS. (W. H. C.)

vegetables where it nestles. Of the plants which, though they grow in the dark, only make long shoots, and refuse to seek their flower.

"There was a time when one such fact would have made my day brilliant with thought. But now I seek the divine rather in Love than law." [1]

If even these simpler thoughts show a tendency to link themselves with something a little far-fetched and fantastic, we must remember that this was a period when German romance was just invading us; when Carlyle was translating the fantasy-pieces of Tieck, Hoffmann, and Musæus; and when some young Harvard students spent a summer vacation in rendering into English the mysteries of " Henry of Ofterdingen," by Novalis. Margaret Fuller took her share in this; typified the mysteries of the soul as " Leila," in the " Dial," and wrote verses about herself, under that name, in her diary : —

> " Leila, of all demanding heart
> By each and every left apart ;
> Leila, of all pursuing mind
> From each goal left far behind ;
> Strive on, Leila, to the end,
> Let not thy native courage bend ;
> Strive on, Leila, day by day,
> Though bleeding feet stain all the way ;
> Do men reject thee and despise ? —
> An angel in thy bosom lies
> And to thy death its birth replies." [2]

These were her days of thought and exaltation. Other days were given to society, usually in Bos-

[1] MS. (W. H. C.)   [2] MS. Diary, 1844.

ton, where she sometimes took a room for the winter. Hawthorne, in his " American-Note Books," records, under the date, November, 1840: —

" I was invited to dine at Mr. Bancroft's yesterday with Miss Margaret Fuller; but Providence had given me some business to do, for which I was very thankful." [1]

It must be remembered that Hawthorne was always grateful for any dispensation which saved him from a formal dinner-party. That he enjoyed a conversation with Margaret Fuller personally is plain from an entry in his " American Note-Books," describing an interview between them during one of her visits to Concord: —

" *August* 22, 1842.

. . . " After leaving the book at Mr. Emerson's I returned through the woods, and, entering Sleepy Hollow, I perceived a lady reclining near the path which bends along its verge. It was Margaret herself. She had been there the whole afternoon, meditating or reading; for she had a book in her hand, with some strange title, which I did not understand, and have forgotten. She said that nobody had broken her solitude, and was just giving utterance to a theory that no inhabitant of Concord ever visited Sleepy Hollow, when we saw a group of people entering its sacred precincts. Most of them followed a path which led them away from us; but an old man passed near us and smiled to see Margaret, reclining on the ground, and me sitting by her side. He made some remark about the beauty of the afternoon, and withdrew himself into the shadow of the wood.

[1] *American Note-Books*, i. 221.

Then we talked about autumn, and about the pleasures of being lost in the woods, and about the crows, whose voices Margaret had heard; and about the experiences of early childhood, whose influence remains upon the character after the recollection of them has passed away; and about the sight of mountains from a distance, and the view from their summits; and about other matters of high and low philosophy. In the midst of our talk, we heard footsteps above us, on the high bank; and while the person was still hidden among the trees, he called to Margaret, of whom he had gotten a glimpse. Then he emerged from the green shade, and, behold! it was Mr. Emerson. He appeared to have had a pleasant time; for he said that there were Muses in the woods to-day, and whispers to be heard in the breezes. It being now nearly six o'clock, we separated, — Margaret and Mr. Emerson towards his home, and I towards mine." [1]

Such scenes were but joyful interludes in her life at Jamaica Plain; at other times there were what she calls the "rye-bread days" given to domestic cares and country cousins, as in this description : —

"Saturday. This was one of the rye-bread days, all dull and damp without. I accomplished many trifles, and a little writing within. Cousin —— came to see me; —— came home to stay a fortnight. I passed the evening with the Farrars. Around my path how much humble love has flowed. These every-day friends never forget my heart, never censure me, make no demands on me, load me with gifts and services, and, uncomplaining, see me prefer my intellectual kindred. I

[1] *American Note-Books,* ii. 85.

am ungrateful, as Timon was to his servants. Yet, Heaven be praised, though sometimes forgetful of them in absence, I make it up in presence, so far that I think I do not give pain, as I pass along this world." [1]

Other rye-bread days were spent in writing letters of counsel to her younger brothers, who were, during a portion of this time, away at school. There is the whole range of a New England elder-sister's life in the two following extracts from the same letter to Richard Fuller (May 12, 1842). First, the love of Greek, perhaps flagging, must be stimulated : —

" While here I have been reading (only in translation, alas !) the ' Cyropædia,' and other works of Xenophon, and some dramas of Euripides ; and, were envy ever worth our while, I should deeply envy those who can with convenience gain access to the Greek mind in its proper garb. No possession can be more precious than a knowledge of Greek." [2]

But the boyish wardrobe, a severer problem than even Greek, must be also supervised ; she must even encounter the dawning sensitiveness as to shirt-collars, from which no sister can escape.

" Out of this money I wish you and Arthur both to give your aunt some to buy linen for your shirt-bosoms. No one here understands how you wish them made ; whether you wish to have bosoms and collars sewed on or separate ; and you must each leave with her separate,

[1] MS. Diary.   [2] Fuller MSS. ii. 691.

precise written directions, signed with your separate names, or they will not be done so as to suit you." [1]

Then comes a letter about the use of money itself; — a letter whose clear good sense would have surprised those who fancied her, in those days, a dreamer or a pedant.

" I wish you had said distinctly how much money you want. I send five dollars, which, perhaps, is not enough. Yet this makes twenty I have sent you since mother went away. So you see even your frugality does not enable you wholly to dispense with the circulating medium you so much despise, and whose use, when you have thought more deeply on these subjects, you will find to have been indispensable to the production of the arts, of literature, and all that distinguishes civilized man. It is abused like all good things, but without it you would not have had your Horace and Virgil, stimulated by whose society you read the woods and fields to more advantage than —— or —— [certain uneducated neighbors]. Well, enjoy your fields and trees, supplicating the Spirit of all to bring you clear light and full sight." [2]

Then deeper chords are struck, this time in her diary: —

" October 1st [1842]. Anniversary of my father's death. Seven years have passed, — a generation, — unspotted by regrets, and rich in thought and experience, though its gifts were bathed in tears oftentimes.

" October 2, Sunday. Dr. Channing left this world. A blameless life came to an end, — a high aspiration was transferred elsewhere. He could not have died at

---

[1] Fuller MSS. ii. 689.   [2] Fuller MSS. ii. 701.

a better time; it was indeed for him the fullness of time; but it is sad that we shall see him no more, — meet no more the pale benignant countenance, be greeted no more by the gentle formal courtesy; nay, it is even sad that we shall be catechised no more for great truths to feed his earnest mind." [1]

The Fuller family resided at Jamaica Plain from the spring of 1839 to that of 1842, when Margaret took the responsibility of purchasing a house in Ellery Street, Cambridge (now No. 8), not far from the site of her old abode, the Dana House. Here they lived until July, 1843, when the house was sold; but the family, now greatly lessened, bought another house on Prospect Street, which they occupied [2] until after Margaret had transferred herself to New York, in the autumn of 1844, to begin what she called her "business life." But before passing to that, we must consider the various literary and other enterprises which engrossed her about this time; and meanwhile this record of suburban life may well close with a graphic description of her as she seemed, at this period of her career, to a childish neighbor, who writes thus to me: —

"I had known Miss Fuller in my childhood when she was our next-door neighbor in Ellery Street, Cambridge. She made a pet of me; and the isolated little German girl was indebted to her for a thousand trifles that make a child happy. I often sat by her and looked

[1] Fuller MSS. i. 425.
[2] Compare *Memoirs*, i. 319, 371, 382; ii. 120.

at her eyes — the only part of her face I remember —
with a strong fascination. They were wide, and full,
and blue ; whether fine or not, I could not at seven
years old decide ; but they always seemed to look far
off, out of and beyond the story she was telling or the
picture she was showing me ; and in looking at her eyes
I seemed to travel with her fancy through fairy-land.
She was very sweet and good to me, and I missed her
very much when, after a time, my father moved to Boston and I could no longer crawl under or climb over
the fence to my Miss Margaret; for I scorned the gate,
which was just as near, but had not that touch of romance."

VIII.

CONVERSATIONS IN BOSTON.

IT was in the suburban quiet of Jamaica Plain that the project of holding literary conversations first shaped itself. When Madame de Staël asked the Comte de Ségur which he liked best, her conversation or her writings, he is reported to have replied, "Your conversation, madame, for then you have not the leisure to become obscure." It was really in the effort to avoid obscurity and clarify her own thoughts that Margaret Fuller began by talking instead of writing. Conversations on literary and philosophical themes have since become such common things, that we can hardly appreciate the sort of surprise produced when she first attempted them. It fell in with the convenient theory of her vanity and presumption, while it is evident from her own diaries that the enterprise was undertaken in a very modest way. She felt a desire to do her part in the world, but knew herself not yet mature enough in intellect to write, even if there were any periodical to welcome her. Mere talking, which seemed to other people such an audacious enterprise, seemed to her the very easiest form of intellectual action. Her general feeling on the subject is best to be seen in a letter written a few years later to the Rev. W. H. Channing, not on this express theme, but in regard to a sermon that she had just heard : —

"CAMBRIDGE, *February* 27, 1843.

. . . " Many thoughts had risen in my mind during the discourse. But when we cannot gratify these wishes to express ourselves, it is probably as well. If we are prevented from gathering and giving away the flower, it withers indeed unenjoyed, but leaves a seed on the stalk. My thoughts generally seem too slight or too much in need of more to be written down, so I like to speak them, but if they lie in the mind, they attract the *more* they want. Some degree of expression is necessary for growth, but it should be little in proportion to the full life.

" As fire lays open, and the plow awakes a virgin soil, successions of seeds are called into development, which the powers of nature had generated in different moods and left there in the cold dark, perhaps for ages, quite forgotten. So shall it be with a mind that works lonely, unsolicited, unutterable; the destined hour of tillage shall find it rich.

" I will rejoice in every gladsome spring day, eloquent with blooms, or autumn with its harvests, but the silent fields of stubble or snow shall be no less prized." [1]

In this letter she clearly defines the power of oral utterance, not as a sign of supreme strength, but as rather, in her case at least, a resource of

[1] MS. (W. H. C.)

weakness. Longing for expression, she yet finds her thoughts, she says, too slight or inadequate to be written down ; and therefore likes to speak them, though conscious that even this amount of expression may not always be an advantage. She is going through the experience, in short, which all thinkers have had, and which her favorite Goethe has best formulated "Thought expands, but lames ; action animates, but narrows."

It must be remembered that the feeling of desire to be among men and do her part, rather than linger in solitary self-culture, is still visible at this period. For instance, after spending some delicious days about this time with her friend Miss Sturgis on the Merrimack, she writes : —

"I should not like such a life constantly. There are few characters so vigorous and of such self-sustained self-impulse that they do not need frequent and unexpected difficulties to awaken and keep in exercise their powers." [1]

Still longing for action, conscious of her fitness for it, she took this method of conversation as her best way of bringing to bear some influence upon her age and time. How much more than this she desired is to be seen in this fine piece of aspiration occurring in a letter to the Rev. W. H. Channing : —

"Like a desperate gamester I feel, at moments, as I cling to the belief that he [the Deity] cannot have lost

[1] Fuller MSS. ii. 645.

this great throw of Man, when the lesser hazards have ended so successfully. Men disappoint me so, I disappoint myself so, yet courage, patience, shuffle the cards, Durindarte. There was an Epaminondas, a Sidney, — we need the old counters still.

" I wish I were a man, and then there would be *one.* I weary in this play-ground of boys, proud and happy in their balls and marbles. Give me heroes, poets, law-givers, Men.

" There are women much less unworthy to live than you, Men; the best are so unripe, the wisest so ignoble, the truest so cold !

" Divine Spirit, I pray thee, grow out into our age before I leave it. I pray, I prophesy, I trust, yet I pine." [1]

With these strong aspirations, she was not content to do nothing, and she could at least talk. The conversations did not begin with the blowing of a trumpet ; there was not even a printed circular, but only a manuscript letter to her friend, Mrs. Ripley, of which the following is a part : —

" MY DEAR FRIEND, — I feel it more difficult to give on paper a complete outline of my plan for the proposed conversations than I expected. I find so much to say that I cannot make any statement satisfactory to myself, within such limits as would be convenient for your purpose. As no one will wish to take the trouble of reading a long manuscript, I shall rather suggest than tell what I propose to do, and defer a full explanation till the first meeting. The advantages of a weekly meeting for conversation might be great enough to

[1] MS. (W. H. C.), Sunday, February 21. 1841.

repay attendance, if they consisted only in supplying a point of union to well-educated and thinking women, in a city which, with great pretensions to mental refinement, boasts at present nothing of the kind; and where I have heard many of mature age wish for some such place of stimulus and cheer; and those younger, for a place where they could state their doubts and difficulties, with a hope of gaining aid from the experience or aspirations of others. And if my office were only to suggest topics, which would lead to conversation of a better order than is usual at social meetings, and to turn back the current when digressing into personalities or commonplaces, so that what is most valuable in the experience of each might be brought to bear upon all, I should think the object not unworthy of the effort. But my ambition goes much farther. It is to pass in review the departments of thought and knowledge, and endeavor to place them in due relation to one another in our mind. To systematize thought and give a precision and clearness in which our sex are so deficient, chiefly, I think, because they have so few inducements to test and classify what they receive. To ascertain what pursuits are best suited to us, in our time and state of society, and how we may make the best use of our means for building up the life of thought upon the life of action. . . .

"I believe I have written as much as any one will wish to read. I am ready to answer any questions which may be put, and will add nothing more here except, Always yours truly,

"S. M. Fuller." [1]

The conversations began November 6, 1839, at

[1] MS.

Miss Peabody's rooms in West Street — those rooms where many young men and women found, both then and at a later day, the companionship of cultivated people, and the best of French, German, Italian, and English literature. The conversations continued for five winters, closing in April, 1844. Their theory was not high-flown but eminently sensible, being based expressly on the ground stated in the circular, that the chief disadvantage of women in regard to study was in not being called upon, like men, to reproduce in some way what they had learned. As a substitute for this she proposed to try the uses of conversation, to be conducted in a somewhat systematic way, under efficient leadership. Accordingly these meetings, although taking a wide range, were always concentrated, and with a good deal of effect, on certain specified subjects ; the most prominent of these being, perhaps, that of Mythology, or the reappearance of religious ideas under varying forms. It is a theme which has since assumed great importance and commanded a literature of its own ; but it was then new, and had to be studied at great disadvantage. Through early versions of the "Bhagvat Geeta" and the "Desatir," Margaret Fuller had made advances into this realm : and for her, as for her early companion and life-long friend, Lydia Maria Child, it had great fascinations. She writes in her journal, for instance (February 21, 1841) : —

"This Hindoo mythology is like an Indian jungle,

The growth is too luxuriant for beauty and leaves a lair
for monsters. Being cleared away, here is an after-
growth of fair proportioned trees, and beauteous flowers, the Greek myths.

"Oh, Nature, — History of man, last birth of Nature, — how I see the fibres of God woven all through
every part as far as the eye can stretch!" [1]

While Mrs. Child was making preparations to
develop this new thought in her "Progress of
Religious Ideas," Margaret Fuller made it a frequent theme of her conversations; beginning with
the Greek mythology, and following up with illustrations from other sources, the rich materials for
which are scattered everywhere in her note-books.
In later years, however, following the constant
current which led her toward life and action, she
had for her themes a variety of points in ethics
and education.

The usual hour for these conversations was
eleven in the morning. The persons present were
usually twenty-five or thirty in number, rarely
less, sometimes more; and they were among the
most alert and active-minded women in Boston.
Ten or a dozen, besides Miss Fuller, usually took
actual part in the talk. Her method was to
begin each subject with a short introduction,
giving the outline of the subject, and suggesting
the most effective points of view. This done, she
invited questions or criticisms: if these lagged,
she put questions herself, using persuasion for the

[1] MS.

timid, kindly raillery for the indifferent. There
was always a theme, and a thread. One whole
winter was devoted — through thirteen conversations — to the Fine Arts; another to Ethics, in
different applications; another to Education, in
various respects; another to the proper influence
of women on family, school, church, society, and
literature. On some of these subjects she had, in
her circle, undoubted experts, who knew on certain particular points more than she did. Of these
she availed herself, but kept the reins in her own
hands. We all know that the best-planned talk
is a lottery; to-day blanks, to-morrow prizes;
and there were times when the leader could
bring out no coöperation, and had to fall back on
monologue. But this was not common, and even
the imperfect fragments in the way of report given
by Mr. Emerson in the "Memoirs" [1] are enough
to show the general success of these occasions.
When the subject was "Life," and she called
upon one of her favorite pupils to answer, "What
is life?" the lively girl replied, "It is to laugh or
cry, according to our constitution." In such a
repartee, we can see that the most philosophic
teacher met her match and had original minds to
deal with. Yet, after all, reports of conversation
are failures; and in this case their defects can
only be supplied by more general reminiscences
from pupils or friends, trying to give the secret of
her acknowledged power. Two of these testimo-

---

[1] *Memoirs,* i. 324.

nials I shall cite; the first from one of her life-long intimates, — an artist by profession and a woman of singularly clear and dispassionate nature, — Miss Sarah Freeman Clarke : —

"In looking for the causes of the great influence possessed by Margaret Fuller over her pupils, companions, and friends, I find something in the fact of her unusual truth-speaking power. She not only did not speak lies after our foolish social customs, but she met you fairly. She broke her lance upon your shield. Encountering her glance, something like an electric shock was felt. Her eye pierced through your disguises. Your outworks fell before her first assault, and you were at her mercy. And then began the delight of true intercourse. Though she spoke rudely searching words, and told you startling truths, though she broke down your little shams and defenses, you felt exhilarated by the compliment of being found out, and even that she had cared to find you out. I think this was what attracted or bound us to her. We expected good from such a new condition of our relations, and good usually came of it.

"No woman ever had more true lovers among those of her own sex, and as many men she also numbered among her friends. She had an immense appetite for social intercourse. When she met a new person she met him courageously, sincerely, and intimately. She did not study him to see beforehand how he might bear the shock of truth, but offered her best of direct speech at once. Some could not or would not hear it, and turned away; but often came back for more, and some of these became her fast friends.

" Many of us recoiled from her at first; we feared her too powerful dominion over us, but as she was powerful, so she was tender; as she was exacting, she was generous. She demanded our best, and she gave us her best. To be with her was the most powerful stimulus, intellectual and moral. It was like the sun shining upon plants and causing buds to open into flowers. This was her gift, and she could no more help exercising it than the sun can help shining. This gift, acting with a powerful understanding and a generous imagination, you can perceive would make an educational force of great power. Few or none could escape on whom she chose to exercise it. Of her methods of education she speaks thus simply : —

" ' I have immediate and invariable power over the minds of my pupils; my wish has been more and more to purify my own conscience when near them, to give clear views of the aims of this life, to show them where the magazines of knowledge lie, and to leave the rest to themselves and the spirit that must teach and help them to self impulse.'

" ' The best that we receive from anything can never be written. For it is not the positive amount of thought that we have received, but the virtue that has flowed into us, *and is now us*, that is precious. If we can tell no one thought, yet are higher, larger, wiser, the work is done. The best part of life is too spiritual to bear recording.' " [1]

Another friend equally warm, and also of judicial nature, has borne her testimony to the value of these conversations in terms so admirable that they must be cited. This is the late Elizabeth

[1] MS.

Hoar, of whom Emerson once wrote : "Elizabeth consecrates ; I have no friend whom I more wish to be immortal than she." A letter has already been quoted from this noble woman, describing her first impressions of Margaret Fuller at Concord ; and the following fragment gives her maturer opinion : —

"Her friends were a necklace of diamonds about her neck. The confidences given her were their best, and she held them to them ; the honor of the conversations was the high tone of sincerity and culture from so many consenting individuals, and Margaret was the keystone of the whole. She was, perhaps, impatient of complacency in people who thought they had claims, and stated their contrary opinion with an air. For such she had no mercy. But, though not agreeable, it was just. And so her enemies were made." [1]

To show that Margaret Fuller encountered among her friends and pupils natures as heroic as her own, I will yield to the temptation of quoting a passage from another letter of this same lady ; a bit of philosophy as fine as any that one finds in Epictetus or Antoninus, — stoicism in this case softened and enriched by Christianity without losing a fibre of its force : —

"When I was a little one I suffered agonies of terror at the barking of a dog, yet was ashamed to run away and avoid passing him. It suddenly occurred to my thought, 'What is it to fear ? That the dog should bite me — should inflict just so much pain as a dog's bite

[1] MS.

can, upon me. Well, I can bear so much pain bravely, I am sure, so I will take no further thought about it, but walk boldly on, and be ready for the bite when it comes' — and my fear was gone. The story sounds trifling, but it is not so in my life, because the philosophy I learned from that moment's thought has been of so much use to me since, in carrying me straight up to the ghosts of possible evils, showing their real power. And better than this philosophy is the trust which, by 'always thinking unto it,' we hope to make our *home* — the assurance that we might and surely shall be so cared for as we *could* not care for ourselves." [1]

It is evident, from Margaret Fuller's letters, that the effect of these occasions on herself varied with mood, health, and external influences. She enjoyed with eagerness the intellectual exercise ; she felt that she was, perhaps, doing some good ; and the longing for affection, which was one of the strongest traits of her nature, was gratified by the warm allegiance of her pupils. She went back to Jamaica Plain, every now and then, to rest, and, while rejoicing in that respite, still felt that her field was action, and that she could not, like Mr. Emerson, withdraw from the world to a quiet rural home. She wrote thus, on one occasion, to the Rev. W. H. Channing : —

"10*th December,* 1840.

"Two days in Boston ; how the time flies there and bears no perfume on its wings, — I am always most happy to return to my solitude, yet willing to bear the contact of society, with all its low views and rash blame,

[1] MS.

for I see how the purest ideal natures need it to temper them and keep them large and sure. I will never do as Waldo [Emerson] does, though I marvel not at him." [1]

The tone of this passage is saddened, no doubt, by some ungenerous criticisms upon herself and one of her favorite pupils, which she goes on to refute in detail, ending in the following high tone of aspiration : —

" How, when I hear such things, I bless God for awakening my inward life. In me, my Father, thou wouldst not, I feel, permit such blindness. Free them also, help me to free them, from this conventional standard, by means of which their eyes are holden that they see not. Let me, by purity and freedom, teach them justice, not only to my individual self, — of that small part of myself I am utterly careless, — but to this everflowing Spirit. Oh, must its pure breath pass them by ? " [2]

The criticisms which her conversations brought upon themselves, in their day, were mostly so trivial that they are not now worth recalling ; but there has been one curious effort to pervert these occasions from their true character, and this occurs in the posthumous autobiography of a woman of great prominence, who had, at one time, a distinct influence over Margaret Fuller. Posthumous attacks are always the hardest to meet, because in them the accuser still lives and testifies without cross-examination, while it often happens that the accused and his witnesses are alike dead.

[1] MS. (W. H. C.)   [2] MS. (W. H C.)

In this case the charge has an especial interest, because Margaret Fuller lived in the day when a great moral agitation was beginning to sweep over the land, and she, like all her contemporaries, must be judged in part by the test it applied.

It is a point never yet wholly cleared up, either by her printed memoirs or private letters, why she entered with somewhat tardy sympathy into the anti-slavery movement. Her personal friends were identified with it, including Dr. Channing, and more especially Mr. and Mrs. Ellis Gray Loring ; also her nearest intimates of her own age, Messrs. Clarke and Channing. Miss Martineau, whom she admired, had entered ardently into it; but it was not until the agitation in regard to the annexation of Texas in 1844 that Miss Fuller was strongly aroused in regard to the encroachments of slavery. It is possible that the influence of her father, as a Jeffersonian Democrat, worked the other way ; yet he had opposed the Missouri Compromise of 1820 ; and the anti-slavery tradition was strong in the family. It certainly was not the social influence of those who belonged to her classes and came to her conversations, for their influence tended, as will be presently shown, in a different direction.

In her diary of 1844, she wrote as follows : —

"Mrs. Loring here. They want something of me about Texas. Went to walk, but could not think about it. I don't like to do anything else just yet, don't feel ready. I never can do well more than one thing at a time, and the least thing costs me so much thought and feeling; others have no idea of it." [1]

Afterwards she wrote : —

"Might not we women do something in regard to this Texas annexation project? I have never felt that I had any call to take part in public affairs before; but this is a great moral question, and we have an obvious right to express our convictions. I should like to convene meetings everywhere and take our stand." [2]

I wish to dwell especially on this aspect of Margaret Fuller's position, because it has been so very unjustly dealt with in that singularly harsh and unfair book, the "Autobiography of Harriet Martineau." At the time when Miss Martineau's "Society in America" was published, Margaret Fuller wrote her a letter on the subject — a letter of great dignity and courage. There is in it no conceit, no arrogance, but only courteous, deferential protest. It is not written *de haut en bas*, but *de bas en haut*. In it she points out that one may criticise even one's superiors: —

"There are many topics treated of in this book of which I am not a judge; but I do pretend, even where I cannot criticise in detail, to have an opinion as to the general tone of thought. . . . When Webster speaks on the currency, I do not understand the subject, but I do understand his mode of treating it, and can see what a blaze of light streams from his torch. When Harriet Martineau writes about America, I often cannot test that rashness and inaccuracy of which I hear so much,

[1] MS. Diary, 1844.   [2] *Memoirs*, i. 141.

but I can feel that they exist. A want of soundness, of habits of patient investigation, of completeness, of arrangement, are felt throughout the book, and, for all its fine descriptions of scenery, breadth of reasoning, and generous daring, I cannot be happy in it, because it is not worthy of my friend ; and I think a few months given to ripen it, to balance, compare, and mellow, would have made it so." [1]

And when Miss Fuller came to touch the vexed question of the anti-slavery movement in America, as treated by Miss Martineau, she simply wrote thus : —

"I do not like that your book should be an ' abolition' book. You might have borne your testimony as decidedly as you pleased ; but why leaven the whole book with it ? This subject haunts us on almost every page. It *is* a great subject, but your book had other purposes to fulfill." [2]

This was the head and front of Miss Fuller's offending. But Miss Martineau's reference to this letter gives her the opportunity for one of those curious examples of failing memory and un-failing self-confidence which were pointed out, by the reviewers of her "Autobiography," at the time of its publication. She describes the communication as a letter which Miss Fuller "declares she sent her," but she can only recall having received a very different letter and one "quite unworthy of the writer." [3] Yet Miss Martineau had herself

[1] *Memoirs*, i. 193.   [2] *Memoirs*, i. 194.
[3] Harriet Martineau's *Autobiography*, i. 381.

made an entry in her own diary for November, 1839, — quoted by Mrs. Chapman in her appendix ;[1] and this record says of the letter then received : —

"Tuesday. An immense letter from Margaret Fuller. Sad about herself, and very severe on my book; — righteously so, but with much mistake in it. The spirit is very noble. Do I improve in courage about learning the consequences of what I do ? I commit myself boldly, but I suffer a good deal. But I do not think I go back. I suffered a good deal from her letter."

Now if the letter thus described was not the letter which Margaret Fuller "declared she sent," what was it ? It certainly was not that "unworthy" letter which Miss Martineau imputes to her, or it would not have been praised so highly. The fact is that the letter which Miss Martineau had characterized at the time as "very noble" she afterwards so far forgets as to insinuate that it never was really sent; but she remembers an "unworthy" letter, about which she gives no particulars and of whose existence there is no other memorial.

As to the letter itself, there is nothing unreasonable in it ; nothing which history has not confirmed. Miss Martineau's self-identification with the abolitionists was courageous and noble, but the habitual exaggeration of her mental action, and her liability to error through her temperament and her deafness, followed her into this

[1] Harriet Martineau's *Autobiography*, ii. 319.

sphere also. Her " Martyr Age in the United
States " will always remain the most dramatic
picture of the whole period she depicted.   The
difficulty is that it is not only dramatic but
slightly melodramatic ; there is a theatrical tinge
in it all ; every man she describes is faultless,
every woman a queen ; and even those who, like
myself, knew and reverenced these heroes and her-
oines, must admit this tone of excess.   It was the
same with her larger book.   She saw the sin
which was nearest, and painted it ; but she saw
little else.   Now that slavery is abolished " Society in America " is obsolete ; while De Tocqueville's work, written earlier, is still a classic, and
is frequently cited in regard to the questions that
are before us to-day.

All this prepares us for Miss Martineau's curious and — as the facts prove — utterly unfair criticisms upon Margaret Fuller's conversations.   She
thus describes them : —

" The difference between us was that while she was
living and moving in an ideal world, talking in private
and discoursing in public about the most fanciful and
shallow conceits which the Transcendentalists of Boston
took for philosophy, she looked down upon persons who
acted instead of talking finely, and devoted their fortunes, their peace, their repose, and their very lives to
the preservation of the principles of the republic.   While
Margaret Fuller and her adult pupils sat 'gorgeously
dressed,' talking about Mars and Venus, Plato and
Goethe, and fancying themselves the elect of the earth

in intellect and refinement, the liberties of the republic
were running out as fast as they could go, at a breach
which another sort of elect persons were devoting themselves to repair; and my complaint against the 'gorgeous' pedants was that they regarded their preservers
as hewers of wood and drawers of water, and their work
as a less vital one than the pedantic orations which
were spoiling a set of well-meaning women in a pitiable
way." [1]

To those of us who recall the plain Boston of
those days there is something quite unexpected in
thus fastening upon Margaret Fuller's circle the
sin of gorgeousness. Whence came this vehement epithet, so hopelessly inconsistent with the
well-kept black silk or modest alpaca of that
period. It apparently came from the exuberant
phrase of one young admirer quoted in the "Memoirs" of Margaret Fuller, who went so far as to
say of her idol, "Margaret used to come to the
conversations very well dressed, and altogether
looked sumptuously." [2] Even sumptuousness, it
might be said, is not gorgeousness; and there were,
moreover, young girls in Boston to whom what
has since been called "the gospel of good gowns"
was then very imperfectly revealed, and who so
adored their teacher that she would have looked
superbly in her oldest Groton wardrobe; just as
when she was fifteen, the younger school girls admired her way of coming into school and her half-

[1] *Autobiography of Harriet Martineau,* i. 381.
[2] *Memoirs,* i. 336.

shut eyes. So much for the gorgeousness; and as to the real charge, it requires only the very plainest comparison of Miss Martineau's own statements to correct them. She says that while Margaret Fuller and her pupils were doing so and so, another sort of elect persons, whom the first set despised, were saving the nation. The curious fact is that all this antagonism lies wholly in Miss Martineau's imagination, and that the two sets were almost identically the same. It is easy to show that the " spoiled women " of Margaret's classes were the very women who were fighting Miss Martineau's battles.

The only list known to me of any of these classes is that given in Miss Fuller's " Memoirs." [1] It contains forty-three names. Among these are to be found the two women who taught Miss Martineau her first lessons in abolitionism on her arrival in America: Mrs. Lydia Maria Child and Mrs. Ellis Gray Loring. The list comprises the wives of Emerson and Parker and the high-minded Maria White who afterwards, as the wife of Lowell, did much to make him an abolitionist; it includes the only daughter of Dr. Channing; it comprises Miss Littlehale, now Mrs. Ednah D. Cheney; it includes many family names identified with the anti-slavery movement in Boston and vicinity from its earliest to its latest phase; such names as Channing, Clarke, Hooper, Hoar, Lee, Peabody, Quincy, Russell, Shaw, Sturgis. These

[1] i. 338, note.

names form, indeed, the great majority of the list, while not a person appears on it who was conspicuously opposed to the anti-slavery agitation. Miss Martineau's extraordinary mistake simply calls attention to the fact that it was not upon pedants or dreamers, but upon the women who led the philanthropic thought and action of Boston, that Margaret Fuller's influence was brought to bear. She did not at this time appreciate Garrison; she afterwards lamented in Italy that she had not appreciated him better; but she helped to train many of the women who learned his lessons and stood by his side. That these conversations served as a moral — even more than as a mental — tonic is the uniform testimony of all who took part in them; and the later career of these participants shows how well the work was done.

9

A LITERARY CLUB AND ITS ORGAN.

APART from every word she ever wrote, Margaret Fuller will always be an important figure in American history, for this plain reason: that she was the organizer and executive force of the first thoroughly American literary enterprise. The intellectual and spiritual excitement, popularly called "Transcendentalism," had at least this one merit, that, whatever else it was, it was indigenous. To determine its real worth and weight, beyond this, we must go back to the "Dial." That is its only authentic record. To know what Emerson individually was, we can go to his books; it is the same with Parker, Thoreau, Alcott. But what it was which united these diverse elements, what was their central spirit, what their collective strength or weakness, their maximum and minimum, their high and low water mark, this must be sought in the "Dial." That was the alembic within which they were all distilled, and the priestess who superintended this intellectual chemic process happened to be Margaret Fuller. It is a curious fact that this aspect of her life — being that which will, on the whole, make her most interesting to

coming generations — occupies but two pages and
a half in the two volumes of her published memoirs. It will be the duty of the present biographer, in view of the plan which directs this literary series, to dwell more fully on this aspect of
her life.

We can now see that a great deal of unneces-
sary sympathy used to be wasted on our American writers of fifty years ago. It was habitually
taken for granted that they lived on a peculiarly
barren soil, and that especial credit was to be allowed them if they accomplished anything at all.
The concession was quite needless. They undoubtedly had nature and their own souls to draw
upon; they had few books, but those were the
best; they had some remote glimpse of art through
engravings, at least; they had around them the
inspiration of a great republic, visibly destined to
overspread a continent; and they had two or three
centuries of romantic and picturesque pioneer history behind them. We now recognize that Irving,
Cooper, Bryant, Whittier did not create their material; they simply used what they found; and
Longfellow's fame did not become assured till he
turned from Bruges and Nuremberg, and chose
his theme among the exiles of Acadia. It was
not Irving who invested the Hudson with romance,
but the Hudson that inspired Irving. In 1786,
when Mrs. Josiah Quincy, then a young girl, sailed
up that river in a sloop, she wrote : " Our captain
had a legend for every scene, either supernatural

or traditional, or of actual occurrence during the
war ; and not a mountain reared its head, uncon-
nected with some marvelous story." Irving was
then a child of three years old, but Rip Van Win-
kle and Ichabod Crane — or their equivalents —
were already on the spot, waiting for some one of
sufficient literary talent to tell their tale.

Margaret Fuller grew up at a time when our
literature was still essentially colonial ; not for
want of material, but for want of self-confidence.
As Theodore Parker said in his vigorous vernacu-
lar, somewhat later, the cultivated American literature was exotic, and the native literature was
" rowdy," consisting mainly of campaign squibs,
coarse satire, and frontier jokes.[1] Children were
reared, from the time they learned their letters,
on Miss Edgeworth and Mrs. Trimmer, whose
books, otherwise excellent, were unconsciously sat-
urated with social conventionalisms and distinc-
tions quite foreign to our society. Mrs. Lydia
Maria Child, the leader in the now vast field of
American literature for children, — and afterwards
one of the leaders in that other experiment of the
American novel, — was then a young woman, and
the fellow-student of Margaret Fuller. Charles
Brockden Brown, Irving, Cooper — these were our
few literary heroes. Fortunately for Margaret
Fuller, she had been led by the political tastes of
her father to turn from the weaker side of American intellect, which then was literature, to the

[1] *Mass. Quarterly Review,* iii. 206.

strong side, which was statesmanship. She had
thus learned that there was a department of American life which was not derivative and apologetic,
but strong and self-relying; and she was just in
the mood to be a literary pioneer.

What is called the Transcendental movement
amounted essentially to this: that about the year
1836 a number of young people in America made
the discovery that, in whatever quarter of the
globe they happened to be, it was possible for
them to take a look at the stars for themselves.
This discovery no doubt led to extravagances and
follies; the experimentalists at first went stum-
bling about, like the astrologer in the fable, with
their eyes on the heavens; and at Brook Farm
they, like him, fell into a ditch. No matter.
There were plenty of people to make a stand in
behalf of conventionalism in those very days; the
thing most needed was to have a few fresh thinkers, a few apostles of the ideal; and they soon
made their appearance in good earnest. The first
impulse, no doubt, was in the line of philosophic
and theologic speculation; but the primary aim
announced on the very first page of the "Dial"
was "to make new demands on literature." [1] It
is in this aspect that the movement must especially be treated here.

Even if they had not made this emancipation of
literature one of their prominent objects, they still
would have been laboring for it, even while uncon-

[1] *Dial*, i. 1.

scious. The moment they made the discovery that
they could see the universe with their own eyes,
they ceased to be provincial. " He despises me,"
wrote Ben Jonson, " because I live in an alley.
Tell him his soul lives in an alley." After all,
narrowness or enlargement are in the mind. Mr.
Henry James, turning on Thoreau the reverse end
of a remarkably good telescope, pronounces him
" parochial," because he made the woods and waters of Concord, Massachusetts, his chief theme.
The epithet is curiously infelicitous. To be parochial is to turn away from the great and look at
the little ; the daily newspapers of Paris afford the
best illustration of this fault. It is not parochial,
but the contrary, when Dr. Gould spends his life
in watching the stars from his lonely observatory
in Paraguay ; or when Lafarge erects his isolated
studio among the Paradise Rocks near Newport ;
or when Thoreau studies birds and bees, Iliads
and Vedas, in his little cottage by Lake Walden.
To look out of the little world into the great, that
is enlargement ; all else is parochialism.

It is also to be remembered that people in
America, in those days, if they had access to no
great variety of thought, still had — as in the
Indian's repartee about Time — all the thought
there was. The sources of intellectual influence
then most powerful in England, France, and Germany, were accessible and potent in America also.
The writers who were then remoulding English
intellectual habits — Coleridge, Wordsworth, Shel-

ley — were eagerly read in the United States ; and
Carlyle found here his first responsive audience.
There was a similar welcome afforded in America to Cousin and his eclectics, then so powerful in
France ; the same to Goethe, Herder, Jean Paul,
Kant, Schelling, Fichte, Jacobi, and Hegel. All
these were read eagerly by the most cultivated
classes in the United States, and helped, here as
in Europe, to form the epoch. Margaret Fuller,
so early as October 6, 1834, wrote in one of her
unpublished letters,[1] " our master, Goethe ; " and
Emerson writes to Carlyle (April 21, 1840), " I
have contrived to read almost every volume of
Goethe, and I have fifty-five.[2] To have read
fifty-five volumes of Goethe was a liberal education.

Add to this, that Margaret Fuller, like Emerson, had what is still the basis of all literary
training in the literature of Greece and Rome — a
literature whose merit it is that it puts all its pos-
sessors on a level ; so that if a child were reared in
Alaska and had Æschylus and Horace at his fingers' ends, he would have a better preparation for
literary work, so far as the mere form goes, than
if he had lived in Paris and read only Balzac.
Still again, the vast stores of oriental literature
were just being thrown open ; and the " Dial" was,
perhaps, the first literary journal to place what it
called the " Ethnical Scriptures " in the light now

---

[1] To Mrs. Barlow. Fuller MSS. i. 15.
[2] *Carlyle-Emerson Correspondence,* i. 285.

generally conceded to them; or to recognize what
has been latterly called "the Sympathy of Re-
ligions." Thanks to this general fact, that the
best literature is transportable and carries the
same weight everywhere, these American inno-
vators, living in their little Boston and Cambridge
and Concord, had for literary purposes a cosmopolitan training. This advantage would, however,
have been of little worth to them unless combined with the consciousness that they were living
in a new world and were part of a self-governing
nation. As Petrarch gave an impulse to modern
European literature when he thought himself
reviving the study of the ancient, so the Transcendental movement in America, while actively
introducing French and German authors to the
American public, was really preparing the way
for that public to demand a literature of its own.

The utterances of the "Dial" were often, from
the very outset, tinged with the passing fashion
of a period now gone by. The writers took an
ideal view of things, — sometimes extravagantly
ideal, — and this has not proved a permanent
fashion. No matter; no fashion is permanent;
and the ideal point of view is as sure to have its
turn again, as is the world to roll round — as sure
as the recurrence of Gainsborough hats and Queen
Anne houses. But with this fleeting show there
was achieved a substantial gain, which was not
subject to fashion, and which, when won, was won
forever. Behind all the catchwords, and even

cant, if you please, of the " Transcendentalists,"
lay the fact that they looked immediately around
them for their stimulus, their scenery, their illustrations, and their properties. After fifty years
of national life, the skylark and nightingale were
at last dethroned from our literature, and in the
very first volume of the " Dial " the blue-bird and
the wood-thrush took their place. Since then,
they have held their own ; birds and flowers are
recognized as a part of the local coloring, not as
mere transportable property, to be brought over
by emigrants in their boxes, and good only as
having crossed the ocean. Americans still go to
England to hear the skylark, but Englishmen
also come to America to hear the bobolink.

This effect of the new movement was doubtless partly unconscious ; for the impulse included
some who were illiterate, but thoughtful, and distrusted all literature. In the minds of the leaders,
however, the attitude was conscious and deliber-
ate.

" He who doubts whether this age or this country can
yield any contribution to the literature of the world
only betrays his own blindness to the necessities of the
human soul. Has the power of poetry ceased, or the
need? Have the eyes ceased to see that which they
would have, and which they have not? . . . The heart
beats in this age as of old, and the passions are busy as
ever." [1]

It was this strong conviction in their own

---

[1] Emerson in *Dial*, i. 157, 158 (October, 1840).

minds of the need of something fresh and indigenous, which controlled the criticism of the Transcendentalists; and sometimes made them unjust to the early poetry of a man like Longfellow,
who still retained the European symbols, and
exasperated them by writing about "Pentecost"
and "bishop's-caps," just as if this continent
had never been discovered.

The most striking illustration of the direct literary purpose of this movement is not to be found
in the early writings of Emerson, though they
make it plain enough; but in a remarkable address given at Cambridge by a young man, whose
career was cut short by death, after he had given
promise of important service. Robert Bartlett,
of Plymouth, Massachusetts, graduated at Cambridge in 1836, and in his "Master of Arts"
oration, three years after, took for his theme the
phrase, "No good possible, but shall one day be
real." The address attracted great attention, and
was afterwards published in an English magazine,[1] under the title, "A Voice from America.
The Hope of Literature." Nothing then written
— nothing in even the "Dial" itself — has preserved for us so good a picture of the working of
the new impulse among educated minds, at that
day; but the most remarkable passage was that
in which the young student announced the possi-
bilities of American Literature, as follows: —

"When Horace was affecting to make himself a

[1] Heraud's *New Monthly Magazine*, April, 1840.

Greek poet, the genius of his country, the shade of immortal Romulus, stood over him, 'post mediam noctem visus quum somnia vera,' and forbade the perversion. . . . Is everything so sterile and pigmy here in New England, that we must all, writers and readers, be forever replenishing ourselves with the mighty wonders of the Old World? Is not the history of this people transcendent in the chronicles of the world for pure, homogeneous sublimity and beauty and richness? Go down some ages of ages from this day, compress the years from the landing of the Pilgrims to the death of Washington into the same span as the first two centuries of Athens now fill our memories. Will men then come hither from all regions of the globe — will the tomb of Washington, the rock of the Puritans then become classic to the world? will these spots and relics here give the inspiration, the theme, the image of the poet and orator and sculptor, and be the ground of splendid mythologies? . . . We do not express the men and the miracles of our history in our social action, and correspondingly, ay, and *by consequence*, we do not outwrite them in poetry or art. We are looking abroad and back after a literature. Let us come and live, and know in living a high philosophy and faith, so shall we find now, here, the elements, and in our own good souls the fire. Of every storied bay and cliff and plain, we will make something infinitely nobler than Salamis or Marathon. This pale Massachusetts sky, this sandy soil and raw wind, all shall nurture us :

'O Nature, less is all of thine,
Than are thy borrowings from our human breast.'

Rich skies, fair fields shall come to us, suffused with the immortal hues of spirit, of beauteous act and

thought.   Unlike all the world before us, our own age
and land shall be classic to ourselves." [1]

This oration, be it remembered, was delivered
and printed while the "Dial" was yet unborn;
and before Emerson had published anything but
"Nature" and a few addresses.   These words
which I have quoted were like a trumpet-call to
myself and others, half a dozen years later; and
nothing of Emerson's ever touched us more deeply.
They make it very clear, at any rate, that the intellectual excitement of that day, whatever may
be thought of it as philosophy, produced in literature the effect of emancipation.   The "Dial" was
the embodiment of this movement; and without
Margaret Fuller it is doubtful whether the "Dial"
would ever have been born.

In conducting it, she had to attempt that hardest thing in life, to bring reformers into systematic coöperation.   Reformers are like Esqui-
maux dogs, which must be hitched to the sledge,
each by a separate thong; if put in one common
harness, they turn and eat each other up.   Under the common phrase, " Transcendentalists,"
were comprised, at that day, people of the most
antagonistic temperaments.   Nobody could dwell
higher among the clouds than Alcott; no one
could keep his feet more firmly on the earth than
Parker; yet they must be harnessed to the same
conveyance.   Those who have had to do similar
charioteering amid the milder divergences and

[1] Heraud's *New Monthly Magazine,* iii. 448.

smoother individualities of the present day can best estimate what her task must have been.

Both the magazine and the literary club from which it sprang seem to have been a subject of correspondence among a circle of friends for several years before either took definite shape. Margaret Fuller writes to the Rev. F. H. Hedge, so early as July 4, 1833 : —

"I should be very willing to join such a society as you speak of, and will 'compose a piece,' if you will give me a subject."

This, however, was merely a social club, composed of ladies and gentlemen in Cambridge, and Dr. Hedge has no remembrance of any literary exercises connected with it. But during the winter of 1834–35 there was a good deal of discussion in respect to a possible magazine, and on March 5, 1835, — nearly two years after, — she writes to him, still from Groton : —

"Your periodical plan charms me; I think you will do good and, what is next best, gain favor. Though I have been somewhat jostled in this working-day world, I have still a great partiality for the goddess who

> ' vires [que] acquirit eundo ;
> Parva metu primo ; mox sese attolit in auras
> . . . et caput inter nubila condit.' [1]

I shall feel myself honored if I am deemed worthy of lending a hand, albeit I fear I am merely ' Germanico,' and not 'transcendental.' I go by fits and starts: there

---

[1] The description of "Fama" in Virgil's *Æneid*, iv. 175–177.

is no knowing what I should wish to write upon next January." [1]

Every knot of bright young thinkers is easily tempted to plan a periodical which shall reflect the thoughts of the coterie; and it seemed for some years as if this particular enterprise would go no farther. The Rev. F. H. Hedge, who had urged it most definitely, removed to Bangor, Maine, in 1835, and the project languished. But it so happened that there was held in the autumn of 1836 the bicentennial celebration of Harvard College, and it turned out an important circumstance for this special movement. Four young Unitarian clergymen — Emerson, Hedge, Ripley, and Putnam — meeting after the exercises, got into some conversation about the narrow tendencies of thought in the churches. They adjourned to a room at Willard's Hotel — then a place of some resort in Cambridge, now converted into a horse-railroad office — and talked the matter over at length. It ended in a small meeting for consultation at Rev. George Ripley's in Boston, on September 19, 1836, at which were present Ripley, Emerson, Hedge, Alcott, Clarke, and Francis, and one or two divinity students. This led to a much larger meeting at Mr. Emerson's in Concord, at which were present, besides the above, O. A. Brownson, T. Parker, C. A. Bartol, C. Stetson, and various other men; with Margaret Fuller and Elizabeth P. Peabody. This was the inauguration of a club,

[1] MS.

called " The Transcendental Club " by the world;
sometimes, by Mr. Alcott, " The Symposium
Club ; " and occasionally, by its members, " The
Hedge Club," because its meetings were often
adapted to suit the Rev. F. H. Hedge's occasional
visits to Boston. This association met once a
month or thereabouts for several years.

In 1839 the theme of a much-desired journal
constantly appears in the manuscript diary of Mr.
Alcott, both in connection with this club and with
his own meditations. Thus he writes (March 12,
1839), " Before long a journal will be circulating
the thoughts which are now talked about in private circles," [1] — yet this he says evidently in his
general attitude of prophet and seer, without
more definite forecast.

Soon after (March 27), he writes : —

" Brought home with me Brownson's ' Boston Quarterly Review,' for April. This is the best journal now
current on this side of the Atlantic, but falls far below
the idea of the best minds among us. Its circulation is
limited. A better work will appear before long. Some
of the freest pens now lie idle for want of a channel.
. . . The ' Christian Examiner ' is timid and conserva-
tive." [2]

Again, in his record of a meeting of the club,
May 8, 1839, it appears that the first topic of discussion was " The Present Temper of our Jour-

[1] Alcott's MS. Diary, xii. 464.
[2] Ibid. xii. 542.

nals." He continues, recording his own remarks
but not those of others : —

"I said that they were destitute of proper freshness
and independence. The ' Liberator' was then the only
journal which had root in the soul and flourished." [1]

The Club went on meeting, now at Mr. Emerson's in Concord, now at Dr. Francis's in Watertown, now at Mr. Bartol's in Boston. It was
made up of unusual materials. Hedge supplied
the trained philosophic mind ; Convers Francis,
the omnivorous mental appetite ; James Freeman Clarke, the philanthropic comprehensiveness ;
Theodore Parker, the robust energy ; Orestes A.
Brownson, the gladiatorial vigor ; Caleb Stetson,
the wit ; William Henry Channing, the lofty enthusiasm ; Ripley, the active understanding ; Bartol, the flame of aspiration ; Alcott, the pure ideal-
ism ; Emerson, the *lumen siccum*, or dry light.
Among members or occasional guests were Thoreau, Jones Very, George P. Bradford, Dr. Le
Baron Russell, and a few young theological students from Cambridge, such as William D. Wilson,
now professor at Cornell University, and Robert
Bartlett, whose Harvard "Master of Arts" oration
has been already quoted. Once, and once only, Dr.
Channing and George Bancroft seem to have met
with them at Mr. Ripley's (December 5, 1839).

The project of a magazine, long pending, seems
to have been brought to a crisis by the existence

[1] Alcott's MS. Diary. xii.

of an English periodical, which was at the time thought so good as to be almost a model for the American enterprise; but which seems, on re-reading it in the perspective of forty years, to be quite unworthy of the comparison. There was in England a man named John A. Heraud, author of a Life of Savonarola, and described in one of Carlyle's most deliciously humorous sketches as " a loquacious, scribacious little man of middle age, of parboiled greasy aspect," and by Leigh Hunt, as " wavering in the most astonishing manner between being Something and being Nothing." He seems to have been, if not witty himself, the cause of wit in others, for Stuart Mill said of him: " I forgive him freely for interpreting the Universe, now when I find he cannot pronounce the *h*'s." When Carlyle once quoted to him the saying of Novalis, that the highest problem of authorship is the writing of a Bible, — " ' That is precisely what I am doing,' answered the aspiring, unaspirating." [1]

Nothing was more natural than that Mr. Alcott — who, upon a far higher plane of character, as even Carlyle would have admitted, was engaged in the same rather daring task with Heraud, and even bound up some volumes of his manuscript diary with the label, " Scriptures for 1840," or whatever the date might be — should have looked eagerly toward Heraud, especially when the latter began to publish his " New Monthly Magazine."

---

[1] *Carlyle-Emerson Correspondence*, i. 276, 277.

Dr. Convers Francis, who contrived upon the salary of a poor country clergyman to subscribe to everything and buy everything, of course took Heraud's periodical; and his copy, apparently the only one to be found in these parts, now lies before me. In this magazine it was proposed to publish some other things from American sources besides Bartlett's oration; as, for instance, a review of Jones Very's poems, by Miss Fuller; and one of Tennyson's, by John S. Dwight; but these seem never to have appeared. Besides this monthly, Heraud or his friends planned and announced a still more esoteric periodical, to be called "Aurora;" and his ally, Dr. J. Westland Marston, actually published some numbers of one called "Psyche." All these productions were read with great eagerness by the Boston circle, Mr. Alcott's diary recording from month to month the satisfaction taken by himself, Miss Fuller, and others in Heraud's undertakings, and his own fear that Americans could not support such an enterprise. "It will be some time," he writes in his diary (November 1, 1839), "before our contemplated journal will be commenced, and I question whether we shall find talent or spirit to equal that of our English brethren. We have writers enough, but they are neither accomplished nor free. Half a dozen men exhaust our list of contributors; Emerson, Hedge, Miss Fuller, Ripley, Channing, Dwight, and Clarke are our dependence." [1]   But

[1] Alcott's MS. Diary, xiii. 375.

the trophies of Heraud would not suffer Bosto-
nians to sleep. There was great interchange of
pamphlets and new books, and Mr. Alcott, while
planning to reprint a little work of Heraud's from
an English volume called "The Educator," — a
reprint actually accomplished by him two years
later, in a small volume called "Spiritual Culture," — followed the matter up still further, as
may be seen in the following extract from his
diary: —

"Saturday, 28th [September, 1839].

"I had an agreeable talk with G. Ripley on the
Times, and particularly on my transatlantic friends. He
is much taken with Heraud's journal, which he has read
from January last. He wishes to establish a journal of
like character among ourselves. We need such an organ, but lack the ability to make it worthy of our position. There are but few contributors, and those not at
all free from the influences of the past. Yet such a
journal we must have in due time. Doubtless it would
succeed even now. Brownson's 'Boston Quarterly' is
pledged to a party in politics, and takes narrow ground
both in philosophy and literature. We must have a free
journal for the soul which awaits its own scribes." [1]

Before this, however, as appears from other
memoranda by Mr. Alcott in my possession, Margaret Fuller, at a meeting of the "Symposium"
Club, September 18, "gave her views of the proposed 'Dial,' which she afterwards edited." This
is the first instance I have found of the introduc-

[1] Alcott's MS. Diary, xiii. 264.

tion of the actual title of the American periodical;
but the word was several times used by Mr. Alcott
to describe his own laborious diary ; and he expressly states that it was transferred from his personal use to that of the proposed magazine. " To
these papers," he says, speaking of his own manuscript volumes, " I give the name of ' The Dial,' "
and indorses on a copy of the original prospectus,
" This journal takes its name from a MS. of mine
of like designation, referred to on pages 47 and
50 of this Scripture." [1]

The new magazine now at last impending
moved Mr. Brownson to make a final effort to
unite it with his own, and he came to Mr. Alcott
for that purpose, proposing that instead of estab-
lishing the " Dial " its projectors should write under their own signatures in the " Boston Quarterly
Review." Alcott says of this suggestion (October
19, 1839) : " I shall speak with Emerson and Miss
Fuller about it; " and the next day he and the
lady went together to Concord and discussed the
plan, apparently wisely rejecting it. He writes of
Miss Fuller after his return, " She has a deeper
insight into character than any of her contemporaries, and will enrich our literature."

We find her soon actively at work in writing to
friends and summoning forth contributions. Thus
she writes on New Year's Day, to the Rev. W. H.
Channing, then preaching at Cincinnati : —

[1] Alcott's MS. Diary, xiv. 79.
[2] Ibid. xiii. 320, 321, 326.

"JAMAICA PLAIN, 1*st January*, 1840.

"I write to inform you that there is now every reason to hope that a first number of the much-talked of new journal may be issued next April, and to ask what you will give. I have counted on you for the first number, because you seemed so really in earnest and said you had articles ready written. But I want to know what part you propose to take in the grand symphony, and I pray you to answer me directly, for we must proceed to tune the instruments. Mr. Emerson is warmly interested and will give active assistance for a year. Mr. Ripley and Mr. Dwight are also in earnest; for others I know not yet.

"Will not Mr. Vaughan give us some aid? His article on the ' Chartists ' excited interest here, and we should like some such ' large sharp strokes ' of the pen very much. . . .

"At Newport you prophesied a new literature : shall it dawn in 1840 ? " [1]

On the same day she writes to Rev. F. H. Hedge, at Bangor, Maine: —

"JAMAICA PLAIN, 1*st January*, 1840.

"MY DEAR HENRY, — I write this New Year's Day to wish you all happiness, and to say that there is reason to expect the new journal (in such dim prospect when you were here) may see the light next April. And we depend on you for the first number, and for solid bullion too. Mr. Emerson will write, every number, and so will you if you are good and politic, for it is the best way to be heard from your sentry-box there in Bangor. — My friend, I really hope you will make this the occasion for

[1] MS. (W. H. C.)

assailing the public ear with such a succession of melodies that all the stones will advance to form a city of refuge for the just. I think with the greatest pleasure of working in company with you. But what will it be? will you give us poems or philosophy or criticism, and how much? for we are planning out our first number by the yard. Let me hear from you directly." [1]

Later, she writes to him again: —

"JAMAICA PLAIN, 10*th March*, 1840.

. . . "Henry, I adjure you, in the name of all the Genii, Muses, Pegasus, Apollo, Pollio, Apollyon, ('and must I mention' ——) to send me something good for this journal before the 1st May. All mortals, my friend, are slack and bare; they wait to see whether Hotspur wins, before they levy aid for as good a plan as ever was laid. I know you are plagued and it is hard to write, just so is it with me, for I also am a father. But you can help, and become a godfather! if you like, and let it be nobly, for if the first number justify not the magazine, it will not find justification; so write, my friend, write, and paint not for me fine plans on the clouds to be achieved at some future time, as others do who have had many years to be thinking of immortality.

"I could make a number myself with the help Mr. E. [Emerson] will give, but the Public, I trow, is too astute a donkey not to look sad at *that*." [2]

On March 18, 1840, Emerson writes to Carlyle: —

[1] MS.

[2] MS. The allusion is to the lines in *Rejected Addresses*, —

"And, when that donkey looked me in the face
Its face was sad; and you are sad, my Public!"

"My vivacious friend, Margaret Fuller, is to edit a journal whose first number she promises for the first of July next, — which, I think, will be written with a good will, if written at all."[1]

Again he says, April 22, 1840 : —

"I have very good hope that my friend Margaret Fuller's journal — after many false baptisms now saying it will be called 'The Dial' and which is to appear in July — will give you a better knowledge of our young people than any you have had."[2]

On April 19, 1840, she writes to the Rev. W. H. Channing again : —

"I do not expect to be of much use except to urge on the laggards and scold the lukewarm, and act like Helen McGregor to those who love compromise, by doing my little best to sink them in the waters of oblivion."[3]

On May 31, 1840, she writes to Emerson : —

"There are only thirty names on the Boston subscription list of the 'Dial.' I hope you will let me have your paper by next Friday or Saturday."[4]

Upon such modest encouragement did a periodical proceed which was to be the beginning of a new era in cis-Atlantic literature. The original prospectus — written, I suspect, by Mr. Ripley — was as follows : —

[1] *Carlyle-Emerson Correspondence*, i. 270.
[2] Ibid. i. 285.   [3] MS.   [4] MS.

"THE DIAL:

A

MAGAZINE

FOR

LITERATURE, PHILOSOPHY, AND RELIGION.

To be Continued Quarterly.

" The purpose of this work is to furnish a medium for the freest expression of thought on the questions which interest earnest minds in every community.

" It aims at the discussion of principles rather than at the promotion of measures ; and while it will not fail to examine the ideas which impel the leading movements of the present day, it will maintain an independent position with regard to them.

" The pages of this journal will be filled by contributors who possess little in common but the love of individual freedom and the hope of social progress ; who are united by sympathy of spirit, not by agreement in speculation ; whose faith is in Divine Providence, rather than in human prescription ; whose hearts are more in the future than in the past, and who trust the living soul more than the dead letter. It will endeavor to promote the constant evolution of truth, not the petrifaction of opinion.

" Its contents will embrace a wide and varied range of subjects, and combining the characteristics of a Magazine and Review, it may present something both for those who read for instruction and those who search for amusement.

" The general design and character of the work may be understood from the above brief statement. It may be proper to add that, in literature, it will strive to exercise a just and catholic criticism, and to recognize every sincere production of genius; in philosophy it will attempt the reconciliation of the universal instincts of humanity with the largest conclusions of reason; and in religion it will reverently seek to discover the presence of God in nature, in history, and in the soul of man.

"'The Dial,' as its title indicates, will endeavor to occupy a position on which the light may fall; which is open to the rising sun; and from which it may correctly report the progress of the hour and the day.

"'The Dial' will be published once in three months, on the first day of January, April, July, and October. Each number will contain 136 octavo pages, making one volume in a year of 544 pages, which will be furnished to subscribers at *Three Dollars per annum*, payable on the delivery of the second number. The first number will be published on the first day of July next.

"WEEKS, JORDAN & Co.,
"121 *Washington Street.*

"BOSTON, *May* 4, 1840."

X.

THE DIAL.

NOTHING but the launching of a ship concentrates into short space so much of solicitude as the launching of a new magazine. Margaret Fuller writes to her friend Mrs. Barlow: "I have the pleasure of sending you the first number of a periodical some of us, your old friends, are going to scribble in. The introduction is by Mr. Emerson; pieces on 'Critics' and the 'Allston Gallery' by me. The next number will be better." [1]

To Mr. Emerson, as one of the ship-owners, she writes far more freely (July 5, 1840): —

"Until I shall have seen Mr. R. [Ripley] I cannot answer all your questions; *mais à present,* you can have as many numbers as you want for yourself or your friends of this first number, but our contract with them was that twelve numbers should be given to Mr. R. each quarter for the use of contributors. Of these I receive two. Mr. Thoreau will have it, of course, as we hope his frequent aid. But I did not expect to furnish it to all who may give a piece occasionally. I have not sent it to E. H. [Ellen Hooper] or C. S. [Caroline Sturgis] or N. I sent a list to W. and J. [Weeks & Jordan] of those to

[1] Fuller MSS. i. 23.

whom I wished this number sent. I did not give Mr. Stone's name, but doubtless Mr. R. did. I will see about it, however. I presume Mr. Cranch is a subscriber, as is J. F. Clarke and others who will write; but I will look at the list when in town next Wednesday.

"I desired Mr. Thoreau's ' Persius ' to be sent him, as I was going away to Cohasset at the time it came out, and I understood from Mr. R. that it was sent, and he did not correct it. I do not know how this was; the errors are most unhappy. I will not go away again when it is in press.

"I like the poetry better in small type myself and thought the little page neat and unpretending, but have no such positive feeling about such things that I would not defer entirely to your taste. But now we have begun so, I should think it undesirable to make changes this year, as the first volume should be uniform. I wish I had consulted you at first, but did not know you attached great importance to externals in such matters, as you do so little in others. The marks shall be made and the spaces left as you desire, however, after our respective poems.

"I am glad you are not quite dissatisfied with the first number. I feel myself how far it is from that eaglet motion I wanted. I suffer in looking it over now. Did you observe the absurdity of the last two pages; these are things they had to fill up blanks, and which, thinking 't was pity such beautiful thoughts should be lost, they put in for climax. Admire the winding up, the concluding sentence ! !

"I agree that Mr. Alcott's sayings read well. I thought to write about the expostulation in your last letter, but finally I think I would rather talk with you.

" The next number we will do far better. I want to
open it with your article. You said you might wish to
make some alterations if we kept it — do you wish to
have it sent you, the first part is left in type; they had
printed a good deal before finding it would be too long.
E. H.'s ' Poet,' some of C.'s best, Ellery, and ' The Bard
born out of Time,' we must have for that." [1]

The poem described in these last words will
readily be recognized as Emerson's since celebrated " Wood-Notes." The " Ellery " is an article by Emerson entitled " New Poetry " and
made up chiefly of extracts from Ellery Channing's poems — an essay received with mingled
admiration and rage by the critics, and with especial wrath by Edgar Poe. " E. H.'s ' Poet ' " was
a strong poem, also contained in the second number of the " Dial," by Mrs. Ellen Hooper, wife of
Dr. R. W. Hooper,— a woman of genius, who gave
our literature a classic in the lines beginning, —

" I slept, and dreamed that life was beauty."

Margaret Fuller wrote of her long afterwards
from Rome, " I have seen in Europe no woman
more gifted by nature than she." Another of the
" Dial " poets was the sister of this lady, Miss
Caroline Sturgis, afterwards Mrs. William Tappan, " some of whose best " are contained in this
same second number of the " Dial," where her
contributions are signed " Z." The opening
paper of this second number, " Thoughts on Modern Literature," by Emerson, still yields to the

[1] MS.

reader so much in the way of suggestion and criticism as to impart especial interest to the following letter; and this, moreover, shows how fearlessly Miss Fuller and her associate, the Rev. George Ripley, criticised their most revered contributor : —

"19*th July,* 1840.

" I suppose it is too warm for my dear friend to write, at least to so dull a correspondent, or perhaps it is that I have asked so many things. I am sorry you did not send the verses, for I wanted to take one or two for filling the gaps, and now have been obliged to take some not so good. Have you not some distichs to bestow? I have two or three little things of yours which I wished very much to use, but thought I must not without your leave.

" When I wrote the first line of this letter I thought I should fill it up with some notes I wished to make on the Hall of Sculpture. But I was obliged to stop by a violent attack of headache, and now I am not fit to write anything good, and will only scribble a few lines to send with your proof which Mr. R. [Ripley] left with me. He is much distressed at what he thinks a falling off in the end of your paragraph about the majestic artist, and I think when you look again you will think you have not said what you meant to say. The ' eloquence' and ' wealth,' thus grouped, have rather *l'air bourgeois.* — ' Saddens and gladdens' is good. Mr. R. hates prettinesses, as the mistress of a boarding-house hates flower vases.

" ' Dreadful melody' does not suit me. The dreadful has become vulgarized since its natal day.

" So much for impertinence ! I am very glad I am

to own these remarks about the Meister. As to the
genius of Goethe, the statement, though so much better
than others, is too imperfect to be true. He requires
to be minutely painted in his own style of hard finish.
As he never gave his soul in a glance, so he cannot be
painted at a glance. I wish this ' Kosmos Beauty ' was
not here over again. One does not like their friend to
have any way, anything peculiar ; he must be too individual to be known by a cough or a phrase. And is
this *costly* true to the sense of *kostliche ;* that means
' worthy a high price,' the other ' obtained at a high price,'
n'est-ce pas ? I cannot like that illustration of the humors of the eye. I wish the word *whipped* was never
used at all, and here it is twice in nearest neighborhood.

"At this place I was obliged to take to my bed, —
my poor head reminding me that I was in no state for
criticism."

On comparing these criticisms with the paper
under discussion,[1] it will be found that while Emerson has retained the words " humors " and, in one
case " whipped," in spite of criticism, he has
dropped the other causes of offense. The fine
paragraph on Goethe now closes as follows : —

" Let him pass. Humanity must wait for its physician still, at the side of the road, and confess as this
man goes out that they have served it better who assured it out of the innocent hope in their hearts that a
physician will come, than this majestic artist, with all the
treasures of wit, of science, and of power at his command."

It is easy to see that if this last clause originally

[1] *Dial,* i. pp. 136–158.

contained the words " eloquence " and " wealth "
it is greatly strengthened by the change.

As to obtaining a verse from Emerson to fill
the gap at the close of his paper, her appeal seems
to have been successful ; the five lines called
" Silence " being placed there, which, although
not included by him in his published volumes, are
now printed as his by his editor, Mr. Cabot. At
the time of its first appearance the little verse
was regarded as rather grotesque ; and it will
never, perhaps, be placed among his happiest efforts.

The storm of criticism which opened upon the
" Dial," at the very outset, was something formidable. It was directed even at the very moderate
peculiarities of Emerson ; the " Knickerbocker,"
a New York monthly, making great fun of his
opening essay, which it derided as " literary eu-
phuism." But the chief assault fell upon Alcott's
" Orphic Sayings," which provoked numerous par-
odies, the worst of which Mr. Alcott composedly
pasted into his diary, indexing them, with his
accustomed thoroughness and neatness, as " Par-
odies on Orphic Sayings." Epithets, too, were
showered about as freely as imitations ; the Philadelphia " Gazette," for instance, calling the editors
of the new journal "zanies," " Bedlamites," and
" considerably madder than the Mormons."

It will convey some impression of the difficulties which Margaret Fuller, as leading editor, had
to meet, when we consider that, all this time, Mr.

Alcott and, perhaps, others of the stricter school
of Transcendentalism, were shaking their heads
over the "Dial" as being timid, compromising, and,
in fact, rather a worldly and conventional affair.
Even before its actual birth we find him writing
in his diary, "I fear that the work will consult
the temper, and be awed by the bearing of existing
things." [1]   After the first number he writes to Dr.
Marston in England, "It is but a twilight 'Dial;'"
and to Charles Lane, "This 'Dial' of ours should
have been a truer. It does not content the public,
nor even ourselves. Yours, the 'Monthly Magazine' [Heraud's], pleases me better in several aspects."   To Heraud he writes at the same time:
"The 'Dial' partakes of our vices, it consults the
mood and is awed somewhat by the bearing of
existing orders, yet is superior to our other literary organs, and satisfies in part the hunger of our
youth. It satisfies me not, nor Emerson. It
measures not the meridian but the morning ray;
the nations wait for the gnomon that shall mark
the broad noon." [2]

These remarks are of value as illustrating the
difficulty that Margaret Fuller had to encounter
in endeavoring to keep her magazine somewhere
midway between the demands of Theodore Parker on the one side and those of Alcott on the
other. What Theodore Parker alone would have
made it may be judged by his "Massachusetts

---

[1] Alcott's MS. Diary, xiv. 65.
[2] Ibid. xiv. 65, 146, 150, 157.

Quarterly Review," which followed it; which, as
he said, was to be the "Dial" with a beard, but
which turned out to be the beard without the
"Dial." What Mr. Alcott alone would have
made of it may be judged by Heraud's "Monthly
Magazine," which did not, any more than Parker's "Quarterly," bear comparison in real worth
and suggestiveness with the "Dial" itself. That
on Alcott, at least, some gentle restrictive pressure had to be exercised may be seen by his
rather indignant introduction to "Days from a
Diary," in the last number that Margaret Fuller
edited. Here he chafes at some delay in publishing his contribution, and adds significantly: "The
'Dial' prefers a style of thought and diction not
mine; nor can I add to its popularity with its
chosen readers. A fit organ, for such as myself,
is not, but is to be. The times require a free
speech, a wise, brave sincerity, unlike all examples
in literature; of which the 'Dial' is but the pre-
cursor. A few years more will give us all we
desire — the people all they ask." [1]

When we consider with what fidelity the editors
had held to him, although by all odds their least
popular contributor, it must be admitted that this
affords a new illustration of the difficulty of keeping radicals in a common harness.

After the third number, Margaret Fuller thus
writes to the Rev. W. H. Channing: —

[1] *Dial*, ii. 409.

11

"February 2, 1841.

"Write to me whatever you think about the 'Dial.' I wish very much to get interested in it, and I can only do so by finding those I love and prize are so. It is very difficult to me to resolve on publishing any of my own writing: it never seems worth it, but the topmost bubble on my life; and the world, the Public! alas! — give me to realize that there are *individuals* to whom I can speak!"[1]

She appears, by her correspondence, to have had the usual trials of an editor in respect to the procrastination of others; and we find her actively angling for contributions from Emerson, Parker, Hedge, Alcott, Channing, Clarke, Dwight, Cranch, and the rest. Parker even sent her poetry, as appears by the following letter from him: —

"Herewith I send you a couple of little bits of verse, which I confess to you, *sub rosâ rosissimâ*, are mine. Now, I don't think myself made for a poet, least of all for an *amatory poet*. So, if you throw the lines under the grate, in your critical wisdom, I shall not be grieved, vexed, or ruffled; for, though I have enough of the *irritabile* in my composition, I have none of the *irritabile vatis*."[2]

These distrusted love verses were, as I learn from Mr. G. W. Cook, those printed in the "Dial" for July, 1841, under the name of "Protean Wishes."[3]

[1] MS. [2] Weiss's *Parker*, ii. 303.
[3] *Dial*, ii. 77.

Besides these well-known contributors, she also applied to other literary friends, whose response apparently never came. Among them was her old friend at Providence, Albert G. Greene, then the recognized head of the literary society of that city. To him she writes, October 2, 1840: "Where are the poems and essays, 'Pumpkin Monodies,' and 'Militia Musters,' we were promised? Send them, I pray, forthwith." These were humorous poems, in which Mr. Greene was prolific, though only one of this class of his productions, "Old Grimes," has survived to posterity. They would have been oddly out of place in the "Dial," had they arrived.

In her first two years of editorship she brought into prominence a series of writers each of whom had his one statement to make, and, having made it, discreetly retired. Such were the Rev. W. D. Wilson, who wrote "The Unitarian Movement in New England;" the Rev. Thomas T. Stone, who wrote "Man in the Ages;" Mrs. Ripley, the gifted wife of the Rev. George Ripley, who wrote on "Woman;" Professor John M. Mackie, now of Providence, R. I., who wrote of "Shelley;" Dr. Francis Tuckerman, who wrote "Music of the Winter;" John A. Saxton, father of the well-known military governor of South Carolina, who wrote "Prophecy — Transcendentalism — Progress;" the Rev. W. B. Greene, a West Point graduate, and afterwards colonel of the Fourteenth Massachusetts Volunteers, who wrote "First Princi-

ples." Miss Fuller herself wrote the more mystical sketches — "Klopstock and Meta," "The
Magnolia of Lake Pontchartrain," "Yucca Filamentosa," and "Leila ; " as well as the more
elaborate critical papers — "Goethe," "Lives of
the Great Composers," and "Festus." Poetry was
supplied by Clarke, Cranch, Dwight, Thoreau,
Ellery Channing, and, latterly, Lowell ; while Parker furnished solid, vigorous, readable, common-
sense articles, which, as Mr. Emerson once told
me, "sold the numbers." It is a curious fact that
the only early "Dial" to which Parker contributed nothing was that which called down this
malediction from Carlyle : —

"The 'Dial,' too, it is all spirit-like, aeriform, aurora-
borealislike. Will no *Angel* body himself out of that ;
no stalwart Yankee *man* with color in the cheeks of him,
and a coat on his back ? " [1]

Yet Theodore Parker was a good deal more stalwart than Carlyle, had more color in his cheeks,
and wore a more presentable coat on his back ; and
he had written an exceedingly straightforward
paper for every number before that of October,
1841. This, as it happened, was prepared under
difficulties, and Margaret Fuller herself had to
write eighty-five of its one hundred and thirty-six
pages. It is plain, from the reluctance to write
which she so often expresses, that she occupied this
occasional prominence against her will. Instead of
being a monopolist, she appears as the scapegoat

[1] *Carlyle-Emerson Correspondence*, i. 352

of the procrastination of others. To fill with first-class material a magazine which does not pay a dollar, and has only twelve free copies for all contributors put together, is not so easy. In case of gaps, she must supply them. In such event, at the last moment she must revert to her copious note-books, and do that from which every careful writer shrinks — treat hurriedly and superficially some theme that had been reserved for the careful elaboration of more fortunate months. Mr. Emerson testifies to his "grateful wonder"[1] at the courage with which she could do this; and we see it recorded in such passages as the following, which is taken from a letter to her mother, written on Christmas Day, either in 1840 or 1841: —

"I am in a state of extreme fatigue; this is the last week of the 'Dial,' and, as often happens, the copy did not hold out, and I have had to write in every gap of time. M. and J. [two young ladies, her pupils] have been writing for me extracts, etc., but I have barely scrambled through, and am now quite unfit to hold a pen."[2]

She had one essential attribute of an editor, in a keen and impartial judgment of her contributors. "I wish," she writes in her diary, "I could overcome my distrust of Mr. Alcott's mind."[3] Of Theodore Parker she says: "He cannot be the leader of my journal, . . . but his learning and just way of thinking will make him a very valu-

---

[1] *Memoirs*, i. 324.   [2] Fuller MSS. ii. 287.
[3] Fuller MSS. i. 599.

able aid." [1] This capital remark is also made, in one case, upon a rather elaborate contributor : "It was pity to break Mr. Lane's piece. He needs to fall his whole length to show his weight." [2] But best of all is this clear statement, in which, even against the authority of Emerson, she pleads for breadth of judgment : —

"CAMBRIDGE, 12*th November,* 1843.

. . . "When I had the care of the ' Dial,' I put in what those connected with me liked, even when it did not well please myself, on this principle, that I considered a magazine was meant to suit more than one class of minds. As I should like to have writings from you, Mr. Ripley, Mr. Parker, etc., so I should like to have writings recommended by each of you. I thought it less important that everything in it should be excellent, than that it should represent with some fidelity the state of mind among us, as the name of ' Dial ' said was its intent.

"So I did not regard your contempt for the long *prosa* on ' Transcendentalism — Progress,' etc., any more than Parker's disgust at Henry Thoreau's pieces.

"You go on a different principle ; you would have everything in it good according to your taste, which is, in my opinion, though admirable as far as it goes, far too narrow in its range. This is *your* principle ; very well ! I acquiesce, just as in our intercourse I do not expect you to do what I consider justice to many things I prize. . . .

"I do not care for your *not liking* the piece, because,

[1] Fuller MSS. i. 599.
[2] MS. letter to Emerson, August 5, 1843.

when you wrote in your journal that I cared for tal
ent as well as genius, I accepted the words written in
dispraise as praise. I wish my tastes and sympathies
still more expansive than they are, instead of more severe. Here we differ." [1]

It was in reference to this same point that she
wrote in her journal thus : —

" My friend spoke it in blame that I could prize talent
as well as genius ; but why not ? Do not Nature and
God the same? The criticism of man should not dispar-
age and displace, but appreciate and classify what it finds
existent. Let me recognize talent as well as genius, understanding as well as reason, — but each in its place.
Let me revere the statue of Moses, but prize at its due
rate yon rich and playful grotesque. Also, cannot one
see the merit of a stripling, fluttering muse like that
of Moore, without being blind to the stately muse of
Dante ? " [2]

It is to be remembered that although Miss Fuller's salary, as editor of the "Dial," was nominally $200, she practically had nothing ; and early
in its second year she writes to her brother Richard (November 5, 1841) : " I have begun with a
smaller class this year than usual, and the 'Dial' is
likely to fall through entirely." In the same letter, and at a time of such discouragement as this,
she proposes to her brother that they should unite
in advancing $300 to an older brother in Louis-
iana ; she pledging herself, however, to become
responsible for the whole amount, if necessary,

[1] MS.   [2] Fuller MSS. i. 589.

though then possessed of but about $500 in the world.[1] Such acts of sisterly devotion were common things with her ; and this is mentioned only to show out of what patient self-denial the "Dial" was born.

Four months later she was compelled to lay down her task ; her own statement of circumstances being as follows, in a letter to Mr. Emerson, and briefly indorsed by him " Margaret Fuller — March, 1842. Stop the " Dial ! ' "

"MY DEAR WALDO, — I requested Miss Peabody to write to you, but, after looking over her letter, I want to add some lines myself. I hoped they would get at these particulars before you returned from New York, that you might hear them on your way and not be teased as soon as you arrive at your quiet home, but you came earlier than I had expected. Yesterday I found myself so unwell, and really exhausted, [while] letters received from the family made my stay here so uncertain, that I wrote the little notice with regard to the possibility of suspending the 'Dial' for a time, feeling that I must draw back from my promise that I would see to the summer number ; but this morning after J. Clarke and Miss P. had at last the means of almost entirely examining the accounts, they give me the result you find in her letter to you, which makes it impossible for me to go on at all.

"I could not do it, in future, if I have the same burden on me as I have had before, even as well as I have done. There is a perceptible diminution of my strength, and this winter has been one of so severe labor, I shall not recover fully from it for two or three months. Then, if I must take up a similar course next winter, and have this tie upon me for the summer, I think I should sink under it entirely.

" I grieve to disappoint you after all the trouble you have taken. I am also sorry myself, for if I could have received a maintenance from this 'Dial,' I could have done my duties to it well, which I never have all this time, and my time might have been given to my pen; while now, for more than three months I have been able to write no line except letters. But it cannot be helped. It has been a sad business.

" I think perhaps Mr. Parker would like to carry it on even under these circumstances. For him, or for you, it would be much easier than for me, for you have quiet homes, and better health. Of course, if you do carry it on, I should like to do anything I can to aid you.

" There must be prompt answer, as the press will wait.

" Your affectionate   MARGARET." [1]

The following month, after the appearance of a circular from Mr. Emerson announcing the continuance of the magazine, she writes as follows : —

"CANTON, *April* 18 [1842].

" DEAR FRIEND, — I received your letter before I left Boston, but in the hurry of the last hours could not write even a notelette with the parcel I requested J. Clarke to make up for you of Borrow, Longfellow, some more shreds of 'Dial,' including the wearifu' Napoleon, and the Prayer Book, if Dorothea Dix could be induced to grant the same. What awkward thing could I have

[1] MS.

said about your advertisement? I can't think. — All was understood, except that you had said ' I should put my name on the cover and announce myself as editor, only that I am not sure I can bind myself for so long as a year,' and so when I saw the advertisement I was glad, and only so far surprised as that I had not felt sure you would do it. — How many tedious words !

"I think I shall like being here much and find the rest I need. The country is tolerably pretty, gentle, unobtrusive — within the house plain kindness, and generally a silence unbroken except by the sounds from the poultry, or the wind; to appreciate which blessing one should have lived half a year in a boarding-house with as infirm a head as mine, and none to ward off interruptions, sick or well."

Emerson wrote thus to Carlyle (March 31, 1842) in regard to the final transfer of editorship to himself : —

"I should tell you that my friend Margaret Fuller who has edited our little ' Dial ' with such dubious approbation on the part of you and other men, has suddenly decided a few days ago that she will edit it no more. The second volume was just closing; shall it live for a third year ? You should know, that if its interior and spiritual life has been ill-fed, its outward and bibliopolic existence has been worse managed. Its publishers failed, its short list of subscribers became shorter, and it has never paid its laborious editor, who has been very generous of her time and labor, the smallest remuneration. Unhappily, to me alone could the question be put whether the little aspiring starveling should be reprieved for another year. I had not the cruelty to kill ft, and so must answer with my own proper care and nursing for its new life. Perhaps it is a great folly in me who have little adroitness in turning off work to assume this sure vexation, but the ' Dial ' has certain charms to me as an opportunity, which I grudge to destroy. Lately at New York I found it to be to a certain class of men and women, though few, an object of tenderness and religion. You cannot believe it ? " [1]

It is to be noticed that Emerson in his printed letters to Carlyle habitually speaks of the magazine as " Margaret Fuller's," and speaks of giving his lectures to her for publication rather than make any other use of them.[2] His loyalty to it seemed inseparably connected with his loyalty to her, and this seems to have been true in a measure with all its contributors. She continued to write much for it even after her editorship had ceased ; but is sometimes found so discontented with her own work as to withhold it. After the death of Dr. Channing she thus writes to Mr. Emerson (November 8, 1842) : —

" Should you write some notice of Dr. C. for your ' Dial ' if I did not ? I have written, but the record seems best adapted for my particular use, and I do not know whether I shall come to anything more general. If you should not write more than you have, will you send me your one stroke on the nail-head for me to look at ? " [3]

Nothing could be better than this recognition

---

[1] *Carlyle-Emerson Correspondence*, i. 366.
[2] Ibid. i. 287, 320.   [3] MS.

of the extraordinary precision and vigor of Emerson's single strokes.

The "Dial" expired after four years of precarious life. Perhaps those who best recognized its power were not those who created it, and who, as parents, recognized with anxious eyes the defects of their child, — but rather those who, like myself, came too late upon the scene to do more than have some boyish copy of verses judiciously rejected from the last numbers, and who yet drew from the earlier volumes a real and permanent impulse. When one considers the part since played in American literature and life by those whose youthful enthusiasm created this periodical, it is needless to say that their words kindled much life in the hearts of those still younger. It is a sufficient proof of the advantage of this potent influence that it worked itself clear, at last; and those who were reared on the "Dial" felt the impulse of its thought without borrowing its alleged vagueness. Nor was this influence limited to America, for on visiting England in 1846 Margaret Fuller had the pleasure of writing to Emerson, "On my first arrival I encountered at Liverpool and Manchester a set of devout readers of the 'Dial,' and still more of Emerson." [1]

[1] Fuller MSS. i. 209.

XI.

BROOK FARM.

A CHAPTER on Brook Farm would be hardly needed, in a life of Margaret Fuller, but for one single cause, — the magic wielded by a man of genius. Zenobia in Hawthorne's "Blithedale Romance" has scarcely a trait in common with Margaret Fuller; yet will be identified with her while the literature of the English language is read. Margaret Fuller had neither the superb beauty of Zenobia, nor her physical amplitude, nor her large fortune, nor her mysterious husband, nor her inclination to suicide ; nor, in fine, was she a member of the Brook Farm community at all. These points of difference would seem to be enough, but were these ten times as many they would all be unavailing, and the power of the romancer would outweigh them all. It is impossible to make the readers of fiction understand that a novelist creates his characters as spiders their web, attaching the thread at some convenient point and letting it float off into free air ; perhaps to link itself at last to something very far away. George Sand has well said that to copy any character precisely from nature would be to make it unnatural; since you cannot also transfer to your book all the surroundings that have made that character what it is. The author gets his first hint from some real person, — perhaps from several, — and all the rest is his own; or it might almost be said the character's own, so astounding is the way in which these visionary people take their fates into their own hands and perhaps do the precise things which their creator intended to prevent. If all this is true of the most commonplace novelist, it is especially true of the most ideal of all writers of fiction, Hawthorne. Even his real people, when he writes what he means for sober history, become almost ideal in the atmosphere he paints; how much more with those in his romances. That there was a certain queenliness about Margaret Fuller, that she sometimes came to Brook Farm, and that a cow which was named after her lorded it over the other cows; this was all that she really contributed to Hawthorne's Zenobia; and much less than this would have been sufficient for his purpose.

Nevertheless Brook Farm was for a few years a fact so large among the circle to which she belonged that it is well to have some good reason for introducing it here. It was one of the best — probably the best — incarnation of the ardent and wide-reaching reformatory spirit of that day. It was a day when it certainly was very pleasant to live, although it is doubtful whether living would have remained as pleasant, had one half the proj-

ects of the period become fulfilled. The eighty-
two pestilent heresies that were already reckoned
up in Massachusetts before 1638, or the " generation of odd names and natures " which the Earl of
Strafford found among the English Roundheads,
could hardly surpass those of which Boston was
the centre during the interval between the year
1835 and the absorbing political upheaval of 1848.
The best single picture of the period is in Emerson's lecture on "New England Reformers," delivered in March, 1844 ; but it tells only a part
of the story, for one very marked trait of the
period was that the agitation reached all circles.
German theology, as interpreted by Brownson,
Parker, and Ripley, influenced the more educated
class, and the Second Advent excitement equally
prepared the way among the more ignorant. The
anti-slavery movement was the profoundest moral
element, on the whole, but a multitude of special
enterprises also played their parts. People habitually spoke, in those days, of " the sisterhood of.
reforms," and it was in as bad taste for a poor
man to have but one hobby in his head as for a
rich man to keep but one horse in his stable. Mes-
merism was studied ; gifted persons gave private
sittings for the reading of character through handwriting ; phrenology and physiology were ranked
together ; Alcott preached what Carlyle called a
" potato gospel ; " Graham denounced bolted flour ;
Edward Palmer wrote tracts against money. In a
paper published in the " Dial " for July, 1842, on

the " Convention of Friends of Universal Reform "
in Boston, Emerson says of that gathering : —

" If the assembly was disorderly, it was picturesque.
Madmen, madwomen, men with beards, Dunkers, Mug-
gletonians, Come-outers, Groaners, Agrarians, Seventh-
Day Baptists, Quakers, Abolitionists, Calvinists, Unita-
rians, and Philosophers — all came successively to the
top." [1]

Having myself attended similar meetings soon
after, I can certify that this is not an exaggeration,
but, on the contrary, a plain, unvarnished tale. It
is to be remembered, too, that all this stir came
upon a society whose previous habit of life was
decidedly soberer and better ordered than that of
to-day ; stricter in observance, more conventional
in costume. There could hardly be a better illustration of this fact than when Emerson includes
in his enumeration of eccentricities " men with
beards ; " for I can well remember when Charles
Burleigh was charged with blasphemy, because
his flowing locks and handsome untrimmed beard
was thought to resemble — as very likely he intended — the pictures of Jesus Christ ; and when
Lowell was thought to have formally announced
a daring impulse of radicalism, after he, too, had
eschewed the razor. The only memorial we retain unchanged from that picturesque period is
in some stray member of the " Hutchinson Family " who still comes before the public with now
whitening locks and vast collar that needs no

[1] *Dial,* iii. 101.

whitening ; and continues to sing with unchanged sweetness the plaintive melodies that hushed the stormiest meeting when he and his four or five long-haired brothers stood grouped round their one rose-bud of a sister like a band of Puritan Bohemians.

Amid all these wild gospellers came and went the calm figure of Emerson, peaceful and undisturbed. I can remember that, after certain of his lectures in Boston, his chosen hearers habitually gathered to meet him at the rooms of one young man, an ardent Fourierite, though not actually a Brook-Farmer. Outside the door was painted in flaming colors a yellow sun, at the centre of whose blazing rays was the motto " Universal Unity," while beneath it hung another inscription in black and white letters, " Please wipe your feet." This emblazonment and this caution symbolized the whole movement. The gateway of Brook Farm might have been similarly inscribed. There was a singular moral purity about it which observers from the point of view of Paris or even London have since found a little contemptible. With the utmost freedom in all things, and a comprehensiveness to which that of " the latitude-men about Cambridge " in England was timid conservatism, Brook Farm, like all other haunts of the " come-outers " of the period, was as chaste as a Shaker household.

But it will readily be seen that amid this impulse of universal reform some such enterprise as

Brook Farm was inevitable. Already at New Harmony, Zoar, and elsewhere in the Western States,
there had been socialistic experiments. But all
the others were more or less imported ; this was
indigenous, except that, like all other profoundly
sincere movements, it borrowed some examples
and incentives from the plains of Galilee. The
very name given to the first proclamation of the
enterprise in the " Dial," " A Glimpse at Christ's
Idea of Society," [1] written by Miss E. P. Peabody, shows that this clear element of religious
impulse came first; the Fourierite gospel arrived
later, and rather marked the decline. To those
who like myself visited " the Community " only as
observant and rather incredulous boys, under guidance of some enlightened cousin, it all seemed a
very pleasant picnic, where youths and maidens
did pretty much what they wished, and sang du-
ets over their labors. The very costume was by
no means that monotony of old clothes which
Hawthorne depicts in the " Blithedale Romance,"
for some of the youths looked handsome as Raphael in flowing blouses of various colors and picturesque little vizor-less caps, exquisitely unfitted
for horny-handed tillers of the soil. Nowhere was
there such good company ; young men went from
the farm to the neighboring towns to teach German classes ; there were masquerades and gypsy
parties, such as would thrive on no other soil ;
whatever might be said of the actual glebe of

---

[1] *Dial,* ii. 214 (October, 1841).

Brook Farm, the social culture was of the richest. Those who ever lived there usually account it to this day as the happiest period of their lives. Even the shy Hawthorne does some justice to this aspect of the society, and there is no reason why any one should object to his making Margaret Fuller a leading figure in its short-lived circle, except the fact — justly trivial to a romancer — that she was not there.

She doubtless, like Emerson, joined occasionally in its merry-makings. In his "American Note-Books," Hawthorne once describes them as appearing together at a festival. But to her, from the beginning, it was simply an experiment which had enlisted some of her dearest friends; and, later, she found at Brook Farm a sort of cloister for occasional withdrawal from her classes and her conversations. This was all; she was not a stockholder, nor a member, nor an advocate of the enterprise; and even "Miss Fuller's cow" which Hawthorne tried so hard to milk [1] was a being as wholly imaginary as Zenobia; although old Brook-Farmers report that Mr. Ripley was fond of naming his cattle after his friends, and may, very likely, have found among them a Margaret Fuller.

Her general attitude toward the associative movement, at the outset, may be seen in these sentences, written to the Rev. W. H. Channing, after a public meeting of the faithful: —

[1] *American Note-Books,* ii. 4.

" I will not write to you of these conventions and communities unless they bear better fruit than yet.   This convention was a total failure, as might be expected from a movement so forced. . . . O Christopher Columbus! how art thou admired when we see how other men go to work with their lesser enterprises." [1]

Again, she writes of an interview with Mr. and Mrs. Ripley, when Brook Farm was being organized (October 28, 1840) : —

" In town I saw the Ripleys.   Mr. R. more and more wrapt in his new project.   He is too sanguine, and does not take time to let things ripen in his mind ; yet his aim is worthy, and with his courage and clear mind his experiment will not, I think, to him at least, be a failure. I will not throw any cold water, yet I would wish him the aid of some equal and faithful friend in the beginning, the rather that his own mind, though that of a captain, is not that of a conqueror.   I feel more hopeful as he builds less wide, but cannot feel that I have anything to do at present, except to look on and see the coral insects at work.

" Ballou was with him to-night ; he seems a downright person, clear as to his own purposes, and not unwilling to permit others the pursuit of theirs." [2]

It appears from Mr. Alcott's MS. diary that in October, 1840, while the whole matter was taking form, he met George Ripley and Miss Fuller at Mr. Emerson's in Concord, for the pur-

[1] MS. (W. H. C.)

[2] MS.   The Rev. Adin Ballou was a well-known leader among the Associationists in that day, yet did not live at Brook Farm, but at Mendon, Mass.

pose of discussing the new theme. Neither Alcott
nor Emerson accepted the project in its completeness.[1] During the following month Alcott enumer-
ates these persons as being likely to join the proposed community, — Ripley, Emerson, Parker, S.
D. Robbins, and Miss Fuller.[2] But I know no
reason to suppose that any of these, except Mr. Ripley himself, had any such serious intention; though
Mr. Emerson himself was so far influenced by the
prevailing tendency as to offer to share his house
with Mr. Alcott and his family, while suggesting
that other like-minded persons should settle near
them in Concord. Mr. Alcott himself speaks of
Brook Farm as " our community; " but perhaps
uses the words in a very general sense.

At any rate, Brook Farm established itself
without them, and though Margaret Fuller often
visited it, this letter to Mr. Emerson shows the
motives, quite remote from Zenobia's, with which
she did so, — that she might be gentle, dull, and
silent !

" CAMBRIDGE, 10th *May*, 1841.

" Your letter, my dear friend, was received just as I
was on the wing to pass a few days with the fledglings
of Community; and I have only this evening returned
to answer it. I will come on Saturday afternoon next
if no cross accident mar the horizon of my hopes, and
the visible heavens drop not down Niagaras. All that
I have to say may best be reserved till I come ; it is
necessary that I should be economical, for I have of late

---

[1] Alcott's MS Diary, xiv. 170.
[2] Ibid. xiv. 199.

been as gentle, as dull, and as silent as the most fussy old bachelor could desire his housekeeper to be. You said, however, I could come and live there, if I had not a mind to talk, so I am not afraid, but will come, hoping there may be a flow after this ebb, which has almost restored the health of your affectionate

"MARGARET." [1]

Again, this extract from a letter to Mr. Emerson (August 10, 1842) illustrates the same point. It seems that Professor Farrar and his wife were to have taken a journey, in which case Margaret Fuller would have remained in their house at Cambridge, a plan that would have "insured several weeks of stillness and solitude" for her; she being "tired to death of dissipation." This failing, she expresses willingness to go to Concord, but, should that be inconvenient, she can go to Brook Farm, as the next best medicine: —

"They will give me a room at Brook Farm, if I wish, let me do as I please, and I think if I went there to stay I could keep by myself, and employ myself, if there is any force in my mind. Beside, I will not give up seeing you. If you do not want me to stay in this unlimited fashion I will come for two or three days, on a visit technically speaking. But I want to know beforehand which it shall be, for, if I come to stay, I shall bring my paper, etc., but if not I shall leave them here, write to Brook Farm to engage my room, and go there so soon as I have seen you satisfactorily." [2]

However she might dream of solitude, she could

[1] MS.   [2] MS.

not wholly maintain it, even in these "retreats" at Brook Farm. She seems to have been in the habit of going there on New Year's Eve; and there are among her papers successive meditations or descriptions at that time, usually introducing some poem of her own. One of these narratives is as follows: —

"*Night preceding New Year's Day*, 1844.

"The moon was nearly full, and shone in an unclouded sky over wild fields of snow. The day was Sunday, a happy Sunday. I had enjoyed being with William *equally* when we were alone or with these many of different ages, tempers, and relationships with us, for all seemed bound in one thought this happy day.

"William addressed them in the morning on the Destiny of the Earth, and then I read aloud Ellery's poem 'The Earth.' [1] . . . But in the night the thoughts of these verses kept coming, though they relate more to what had passed at the Fourier convention, and to the talk we had been having in Mrs. R.'s room, than to the deeper occupation of my mind." [2]

To find how this dream of silence filled her soul, at times, we must turn to another passage in the same letter to the Rev. W. H. Channing which describes her interview with the Ripleys: —

"It is by no means useless to preach. In my experience of the divine gifts of solitude, I had forgotten what might be done in this other way. O that crowd

[1] A fine poem by Ellery Channing beginning —

"My highway is unfeatured air."

[2] MS.

of upturned faces with their look of unintelligent complacency! Give me tears and groans, rather, if there *be* a mixture of physical excitement and bigotry. Mr. Dewey is heard because, though he has not entered into the secret of piety, he wishes to be heard and with a good purpose; can make a forcible statement and kindle himself with his own thought. How many persons must there be who cannot worship alone since they are content with so little. Can we not wake the spark that will weld them, till they take beautiful forms and can assist each alone? Were one to come now who could purge us with fire! . . .

"But all my tendency at present is to the deepest privacy. — Where can I hide till I am given to myself? Yet I love the others more and more, and when they are with me must give them the best from my scrip. When I see their infirmities I would fain heal them, forgetful of my own! But am I left one moment alone, then, a poor wandering pilgrim, yet no saint, I would seek the shrine; would therein die to the world and then if from the poor reliques some miracle might be wrought, that is for them!

"Yet some of these saints were able to work in their generation, for they had renounced all!" [1]

It may have been on one of these New Year's retreats that she wrote her most thoughtful and most artistic poem; almost the only one of hers to which the last epithet could be applied, if, indeed, it be applicable here. The poem was printed in "Summer on the Lakes," and is on a theme which suited her love of mystic colors

[1] MS. (W. H. C.)

and symbols — the tradition of the Rosicrucians. The modern theory is, however, that this word did not come from the cross and the rose, as she assumes, but from the cross and the dew (*ros*); this last substance being then considered as the most powerful solvent of gold, and so used in the effort to discover the philosopher's stone.

SUB ROSA CRUX.

"In times of old, as we are told,
  When men more child-like at the feet
    Of Jesus sat, than now,
  A chivalry was known more bold
  Than ours, and yet of stricter vow,
    Of worship more complete.

" Knights of the Rosy Cross, they bore
  Its weight within the heart, but wore
Without, devotion's sign in glistening ruby bright ;
  The gall and vinegar they drank alone,
  But to the world at large would only own
The wine of faith, sparkling with rosy light.

"They knew the secret of the sacred oil
  Which, poured upon the prophet's head,
    Could keep him wise and pure for aye.
  Apart from all that might distract or soil,
    With this their lamps they fed,
Which burn in their sepulchral shrines unfading night and day.

" The pass-word now is lost
  To that initiation full and free ;
  Daily we pay the cost
  Of our slow schooling for divine degree.
We know no means to feed an undying lamp ;
Our lights go out in every wind or damp.

" We wear the cross of ebony and gold,
  Upon a dark back-ground a form of light,

A heavenly hope upon a bosom cold,
A starry promise in a frequent night;
The dying lamp must often trim again,
For we are conscious, thoughtful, striving men.

" Yet be we faithful to this present trust,
Clasp to a heart resigned the fatal *must;*
Though deepest dark our efforts should enfold,
Unwearied mine to find the vein of gold;
Forget not oft to lift the hope on high;
The rosy dawn again shall fill the sky.

" And by that lovely light, all truth revealed,
The cherished forms which sad distrust concealed,
Transfigured, yet the same, will round us stand,
The kindred angels of a faithful band;
Ruby and ebon cross both cast aside,
No lamp is needed, for the night has died.

" Be to the best thou knowest ever true,
Is all the creed;
Then, be thy talisman of rosy hue,
Or fenced with thorns that wearing thou must bleed,
Or gentle pledge of Love's prophetic view,
The faithful steps it will securely lead."

XII.

BOOKS PUBLISHED.

THE first sign of marked literary talent, in a young person, is apt to be an omnivorous passion for books, followed, sooner or later, by the desire to produce something; this desire often taking experimental and fugitive forms. The study of "Sir James Mackintosh's Life and Works," at Groton, seems to have impressed Margaret Fuller strongly with the danger of miscellaneous and desultory preparation. She writes: —

"The copiousness of Sir J. Mackintosh's reading journals is, I think, intimately connected with his literary indolence. Minds of great creative power take no pleasure in going into detail on the new materials they receive, — they assimilate them by meditation and new creations follow. A Scott, a Goethe, would neither talk out nor write down the reflections suggested by what the day had brought; they would be transfused into new works." [1]

Later, she had a vision of writing romances, like George Sand, and expressed herself thus in her diary: —

[1] Fuller MSS. iii. 27b.

[GROTON, *November*, 1835.]

"These books have made me for the first time think I might write into such shapes what I know of human nature. I have always thought that I would not, that I would keep all that behind the curtain, that I would not write, like a woman, of love and hope and disappointment, but like a man, of the world of intellect and action. But now I am tempted, and if I can but do well my present work and show that I can write like a man, and if but the wild gnomes will keep from me with their shackles of care for bread in all its shapes of factitious life, I think I will try whether I have the hand to paint, as well as the eye to see. But I cannot but feel that I have seen, from the mouth of my damp cave, stars as fair, almost as many, as this person from the ' Flèche of the Cathedral,' where she has ascended at such peril. But I dare boast no more; only, please fate, be just and send me an angel out of this golden cloud that comes after the pelting showers I have borne so long." [1]

The project of fiction went no farther, unless her fragment of an " Autobiographical Romance," written in 1840, was the result of it ; and her first two published books were, naturally enough, translations from the German. She had expected, as early as November 30, 1834, as appears by a letter to the Rev. F. H. Hedge, to print her translation of Goethe's " Tasso." [2] This had failed to find a publisher; but several years later George

[1] Fuller MSS. iii. 303–305. The allusion is to George Sand's *Sept Cordes de la Lyre*.

[2] Published after her death, in her *Art, Literature, and the Drama*.

Ripley and other friends of hers projected and
carried out, to the extent of fifteen volumes, a series of "Specimens of Foreign Literature," composed of translations from the German and French.
As announced in the preface to the first volume,
dated February 22, 1838, the series was to have
included "A Life of Goethe, in preparation for
this work, from original documents;" and of this
memoir, apparently, Margaret Fuller was to have
been the compiler. For some reason this plan was
abandoned, but she was the translator and editor
of the fourth volume of the series, containing Eckermann's "Conversations" with the great German poet. The work was done, as her preface
states, under many disadvantages, much of it being dictated to others, on account of illness; and
these obstacles were the more felt, inasmuch as
she was not content with a literal translation, but
undertook to condense some passages and omit
others. Her preface is certainly modest enough,
and underrates instead of overstating the value of
her own work. She made a delightful book of it,
and one which, with Sarah Austin's "Characteristics of Goethe," helped to make the poet a familiar
personality to English-speaking readers. For one,
I can say that it brought him nearer to me than
any other book, before or since, has ever done.
This volume was published at Boston, by Hilliard,
Gray & Co., in 1839, — her preface being dated
at Jamaica Plain on May 23 of that year, — and
I suspect that she never had any compensation

for it beyond the good practice for herself and the gratitude of others. Her preface contains some excellent things, giving a view of Goethe more moderate than that which Carlyle had just brought into vogue, though she still was ardent and admiring enough. But she points out very well — though perhaps emphasizing them too much — some of the limitations of Goethe's nature. She does not even admit him to be in the highest sense an artist, but says, " I think he had the artist's eye and the artist's hand, but not the artist's love of structure," — a distinction admirably put.

From the subject of Goethe followed naturally, in those days, that of Bettina Brentano, whose correspondence with the poet, translated in an attractive German-English by herself, had appeared in England in 1837, and had been reprinted at Lowell, Massachusetts, in 1841. Margaret Fuller, in the "Dial" in January, 1842,[1] had called attention to another work from the same source: the letters that had passed, at an earlier period than the Goethe correspondence, between Bettina and her friend Caroline von Günderode. These letters were published at Leipzig in 1840, after the death of Günderode. They were apparently written in the years 1805–06, when Bettina was about sixteen; and she in her letters to Goethe's mother, published in " Correspondence of a Child," gives an account of this friend and her tragic death.

[1] *Dial,* ii. 313.

Bettina is now little read, even by young people, apparently, but she then gave food for the most thoughtful. Emerson says: " Once I took such delight in Plato that I thought I never should need any other book ; then in Swedenborg, then in Montaigne, — even in Bettina ; " and Mr. Alcott records in his diary (August 2, 1839), "he [Emerson] seems to be as much taken with Bettina as I am." For the young, especially, she had a charm which lasts through life, insomuch that the present writer spent two happy days on the Rhine, so lately as 1878, in following out the traces of two impetuous and dreamy young women whom it would have seemed natural to meet on any hillside path, although more than half a century had passed since they embalmed their memory there.

When first at work upon this translation, Margeret Fuller wrote thus to the Rev. W. H. Channing : —

" I meant to have translated for you the best passages of ' Die Günderode ' (which I prefer to the correspondence with Goethe. The two girls are equal natures, and both in earnest. Goethe made a puppet-show for his private entertainment of Bettina's life, and we wonder she did not feel he was not worthy of her homage). But I have not been well enough to write much, and these pages are only what I have dictated ; they are not the best, yet will interest you. The exquisite little poem by Günderode read aloud two or three times, that you may catch the music ; it is of most sweet mystery.

She is to me dear and admirable, Bettina only interesting. She is of religious grace, Bettina the fullness of nature." [1]

Again she writes to him, copying at the same time Günderode's poem, " Ist Alles stumm und leer."

" Günderode is the ideal; Bettina, nature; Günderode throws herself into the river because the world is all too narrow. Bettina lives, and follows out every freakish fancy, till the enchanting child degenerates into an eccentric and undignified old woman. There is a medium somewhere. Philip Sidney found it; others had it found for them by fate." [2]

Apart from all other aspects of interest, Margaret Fuller's translation of the first part of these letters is perhaps the best piece of literary work that she ever executed; so difficult was it to catch the airy style of these fanciful German maidens; and so perfectly well did she succeed, preserving withal the separate individualities of the two correspondents. Only one thin pamphlet was published, in 1842, containing about a quarter part of the letters. It appeared without her name; and apparently there was not enough of patronage to lead her on; but, after the death of Bettina von Arnim, the translation was completed by Mrs. Minna Wesselhoeft at the suggestion of Miss Elizabeth P. Peabody, the original publisher, and was printed with Margaret Fuller's

[1] MS. (W. H. C.)   [2] MS. (W. H. C.)

fragment, by a Boston bookseller (Burnham) in
1860. There is nothing in the reprint to indi-
cate the double origin, but the point of transition
between the two translations occurs at the end of
the first letter on page 86; while this volume, as
completed, retains Margaret Fuller's original preface and an extract from her " Dial " essay. Mrs.
Wesselhoeft informs me that she revised Miss
Fuller's part of the translation, but found nothing to correct save two or three colloquial idioms,
pretty sure to be misinterpreted by one not a native of Germany.

Margaret Fuller's first original work was the
fruit of the only long journey she ever took, in
her own country; a summer spent in traveling in
what was then called " the far West " (May 25
to September 19, 1843) with her life-long friends,
James Freeman Clarke and his sister Sarah, under
the guidance of their brother, William H. Clarke,
of Chicago. The last named was one of Margaret Fuller's dearest friends; a man of rare gifts,
a delightful out-door companion and thoroughly
acquainted with the pioneer life to which he introduced his friends. Their mode of traveling
seems of itself to mark a period a hundred years
ago instead of forty; and is graphically described
in a letter to Mr. Emerson, written on the return
journey: —

" CHICAGO, *4th August*, 1843.

" We traveled in a way that left us perfectly free to
idle as much as we pleased, to gather every flower and
13

to traverse every wood we fancied. We were then in a strong vehicle called a lumber wagon which defied all the jolts and wrenches incident to wood paths, mud holes, and the fording of creeks ; we were driven by a friend, who drove admirably, who had the true spirit which animates daily life, who knew the habits of all the fowl, and fish, and growing things, and all the war-like legends of the country, and could recite them, not in a pedantical, but in a poetical manner ; thus our whole journey had the gayety of adventure, with the repose of intimate communion. Now we were in a nice carriage, fit for nothing but roads, and which *would* break even on those, with a regular driver, too careful of his horses to go off a foot-pace, etc., etc.

" However, we had much pleasure and saw many pretty things, of which I must tell you at my leisure. Our time was chiefly passed in the neighborhood of a chain of lakes, fine pieces of water, with the wide sloping park-like banks, so common in this country." [1]

" Summer on the Lakes " was prepared for the press after her return, with the aid of a good deal of study at the Harvard College Library ; where I can well remember to have seen Miss Fuller sitting, day after day, under the covert gaze of the undergraduates who had never before looked upon a woman reading within those sacred precincts, where twenty of that sex are now employed as assistants. She was correcting the press during much of the spring of 1844, when the proof-sheets came in every evening. " I expect it at night," she writes, " as one might some old guardian."

[1] MS.

During this period she had many sleepless nights, as appears by her diary, with such constant headaches that she chronicles not the days when she has them but when she is without them. One day at last she writes, quite exhausted : —

"I begin to be so tired of my book ! It will be through next Thursday, but I'm afraid I shall feel no better then, because dissatisfied with this last part. I ought to rewrite the Indian chapter, were there but time ! It will, I fear, seem desultory and ineffectual, when my materials are so rich ; *owre* rich, perhaps, for my mind does not act on them enough to fuse them."

The work itself is of value as illustrating a truth often noticed, that the ideal books of travel last longer than the merely statistical ; since the details, especially of our newer communities, are superseded in a year, while it may be decades before another traveler comes along who can look beneath them and really picture the new scenes for the mind's eye. A book of facts about Illinois in 1843 would now be of little value, but the things that Margaret Fuller noted are still interesting. Like Mrs. Jameson, who wrote her "Winter Studies and Summer Rambles" about the same time, she saw the receding Indian tribes from a woman's point of view; she sat in the wigwams, played with the children, pounded maize with the squaws. The white settlers, also, she studied, and recorded their characteristics ; " the Illinois farmers, the large, first product of the soil ; " and the varied nationalities represented among the foreign immigrants.   The following extract from a letter to Mr. Emerson shows her careful observation of these types, then so new: —

"Here I am interested in those who have a mixture of Indian blood.   With one lady I may become well acquainted, as she is to travel with us.   Her melancholy eyes, and slow, graceful utterance, and delicate feeling of what she has seen, attract me.   She is married here and wears our dress, but her family retain the dress and habits of their race.   Through her I hope to make other acquaintance that may please me.

"Next week we are going into the country to explore the neighborhood of Fox and Rock rivers.   We are going, in regular western style, to travel in a wagon, and stay with the farmers.   Then I shall see the West to better advantage than I have as yet.

"We are going to stay with one family, the mother of which had what they call a 'claim fight.'   Some desperadoes laid claim to her property, which is large; they were supposed to belong to the band who lately have been broken up by an exertion of lynch law. She built shanties in the different parts; she and her three daughters each took one to defend it.   They showed such bravery that the foe retreated.

"Then there is an Irish gentleman who owns a large property there.   He was married to the daughter of an Irish earl.   His son, a boy who inherits the (her) fortune he has left in Europe, and since the death of his wife lives alone on the Rock River; he has invited us to stay at his house, and the scenery there is said to be most beautiful.

"I hear, too, of a Hungarian count who has a large tract of land in Wisconsin.   He has removed thither with all his tenantry, several hundred persons they say. He comes to market at Milwaukee; they call him there the Count; they do not seem to know his other name. We are to stay at Milwaukee, and I shall inquire all about him. I should like to know how he has modified his life from the feudal lord to the brotherly landlord. I should think he must be a good and resolute man to carry out such a scheme successfully.

"I want to see some emigrant with worthy aims, using all his gifts and knowledge to some purpose honorable to the land, instead of lowering themselves to the requisitions of the moment, as so many of them do." [1]

The book has, doubtless, great defects, as is apt to be the case with a first work; an author feels, at such times, that he may never have another opportunity, and so is tempted to load his book down with episodes in order to lose nothing. This was the case with Miss Fuller. To insert boldly, in the middle of her book of travels, forty pages about Kerner's "Seeress of Prevorst," which she had read in Milwaukee, — this showed the waywardness of a student and talker, rather than the good judgment which she ought to have gained in editing even the most ideal of magazines. These things weighed the book down too heavily for success, and her brother, in reëditing her works, has wisely printed them separately. Yet the value of "Summer on the Lakes" remains; and I found afterwards, in traveling westward, that it had done more than any other book to prepare me for

[1] MS.

some of the most important aspects of that new world. It also excited interest in some quarters through the episodes themselves, especially that of " Mariana," which was taken to be autobiographical, as it partly was; although the character of Sylvain, Mariana's supposed lover, was almost wholly imaginary, as the following letter will show : —

" As to my book, there are complimentary notices in the papers, and I receive good letters about it. It is much read already, and is termed ' very entertaining ! ' Little & Brown take the risk, and allow a percentage. My bargain with them is only for one edition; if this succeeds, I shall make a better. They take their own measures about circulating the work, but any effort from my friends helps, of course. Short notices by you, distributed at Philadelphia, New York, and even Cincinnati, would attract attention and buyers ! ! Outward success in this way is very desirable to me, not so much on account of present profit to be derived, as because it would give me advantage in making future bargains, and open the way to ransom more time for writing. The account of the ' Seeress ' pleases many, and it is pleasing to see how elderly routine gentlemen, such as Dr. Francis and Mr. Farrar, are charmed with the little story of ' Mariana.' They admire, at poetic distance, that powerful nature that would alarm them so in real life. . . . Imagine prose eyes, with glassy curiosity looking out for Mariana ! Nobody dreams of its being like me ; they all thought Miranda was, in the ' Great Lawsuit.' People seem to think that not more than one phase of character can be shown in one life.

"Sylvain is only a suggested picture; you would not know the figure by which it is drawn, if you could see it. Have no desire, I pray thee, ever to realize these ideals. The name I took from Fanny Ellsler's partner. In the bridal dance, after movements of a bird-like joy, and overflowing sweetness, when he comes forward, she retires with a proud, timid grace, so beautiful; it said, 'See what a man I am happy enough to love.' And then came forward this well-taught dancer, springing and pirouetting without one tint of genius, one ray of soul; it was very painful and symbolized much, far more than I have expressed with Sylvain and Mariana." [1]

"Summer on the Lakes" seems to have yielded nothing to the author but copies to give away. It is a pathetic compensation for an unsuccessful book, that the writer at least has an abundant supply of it; and when we consider that Thoreau, eight years later, was carrying up to his garret, as unsold, seven hundred out of the thousand copies of his "Week on the Concord and Merrimack," we may well feel that Miss Fuller's little book of travels was successful, if it cost her nothing. At any rate she distributed it with some freedom, writing to Mr. Emerson, May 22, 1845, "Thirteen copies of 'Summer on the Lakes' were sent to your address in Boston; five for you, four for Caroline [Sturgis], four to be sent to Sarah Clarke, through James, if you will take the trouble." There must have been, at some time, a

[1] MS. (W. H. C.)

hope of a second edition, as Miss Sarah Clarke etched some charming illustrations to accompany it, a series of which I have seen. This re-issue never came, but she sold, apparently, seven hundred copies;[1] the whole edition of a new book at that day being usually five hundred or a thousand.

Before assuming her editorial work she found time to revise and amplify an essay which had been first published in the " Dial," and had attracted far more general attention than any of her previous articles. It had appeared in October, 1843, under the name of " The Great Lawsuit, or Man *vs.* Men, Woman *vs.* Women." This phrase was awkward, but well intentioned, its aim being to avert even the suspicion of awakening antagonism between the sexes. The title attracted attention, and as the edition of the " Dial," in its last year, was even smaller than ever before, this number soon disappeared from the market, and it is not uncommon to see sets of the periodical bound up without it, as is the case with my own.

She added a great deal to the essay before reprinting it, and brought it to a final completion during seven weeks delightfully spent amid the scenery of the Hudson, at Fishkill, N. Y., where she had the society of her favorite out-door companion, Miss Caroline Sturgis, lived in the open air with her when the sun shone, and composed only on rainy days. She wrote to Mr. Emerson (November 17, 1844) : —

[1] Fuller MSS. ii. 755.

"I have been happy now in freedom from headache and all other interruptions, and have spun out my thread as long and many-colored as was pleasing. The result I have not yet looked at; must put some days between me and it first. Then I shall revise and get it into printer's ink by Christmas, I hope." [1]

She wrote more fully, on the same day, to the Rev. W. H. Channing : —

"*Sunday evening,* 17*th November,* 1844.

"At last I have finished the pamphlet. The last day it kept spinning out beneath my hand. After taking a long walk early in one of the most noble, exhilarating sort of mornings, I sat down to write, and did not put the last stroke till near nine in the evening. Then I felt a delightful glow, as if I had put a good deal of my true life in it; as if, suppose I went away now, the measure of my footprint would be left on the earth. That was several days ago, and I do not know how it will look on revision, for I must leave several days more between me and it before I undertake that, but think it will be much better than if it had been finished at Cambridge, for here has been no headache, and leisure to choose my hours.

"It will make a pamphlet rather larger than a number of the 'Dial,' and would take a fortnight or more to print. Therefore I am anxious to get the matter *en train* before I come to New York, that I may begin the 1st December, for I want to have it out by Christmas. Will you, then, see Mr. Greeley about it the latter part of this week or the beginning of next? He is absent now, but will be back by that time, and I will write to

[1] MS.

him about it.   Perhaps he will like to undertake it himself.

" The estimate you sent me last summer was made
expecting an edition of fifteen hundred, but I think a
thousand will be enough.   The writing, though I have
tried to make my meaning full and clear, requires, shall
I say, too much culture in the reader to be quickly or
extensively diffused.   I shall be satisfied if it moves a
mind here and there, and through that others ; shall be
well satisfied if an edition of a thousand is disposed of
in the course of two or three years.   If the expense of
publication should not exceed a hundred or even a hundred and fifty dollars, I should not be unwilling to undertake it, if thought best by you and Mr. G.   But I
suppose you would not think that the favorable way as
to securing a sale.

" If given to a publisher, I wish to dispose of it only
for one edition.   I should hope to be able to make it
constantly better while I live, and should wish to retain
full command of it, in case of subsequent editions." [1]

Of the reception of this book, re-baptized " Woman in the Nineteenth Century," she wrote thus :

" The book is out, and the theme of all the newspapers and many of the journals.   Abuse, public and private, is lavished upon its views, but respect expressed
for me personally.   But the most speaking fact, and the
one which satisfied me, is that the whole edition was sold
off in a week to the booksellers, and $85 handed to me
as my share.   Not that my object was in any wise
money, but I consider this the signet of success.   If one
can be heard, that is enough ; I shall send you two

[1] MS. (W. H. C.)

copies, one for yourself and one to give away, if you like. If you noticed it in a New Orleans paper, you might create a demand for it there; the next edition will be out in May." [1]

On December 10, 1845, we find her recording in her journal the pleasure — rarer in those days than now — of receiving an English reprint, published in Clarke's Cabinet Library.[2] She was then visiting Mrs. Child; and she records, also, her hope of a second American edition, but I am not aware that it ever arrived until the book was reprinted, after her death, by her brother Arthur.

She also published, during her connection with the "Tribune," two thin volumes of her miscellaneous writings, called "Papers on Literature and Art." This work appeared in 1846, just before her departure for Europe, and was, in the judgment of her brother Arthur, the most popular of all her books. He has reprinted it, without alteration, in that volume of her writings called "Art, Literature, and the Drama," including the preface, which was thought to savor of vanity and became the theme of Lowell's satire; although the sentence he apparently had in view, "I feel with satisfaction that I have done a good deal to extend the influence of Germany and Italy among my compatriots," was strictly true.

It was in this volume that she published — being the only part of it that had not previously appeared in print — an essay on "American Liter-

---

[1] Fuller MSS. ii. 769. [2] Fuller MSS. ii. 793.

ature," in which she expressed, more fully than
before, the criticisms on Longfellow and others
which were then not uncommon among the Transcendentalists, and which, as uttered by her,
brought on her head some wrath. It did not
diminish this antagonism that the offending essay
attracted especial attention in England, and was
translated and published in a Paris review; but
this aspect of her career must be considered in a
later chapter.

XIII.

BUSINESS LIFE IN NEW YORK.

(1844–1846.)

THE transfer of Margaret Fuller, at the beginning of December, 1844, to what she called her "business life" in New York, made a distinct epoch in her career. After this her mental maturity began; at any rate, her *Wanderjahre*, in the German sense, as distinct from mere apprenticeship. She had come to be the housemate and literary coadjutor of the man who, among all Americans, then stood closest to the popular heart. The name of his journal was no misnomer; he was a Tribune of the People in the old Roman sense. His newspaper office was just at that time the working centre of much of the practical radicalism in the country; but he was also a person of ideal aims and tastes, and was perhaps the first conspicuous man in America, out of Boston, who publicly recognized in Emerson the greatest of our poets. He brought Margaret Fuller to New York, not only that she might put the literary criticism of the "Tribune" on a higher plane than any American newspaper occupied, but that she might discuss in a similar spirit all philan-

thropic questions. To investigate these subjects
on the practical side she had two coadjutors besides Horace Greeley ; — her early fellow-student,
Lydia Maria Child, then a resident of New York,
and also a later and yet closer friend, William
Henry Channing. This remarkable man, whose
gifts and services have in some degree passed from
the knowledge of the younger generation of Americans, through his long residence in England, was
then the most ardent of social reformers, the lof-
tiest among idealists, and — after Wendell Phil-
lips — the most eloquent of orators upon the anti-
slavery platform. But he was also the most
devoted of city missionaries, in New York and
elsewhere ; and, under his guidance, Margaret
Fuller could penetrate the very recesses of the
Five Points, then the last refuge of poverty and
crime. He had been one of her earliest co-labor-
ers on the " Dial ; " he was the intimate friend
of Horace Greeley; and his companionship thus
bridged for her the interval between the old life
and the new. He moreover preached on Sunday
to a small congregation of cultivated reformers ;
and here she found the needed outlet for the religious element in her nature, always profound,
sometimes mystical, but now taking a most health-
ful and active shape. It is a sign of her changed
life when she keeps her New Year's vigils, not in
poetic reveries, as at Boston and Brook Farm, but
in writing such a note as the following to Mr.
Channing : —

"New Year's Eve [1845].

"I forgot to ask you, dear William, where we shall begin in our round of visits to the public institutions. I want to make a beginning, as, probably, one a day and once a week will be enough for my time and strength.

"Now is the time for me to see and write about these things, as my European stock will not be here till spring.

"Should you like to begin with Blackwell's Island, Monday or Tuesday of next week?"[1]

She was at this time living in full sight of that celebrated penitentiary of which she writes. At the suggestion of Mrs. Greeley, who had known Margaret Fuller in Boston, she was not only invited to become a writer in the "Tribune" but a member of the editor's family; Mr. Greeley expressly stating that he regarded her rather as his wife's friend than his own.[2] He had lately taken up his residence in a large old wooden house, built as a country residence by a New York banker, on what New Yorkers call the East River, at Turtle Bay, nearly opposite the southernmost point of Blackwell's Island. The house had ample shrubbery and gardens, with abundant shade trees and fruit trees; and though the whole region is long since laid out in streets and covered with buildings, it was then accessible, as Mr. Greeley tells us, only by a long winding private lane, wholly dark at night and meeting the old "Boston Road" at Forty-Ninth Street. The only

[1] MS. (W. H. C.)   [2] Parton's *Greeley*, p. 258.

regular communication with the thickly-settled parts of that city — two miles away — was by an hourly stage on the Third Avenue.[1] In this suburban retirement Margaret Fuller must have been almost as much cut off from the evening life of the metropolis as if she had remained at Jamaica Plain; and this fact doubtless abbreviated her stay there; but meanwhile she reveled in its picturesqueness, — the wide hall, the piazza, the garden, the trees, the rocks, the gliding sails. She thus describes her position to her brother Eugene, in New Orleans: —

. . . "For me, I have never been so well situated. As to a home, the place where we live is old and dilapidated, but in a situation of great natural loveliness. When there I am perfectly secluded, yet every one I wish to see comes to see me and I can get to the centre of the city in half an hour. The house is kept in a Castle Rackrent style, but there is all affection for me and desire to make me at home, and I do feel so, which could scarcely have been expected from such an arrangement. My room is delightful; how I wish you could sit at its window with me and see the sails glide by! As to the public part, that is entirely satisfactory. I do just as I please, and as much or little as I please, and the editors express themselves perfectly satisfied; and others say that my pieces *tell* to a degree I could not expect. I think, too, I shall do better and better. I am truly interested in this great field which opens before me, and it is pleasant to be sure of a chance at half a hundred thousand readers.

[1] Greeley's *Recollections of a Busy Life,* p. 177.

"Mr. Greeley I like, nay more, love. He is, in his habits, a — plebeian ; in his heart, a noble man. His abilities, in his own way, are great. He believes in mine to a surprising extent. We are true friends." [1]

It was one result of the absorbing cares of her New York life that they left her, from the beginning, no space for the letters and diaries which before were so abundantly produced. Instead of soliloquizing or talking to her friends, she had to deal with the larger public of the "Tribune." She indeed almost ceased letter-writing, as we know from this brief note to the younger brother to whom she had heretofore written so freely : —

"I am very busy, and I receive, now I am separated from all my friends, letters in great number, which I do not attempt to answer, except in urgent cases. Nor do they expect it, but write to me again and again. They know that if I had the time and strength, which I have not, I must not fritter away my attention on incessant letter-writing. I must bend it on what is before me, if I wish to learn or to do." [2]

We are therefore left to know her, at this period, mainly through the testimony of Horace Greeley, her chief and her first host. He never could overcome a slight feeling of professional superiority to the woman who could not write more than a column of matter to his ten ; and who was sometimes incapacitated from work by headaches, whereas he plodded on, ill or well, doing always his daily share. But to her public spirit, her love

[1] Fuller MSS. ii. 765–767.   [2] Fuller MSS. ii. 749.

of children, her generous attitude to all comers, he
bears explicit testimony in his " Recollections."
He describes the involuntary testimony paid to
her by the women who visited the Greeley house;
the naturalness with which she took the lead
among them without exciting jealousy, and the
" almost oriental adoration " which she often
inspired among them.　He expresses constant
amazement at the way in which those who had
known her but a day insisted on telling her their
secrets and asking counsel.　" I judge," he says,
" that she was the repository of more confidences
than any contemporary, and I am sure no one had
ever reason to regret the imprudent precipitancy
of these trusts."　Chambermaids and seamstresses
came to her and unburdened their souls ; and all
children loved her.　" As the elephant's trunk,"
Mr. Greeley says, " serves either to rend a limb
from the oak or pick up a pin, so her wonderful
range of capacities, of experiences, of sympathies,
seemed adapted to every condition and phase of
humanity."　He speaks especially of her " marvelous powers of personation and mimicry ; "
thinks she might, had she chosen, have been the
first actress of the century, but declares that she
seemed quite absorbed, while living, in the simple
effort to leave some small corner of the world
better than she found it.[1]

　　She did not, however, dwell permanently at the
house of Horace Greeley, but afterwards at sev‹

[1] Greeley's *Recollections,* p. 181.

eral different abodes, nearer the "Tribune" office. She resided, for a month or two, in the family of Mr. and Mrs. Cranch; having, during a part of this time, the companionship of a favorite friend, Miss Caroline Sturgis, with whom she enjoyed to the utmost the social and artistic delights of New York. We find her writing in the "Tribune" about picture-galleries, the theatre, the Philharmonic concerts, the German opera, Ole Bull's performances on the violin, and Mr. Hudson's lecture on Shakespeare. Later she had lodgings for a long time at the house of Mrs. McDowell, where she had opportunity to give receptions to her literary friends and to preside as a gracious hostess with a white japonica in her hair. She did most of her writing and proof-reading at home, not keeping regular office-hours: and she evidently worked very hard in her own way, which was not always Mr. Greeley's method. Her researches into poverty and crime took many of her leisure hours; and she sometimes, in the prosecution of these researches, stayed a day or two with Mrs. Child, who, like herself, was equally ready to be absorbed in the music of the spheres and in the sorrows of the streets. Her practical aims were at this time well described in a letter written to her old friend Miss Mary Rotch of New Bedford, Massachusetts, one of those saints who are "Aunt Mary" to a wide circle: —

"New York, *January* 15, 1845.

"Always dear Aunt Mary, — . . . This stopped me, just as I had begun to visit the institutions here, of a remedial and benevolent kind. So soon as I am quite well, I shall resume the survey. Mr. Greeley is desirous I should make it, and make what use of it I think best, in the paper. I go with William C. [Channing]. It is a great pleasure to us to coöperate in these ways. I do not expect to do much, practically, for the suffering, but having such an organ of expression [the 'New York Tribune'], any suggestions that are well grounded may be of use. I have always felt great interest for those women who are trampled in the mud to gratify the brute appetites of men, and wished I might be brought naturally into contact with them. Now I am so, I think I shall have much that is interesting to tell you when we meet.

"I go on very moderately, for my strength is not great, and I am now connected with a person who is anxious I should not overtask it; yet I shall do more for the paper by and by. At present, beside the time I spend in looking round and examining my new field, I am publishing a volume of which you will receive a copy, called 'Woman in the Nineteenth Century;' a part of my available time is spent in attending to it as it goes through the press; for really the work seems but half done when your book is *written*. I like being here; the streams of life flow free, and I learn much I feel so far satisfied as to have laid my plans to stay a year and a half, if not longer, and to have told Mr. G. that I probably shall. That is long enough for a mortal to look forward and not too long, as I must look forward in order to get what I want from Europe.

"Mr. Greeley is a man of genuine excellence, honorable, benevolent, of an uncorrupted disposition, and, in his way, of even great abilities." [1]

The breadth of her work in practical directions — the proof that she was now obtaining what she had always sought, a working-place for something beyond self-culture — is to be seen in the very titles of her papers in the "Tribune." She wrote, Mr. Parton tells us, about three articles a week, these discussing such themes as "The Rich Man," "The Poor Man," "Woman in Poverty," "What fits a Man to be a Voter?" "The Condition of the Blind," "Prison Discipline," "Appeal for an Asylum for discharged Female Convicts," "Politeness to the Poor," "Capital Punishment." Then there are Meditations for special days, as Thanksgiving, Christmas, New Year's, St. Valentine's Day, the Fourth of July, the first of August; these having always some practical bearing. Thus her St. Valentine's Eve was passed at the Bloomingdale Asylum for the Insane, and she describes it. Mr. Greeley thus testifies in regard to this practical tendency of her work : —

"For every effort to limit vice, ignorance, and misery she had a ready, eager ear, and a willing hand; so that her charities — large in proportion to her slender means — were signally enhanced by the fitness and fullness of her wise and generous counsel, the readiness and emphasis with which she, publicly and privately, commended to those richer than herself any object de-

[1] Fuller MSS. i. 43.

serving their alms. She had once attended, with other noble women, a gathering of outcasts of their sex; and, being asked how they appeared to her, replied, 'As women like myself, save that they are victims of wrong and misfortune.' No project of moral or social reform ever failed to command her generous, cheering benediction, even when she could not share the sanguine hopes of its authors: she trusted that these might somehow benefit the objects of their self-sacrifice, and felt confident that they must, at all events, be blessed in their own moral natures. I doubt that our various benevolent and reformatory associations had ever before, or have ever since received such wise, discriminating commendation to the favor of the rich, as they did from her pen during her connection with the 'Tribune.' " [1]

Her sympathy was strong for these women, betrayed into a life of crime by the sins of others; and Mr. Greeley expresses confidently his belief that "If she had been born to large fortune, a house of refuge for all female outcasts desiring to return to the ways of virtue would have been one of her most cherished and first realized conceptions." [2] And to show the strength and discrimination with which she handled another difficult class of questions, I will quote a passage that particularly pleased Mr. Greeley, in regard to the vexed question of Irish immigration: —

" When we consider all the fire which glows so untama-

---

[1] Greeley's *Recollections*, pp. 179, 180.
[2] Parton's *Greeley*, p. 260.

bly in Irish veins, the character of her people, — considering the circumstances, almost miraculous in its goodness, — we cannot forbear, notwithstanding all the temporary ills they aid in here, to give them all a welcome to our shores. Those ills we need not enumerate ; they are known to all, and we rank among them what others would not, that by their ready service to do all the hard work they make it easier for the rest of the population to grow effeminate and help the country to grow too fast. But that is her destiny, to grow too fast ; it is useless talking against it. Their extreme ignorance, their blind devotion to a priesthood, their pliancy in the hands of demagogues, threaten continuance of these ills ; yet, on the other hand, we must regard them as a most valuable element in the new race. They are looked upon with contempt for their want of aptitude at learning new things, their ready and ingenious lying, their eye-service. These are the faults of an oppressed race which must require the aid of better circumstances through two or three generations to eradicate. Their virtues are their own, — they are many, genuine, and deeply rooted. Can an impartial observer fail to admire their truth to domestic ties, their power of generous bounty and more generous gratitude, their indefatigable good-humor (for ages of wrong which have driven them to so many acts of desperation could never sour their blood at its source), their ready wit, their elasticity of nature ? They are at bottom one of the best nations in the world. — Would they were welcomed here, not to work, merely, but to intelligent sympathy and efforts, both patient and ardent, for the education of their children. No sympathy could be better deserved, no efforts wiselier timed."

But while her articles on public questions, signed always with an asterisk (*), were those most read in New York, it was her literary criticism that traveled farthest and brought forth most praise or blame. Her first paper in the "Tribune" was a review of Emerson's "Essays," which appeared December 7, 1844.[1] Here she was, in a manner, on her own ground; but she soon had to plunge, so far as literature was concerned, into a sea of troubles. She entered on her work at a time when the whole standard of literary criticism, not only in America but in England, needed mending. The tomahawk theory still prevailed among editors and even among authors; men revenged literary slights by personal abuse; the desire to "make an example" of a person or to "get even with him" had not then vanished from literature, as it has not yet disappeared from politics. Poe's miscellaneous writings were full of this sort of thing; Lowell's "Fable for Critics" was not at all free from it. At such a time it was no easy thing for a woman to pass from a comparatively secluded life in Boston and her circle of personal friends in the "Dial," to what then seemed the metropolitan life of New York and the hand-to-mouth existence of a daily newspaper.

To the bad tendencies of the time her work furnished an excellent antidote. From some experiences of the daily journal she recoiled at first and perhaps always; the break-neck speed, the

[1] Parton's *Greeley*, p. 255.

necessity of reviewing every book while fresh, no matter though the calm reflection of many days may be needed to do it justice. Horace Greeley, a born gladiator, whose words came swift and hard as blows, records his own impatience at her too cautious habits. If an author's case was pressing, he thought she should sit up an hour later that night and give him the finishing stroke; and the papers that brought her most criticism were those in which she yielded to these importunities, against her own better judgment.

The editorial "we" brings its temptations alike to women and men ; and sometimes her very utterances of deprecation were ill-expressed and taken for new assertion of herself. When she denied to Lowell the genuine poetic gift and said that she must assert this "although to the grief of many friends and the disgust of more," it was unquestionably meant as a bit of sincere humility, and she must have been amazed to find it taken as a phrase of conceit. But she kept higher laws than she broke. In that epoch of strife which I so well remember, that storm-and-stress period, that *Sturm-und-Drangzeit*, she held the critical sway of the most powerful American journal with unimpaired dignity and courage. By comparing a single page of her collected works with any page, taken almost at random, of Edgar Poe's, we see the difference more clearly than it can be expressed in words. On this we have the distinct testimony of the most mercilessly honest of all critics, Horace Greeley : —

" But, one characteristic of her writings I feel bound
to commend, — their absolute truthfulness. She never
asked how this would sound, nor whether that would do,
nor what would be the effect of saying anything; but
simply, 'Is it the truth? Is it such as the public should
know?' And if her judgment answered, 'Yes,' she uttered it; no matter what turmoil it might excite, nor what
odium it might draw down on her own head. Perfect
conscientiousness was an unfailing characteristic of her
literary efforts. Even the severest of her critiques, —
that on Longfellow's Poems, — for which an impulse in
personal pique has been alleged, I happen with certainty to know had no such origin. When I first
handed her the book to review, she excused herself, assigning the wide divergence of her views of poetry from
those of the author and his school, as her reason. She
thus induced me to attempt the task of reviewing it
myself. But day by day sped by, and I could find no
hour that was not absolutely required for the perform-
ance of some duty that *would not* be put off, nor turned
over to another. At length I carried the book back to
her in utter despair of ever finding an hour in which
even to look through it; and, at my renewed and earnest request, she reluctantly undertook its discussion.
The statement of these facts is but an act of justice to
her memory." [1]

Meanwhile, she was always saving up money
for her long-desired trip to Europe; though this
fund was again and again depleted by the needs of
her family and friends. Several hundred dollars
went at once, for instance, to publish for a Danish

[1] Parton's *Greeley*, p. 259.

exile, Harro Harring, a novel called "Dolores," which the publisher had been frightened out of issuing at the last moment, on theological grounds, and which never yielded a dollar to anybody. At last, receiving an invitation from her friends, Marcus and Rebecca Spring, to accompany them and their young son on their voyage, she left New York after twenty months of residence ; "modifying but not terminating her connection with the 'Tribune,' " — in Mr. Greeley's phrase, — and sailed for England on the first of August, 1846.

XIV.

EUROPEAN TRAVEL.

(1846–1847.)

THIS was Margaret Fuller's last note to Mr. Emerson before her departure for Europe: —

"NEW YORK, 15*th July,* 1846.

"I leave Boston in the Cambria, 1st August. Shall be at home at my mother's in Cambridgeport the morning of the 30th July. Can see you either that day or the next there, as I shall not go out. Please write to care of Richard [Fuller], 6 State Street, Boston, which day you will come.

"I should like to take the letter to Carlyle, and wish you would name the Springs in it. Mr. S. has been one of those much helped by Mr. C. I should like to see Tennyson, but doubt whether Mr. C. would take any trouble about it. I take a letter to Miss Barrett. I am likely to see Browning through her. It would do no harm to mention it, though. I have done much to make him known here." [1]

Sailing on the appointed day, she landed at Liverpool, August 12th. A note-book lies before me, kept by her during the first weeks of her European life. It contains hints that were often

[1] MS.

amplified for her " Tribune " letters; but for myself, I always find the first note-book more interesting. " Memory," says the poet Gray, "is ten
times worse than a lead pencil," and it is really
of more value to know what struck a traveler
at the outset than what was afterwards added
to his knowledge. Nothing tests one's habits of
mind and independence of character like the first
glimpse of a foreign country; and it must be remembered that Europe was far more foreign to
Americans forty years ago than to-day. Omitting
a few preliminary passages, the note-book goes on
as follows, being here printed precisely as it is
written; the exact dates being rarely given in
it, but the time being the latter part of August,
1846, and thenceforward: —

" Went to the Paradise-street chapel to hear James
Martineau. His over-intellectual appearance. His con-
servative tendencies, liberality only in spots. Mr. Ireland, a most liberal man, a devout reader of the ' Dial.'
His early record of Waldo [Emerson]. Delight at seeing these impressions confirmed by the stand he has
taken since. Mr. Ireland, declining all stimulants on
the most ultra ground, takes four or five strong cups of
tea, which he does not need. — Monday morning. Me-
chanics' Institute, — method of instruction — seventeen
hundred pupils. Provision for the girls. Fine building
bought for them, at seven thousand pounds. Woman
nominally, not really, at the head. Royal Institute.
Series of works of early Italian art collected by Roscoe. Statue of Roscoe by Chantrey.

" Afternoon. Sweet place on the banks of the Mersey, called 'the Dingle.' Feeling of the man of letters toward the man of money. Park laid out by Mr. Gates for use of the public, a very good means of doing good. Marriage of Mr. J. at Dr. H.'s. Peculiar management of Fleas! Mrs. H. the translator of 'Spiridion.' Fine heads of Godwin, Herwegh, Hoffmann von Fallersleben, Rachel. Splendid full length of Goethe, which I want for myself. Mem. to get a fine head of Rachel for Caroline. Herwegh, too, perhaps. Head of Catharina of Russia. Colossal and Ideal head of Beethoven.

" Early letters of Carlyle, written in the style of the 'Life of Schiller,' occasionally swelling into that of Dr. Johnson. Very low views of life, comfortable and prudential advice as to marriage, envy of riches, thirst for fame avowed as a leading motive.

"Tuesday. Pay up bill. Great expensiveness of the Adelphi. Route from Liverpool to Lancaster. From the latter canal boat to Kendal. Beautiful picture presented by the young Bengalese, our fellow-traveler. Cordial talk of English gentleman. Silly German, with his horrid chat and smirk. His foolish way of addressing an intelligent child. Kendal, the Castle. To Ambleside. Drive presents a landscape for once, lit up by sunshine as exquisite as I had hoped even. Man and Nature go hand in hand here in England. Blue bell, Campanula.

" The fuchsia grows here to great size in the open air. Directions for its culture, note in letter to mother. Make a bed of bog-earth and sand, plant the fuchsias, and give them constantly a great deal of water — this is all that is needful.

" Ambleside. Miss Martineau's house. The look of

health in her face, but a harried, excited, over-stimulated state of mind. Home at the confectioner's, a sweet little English home, with modest, gentle, English Jane to wait. Her courtesy about Eddie [Edward Spring]. Many such little things show us how natural is the disgust of the English to the bad manners and careless habits they find in America. Their ways of driving over these excellent roads are even amusing from their care.

"Evening at Mrs. Derby's, sister-in-law of Sir Humphrey. Her mother, aged seventy-six, a fine specimen of what I have heard of the Scotch lady. Next day drive with Mrs. P. Handsome dwellings on the banks of Windermere. Evening at Miss M.'s. Mr. Milman, Dr. Gregory. Stories about Hartley Coleridge, and account of Sara C., author of 'Phantasmion.' Note the chapter she has added to the 'Aids to Reflection' now about to be published.

"It seems the cause of Coleridge's separation from his wife and family was wholly with himself: because his opium and his indolence prevented his making any exertions to support them. That burden fell on Southey, who, without means, except from his pen, sustained the four persons thus added to his family. Just as I might do for —— if I would. Hartley Coleridge's bad habits naturally inherited from his father. Waiter offers to keep 'the talking gentleman' to board him, to clothe him. Oh don't, don't take away the 'talking gentleman!' How wicked to transmit these morbid states to children! Mr. Milman's hard and worldly estimate. Introduced to Dr. Gregory. A man of truly large, benevolent mind.

"Next day Grasmere, Rydal Mount. I was disappointed in the habitation of Wordsworth. It is almost the least beautiful spot hereabout. Remarks of our landlady about W. how pleasing, constantly ending with 'And Mrs. Wordsworth, too.' 'And really, ma' am, I think it is because he is so kind a neighbor.'

"Windermere. The professed magnetizer with his *beaux yeux* and extreme sensibility, unable to confer benefit without receiving injury, gave me yet another view of this grand subject." [1]

"Mr. and Mrs. Bracebridge, specimens, we understand, of the first English *hairystocracy*, spoken of as something extra — of their class, — and, indeed, they were very liberal. Mr. B. much engaged in prison and other reforms. Owns a place in Athens, and lives there often.

"Sunday evening with B.'s and G.'s. Gossip about the upper classes, but in a good spirit. It amused me to hear the mechanical, measured way in which they talked of character. With all the abuses of America, we have one advantage which outweighs them all. Most persons reject the privilege, but it is, really, possible for one to grow.

"Monday. Spent the morning in finishing letter for the steamer. Afternoon on the lake of Grasmere. Wet feet. Extraordinary kindness of the ladies of the Clan Campbell. Easedale, Loughrigg, a most enchanting place, dear to Wordsworth.

"Thursday. Romantic story of our landlady's husband, quite in my line. Walk along the hills, little ravine, arched bridge, and brook rushing beneath it. Delightful walk over the fields past Fox How. Speak

[1] This apparently refers to the celebrated H. G. Atkinson, who converted Miss Martineau to his opinions. Another account of him by Miss Fuller will be found in her *Memoirs*, ii. 173.

of Dr. Arnold and the justice done him all around. Said to have made a happy and equal marriage. Visit to Wordsworth. Evening at the Greys'. Cultivated and liberal mind of the manufacturer. Ditto of the country gentleman. Countess Hahn Hahn had just been at Ambleside.

" Wednesday. To Langdale. Scaurfell the scene of the ' Excursion.' Rothay church. First fall lunch in the farm-house. Dungeon Ghyll Force. Most enchanting view at last. As fine a day as I ever had. Account in evening by tedious Miss Briggs of the ease with which one may be lost in the mist. This 26th was Eddie's birthday.

" Thursday. Farewell to Ambleside. A happy eight days we have had here." [1]

Portions of a more complete narrative, based on these sketches, will be found in her " Memoirs," [2] and other portions in her " Tribune " letters. The instances of alternate contraction and expansion, in these ampler narratives, are very interesting and characteristic, and the total impression of truthfulness and accuracy is strong. There are no signs of retouching for literary effect, but in many cases the single word of memorandum suggests a paragraph, while on other points caution or courtesy dictated a reticence which it is now needless to maintain.

Here is a passage from her Edinburgh diary. David Scott, whose pictures interested her so

[1] MS. Note-Book.
[2] ii. 171. The *Tribune* letters may be found in *At Home and Abroad.*

much, painted a striking portrait of Emerson, which is now in the Concord, Massachusetts, public library: —

[September, 1846.] " At Robert Chambers's. Saw there beautiful book of Highlanders in their costumes. Hopes of chemistry as to making food. Remark of R. C. as to the *clumsiness* of nature's means of providing for that purpose, etc. Mrs. C. with her fifteen children and three pair of twins among them.

"Monday. Visit to the Bank of Scotland. To [David] Scott's room. He is a severe, earnest man with high imaginations. I liked him much, and his pictures from him, though there was not one which, taken by itself, could be called really good.

"Note here, not that it has to do anything with these matters, but because I happen to think of it here, that the tune of 'Scots wha hae' is, according to tradition, the original one of 'Hey Tutti Taiti,' to which the Scots did actually march to the field of Bannockburn. Shoemaker amazed at the N. Y. [New York] shoes. Evening at Mrs. Crowe's. S. B. [Samuel Brown.] D. S. [David Scott.] Mr. De Quincey. Pleasant flow of talk, but the Opium Eater did not get into his gorgeous style. Good story told by S. B. about Burns. Write it out for 'Tribune' and quote the pertinent verse.[1] I was very sorry to leave Edina now; might have had such good times with the two friends."

Her view of Mary Queen of Scots is put in too striking a manner to be omitted : —

[September, 1846.] " Holyrood. Prince Labanoff.

[1] This story may be found in *Memoirs*, ii. 177 ; and the *Tribune* letter in *At Home and Abroad*, p. 139.

The world would not suffer that poor beautiful girl to have the least good time, and now cannot rest for championing her. Singular misery of the lot of a woman with whom all men were dying in love, except her two last husbands ; and with the first, a poor sickly child, she had no happiness. A woman the object of desire to so many, yet never suffered to become the parent of more than two children, and from those separated in so brief a space after birth, and never permitted to take the least comfort in them afterwards. Picture of Montrose charmed my eye. Some noble Vandykes. A full length of George by Wilkie. Hateful old John Knox, with a wife like himself. Came up the Canongate. Were ever people so villainously dirty?"[1]

During her tour in Scotland it is interesting to see how lightly she passes by the night when she was lost on Ben Lomond, of which so full an account is given in her " Memoirs:"[2] —

[September, 1846.] "Inversnaid. In the boat to Rowardennan. Loch Lomond. Boatmen. A fine race. Gaelic songs. Relate their import. Undoubting faith of these people in the story of 'The Lady of the Lake.' 'Oh, yes,' said the boatmen, ' we know they are true, having been handed down from father to son for so many generations.' At Rowardennan. Down in the boat to Luss. Character of the place. Cleanliness for once. The minister, a ' ceevil hamely man.' The Manse. Sunset on Ben Lomond. I was alone. Evening.

[1] MS. Note-Book. There is a passage somewhat similar, but not nearly so well stated, reprinted from the *Tribune*, in *At Home and Abroad*, p. 149.

[2] *Memoirs*, ii. 178; also, *At Home and Abroad*, p. 153.

Dance of the reapers in the barn. Highland strathspey and fling ? Enormous price of fruit in Edinburgh ; total want of it in the country. Quote of Sir W. Scott the feelings of Fitz James about treachery, etc., in his dream ; speak of his character and quote concluding lines in ' Lady of the Lake.'

" Observation on figures of men and women engaged in the Highland dances. Labor alone will not develop the form.

" Next day. Saturday, 12th September. Ascent of Ben Lomond. Lost, and pass the night on a heathery mountain. All the adventures of the eventful twenty-hours to be written out in full. Love Marcus and Rebecca [Spring] forever.

" Sunday. Sick all day from fatigue or excitement. Dinner given by M. [Marcus Spring] to the shepherds. Their natural politeness and propriety of feeling. Peter Cameron. Monday. Still ill, but walked out in the afternoon and saw the purple hills and lake, with what delightful emotions. I seemed to have become acquainted with their genius as I could not in any other way. Inquiring lady thought it must have been ' *awkward*' for me on the hill between 12 and 1 ! Tuesday. Leave Rowardennan. Steamboat with its execrable fiddle, *à l'ordinaire*. Tarbet. Rowed along lochs through pass of Glencrae to Cairndow. Boat to Inverary on Loch Fine. Night there. Read ' Legend of Montrose.'

" Wednesday morning. Duke of Argyle's place. Highland servant in full costume, stupid as the stones he trod on. Noble park. Black Highland cattle. Cross in the market-place from Iona."

Margaret Fuller's note-book closes abruptly, like that of many a traveler, just as she reaches

London, where it would be the most interesting. Her farther progress can be traced by her letters to the " Tribune," which have been reprinted by her brother in the volume of her works called " At Home and Abroad." Over this period I shall pass rapidly, as it is very amply treated in the printed " Memoirs." She had, of course, that peculiar delight of the cultivated American in London, where, as Willis said, he sees whole shelves of his library walking about in coats and gowns. With her boundless love of knowledge, and the scantiness of libraries and museums in the America of that day, she was charmed by the centralization of London; the concentration in one spot of treasures such as may by and by be found scattered through many cities in America, but will never be brought together in one. She saw the heroes of that day, some of whom are heroes still: Wordsworth, Dr. Chalmers, Andrew Combe, the Howitts, Dr. Southwood Smith, De Quincey, Joanna Baillie. Browning, just married, had gone to Italy. Her descriptions of Carlyle [1] are almost as spicy as Carlyle's own letters, and she dismisses Lewes in almost as trenchant a manner as that in which Carlyle dismissed Heraud. Best of all for her, she made acquaintance with Mazzini, whom she was soon to meet again in Italy. She was very cordially received, her two volumes of " Miscellanies " having just been favorably reviewed by the English press; she was inundated

[1] *Memoirs,* ii. 184.

with invitations and opportunities, and could only
mourn, like so many Americans since her day, that
these delightful hospitalities encroached sadly upon
the time to be given to galleries and museums.

In Paris she saw La Mennais, Béranger, and
George Sand; went constantly to the lectures, galleries, and Chamber of Deputies ; saw Rachel act
and heard Chopin play. She found her "Essay
on American Literature" translated and published in " La Revue Indépendante," though the
satisfaction was mitigated by having her name
announced as Elizabeth. She worked away at
learning colloquial French until she spoke it flu-
ently, though not accurately ; and her teacher
pleased her by saying that her accent was like
that of an Italian, though this from French lips
can never be much of a compliment. Yet with
her deep love for Italy she was probably pleased
at the thought of speaking French like an Italian, just as Englishmen are said to be pleased at
speaking it like Englishmen — which, to do them
justice, they usually accomplish. On February
25, 1847, she left Paris for Italy, and in early
spring established herself for a time in Rome.
In summer she went to the different Italian cities,
then to Switzerland. In October she settled herself for the winter in Rome, whose wonderful inspiration she profoundly felt. She says of her
own first experiences there, " All mean things
were forgotten in the joy that rushed over me
like a flood." She felt, as so many Americans

feel in Europe, an impulse to separate herself for a time from all English-speaking people and plunge into a wholly untried atmosphere. She had new and interesting friends, such as the Milanese Madame Arconati, Marchesa Visconti; and a Polish lady, born Princess Radzivill. But unlike, alas! the majority of Americans in Europe, her whole sympathy was with the party of progress, and the rapid unrolling of events in 1848 made an occasion for her, "such a time as I have always dreamed of," she writes. She saw the uprising against Austria; the Austrian arms burned in the public square. She was herself poor, a stranger remote from home; but she was for a time better in health than since she was a child, and her whole heart was with the Italian revolution. When Mazzini returned from his seventeen years of exile, she was able to stand by his side. She saw the republic established; she saw it fall. In April, 1849, Rome was besieged by the French army. Yet already a deeper thread than even the welfare of Italy had mingled itself in her life. In December, 1847, she had been secretly married; in September, 1848, her child had been born. But for this climax of her life I must turn to the narratives of others.

XV.

MARRIAGE AND MOTHERHOOD.

(1847–1850.)

MARGARET FULLER'S profoundest feeling about marriage and motherhood had already been recorded for years in a fragment of her journal. With strong, firm touches, in this confession, she balances what she has against what she would fain possess ; and visibly tries to make the best of the actual : —

"I have no home on the earth, and [yet] I can think of one that would have a degree of beautiful harmony with my inward life.

"But, driven from home to home as a Renouncer, I get the picture and the poetry of each. Keys of gold, silver, iron, and lead are in my casket.

"No one loves me. But I love many a good deal, and see some way into their eventual beauty. I am myself growing better and shall by and by be a worthy object of love, one that will not anywhere disappoint or need forbearance. Meanwhile I have no fetter on me, no engagement, and as I look on others, almost every other, can I fail to feel this a great privilege ? I have no way tied my hands or feet. And yet the varied calls on my sympathy have been such that I hope not to be made partial, cold, or ignorant by this isolation. I have no child, and the woman in me has so craved this experience, that it has seemed the want of it must paralyze me. But now as I look on these lovely children of a human birth, what slow and neutralizing cares they bring with them to the mother! The children of the muse come quicker, with less pain and disgust, rest more lightly on the bosom and have" . . . [here the fragment ends.] [1]

It may naturally be asked why, with such a true woman's longing for home and children, Margaret Fuller had never been married. Loved "with oriental adoration," in Horace Greeley's phrase, by many women, she had also been loved sincerely by many men, while some of each sex had no doubt disliked her. Her letters to the men with whom she was, in maturer years, most intimate are singularly free, I will not merely say from coquettishness or sentimentality, but from anything that could fall short of her high standard of friendship. There is, however, no question that she had in early life at least one deep experience of personal emotion, followed by a reaction of disappointment. It is a satisfaction to know that the same letters which prove this — letters which I am not authorized to publish, nor should I wish to do it — show her only in an unselfish and generous aspect, while they bring her nearer to us by proving that even she, with all her Roman ambition, was still "a very woman" at heart.

[1] MS. (W. H. C.)

With this retrospect for a background, the married life of Margaret Fuller Ossoli may now be studied. It will be portrayed, so far as possible, from original documents ; the first place being given to a letter, relating to her, not included in the " Memoirs," from Mr. Cass, then American *chargé d'affaires* at Rome, and one of the few in whom she put confidence, at the great crisis of her life. The letter is addressed to Mrs. W. Ellery Channing, of Concord, Massachusetts, who, as has already been said, was the younger sister of Madame Ossoli.

" LEGATION DES ÉTATS-UNIS D'AMÉRIQUE.
ROME, *May* 10, 1851.

" MADAM, — I beg leave to acknowledge the receipt of your letter of the —th ult., and to express my regret that the weak state of my eyesight has prevented me from giving it an earlier reply.

" In compliance with your request, I have the honor to state, succinctly, the circumstances connected with my acquaintance with the late Madame Ossoli, your deceased sister, during her residence in Rome.

" In the month of April, 1849, Rome, as you are no doubt aware, was placed in a state of siege by the approach of the French army. It was filled at that time with exiles and fugitives who had been contending for years, from Milan, in the North, to Palermo, in the South, for the Republican cause : and when the gates were closed, it was computed that there were, of Italians alone, thirteen thousand refugees within the walls of the city, all of whom had been expelled from adjacent states, till Rome became their last rallying-point, and to

many their final resting-place. Among these was to be
seen every variety of age, sentiment, and condition, —
striplings and blanched heads ; wild, visionary enthusi-
asts ; grave, heroic men, who, in the struggle for freedom, had ventured all and lost all ; nobles and beggars ;
bandits, felons, and brigands. Great excitement naturally existed ; and, in the general apprehension which
pervaded all classes that acts of personal violence and
outrage would soon be committed, the foreign residents,
especially, found themselves placed in an alarming situation.

"On the 30th of April the first engagement took
place between the French and Roman troops, and a few
days subsequently I visited several of my countrymen,
at their request, to concert measures for their safety.
Hearing on that occasion, for the first time, of Miss
Fuller's presence in Rome, and of her solitary mode of
life, I ventured to call upon her, offering my services in
any manner that might conduce to her comfort and se-
curity. She received me with much kindness, and thus
our acquaintance commenced. Her residence, on the
Piazza Barberini, being considered an insecure abode,
she removed to the Casa Dies, which was occupied by
several American families.

" In the engagements [which succeeded] between the
Roman and French troops, the wounded of the former
were brought into the city, and disposed throughout the
different hospitals, which were under the superintend-
ence of several ladies of high rank, who had formed
themselves into associations, the better to insure care
and attention to these unfortunate men. Miss Fuller
took an active part in this noble work, and the greater
portion of her time, during the entire siege, was passed

in the Hospital of the Trinity of the Pilgrims, which was placed under her direction, in attendance upon its inmates.

"The weather was intensely hot; her health was feeble and delicate; the dead and dying were around her in every form of pain and horror; but she never shrank from the duty she had assumed. Her heart and soul were in the cause for which these men had fought, and all was done that woman could do to comfort them in their sufferings. I have seen the eyes of the dying, as she moved among them, extended upon opposite beds, meet in commendation of her unwearied kindness; and the friends of those who then passed away may derive consolation from the assurance that nothing of tenderness and attention was wanting to soothe their last moments. And I have heard many of those who recovered speak with all the passionate fervor of the Italian nature of her, whose sympathy and compassion throughout their long illness fulfilled all the offices of love and affection. Mazzini, the chief of the Triumvirate, — who, better than any man in Rome, knew her worth, — often expressed to me his admiration of her high character; and the Princess Belgiojoso, to whom was assigned the charge of the Papal Palace on the Quirinal, which was converted on this occasion into a hospital, was enthusiastic in her praise. And in a letter which I received not long since from this lady, who is gaining the bread of an exile by teaching languages in Constantinople, she alludes with much feeling to the support afforded by Miss Fuller to the Republican party in Italy. Here, in Rome, she is still spoken of in terms of regard and endearment; and the announcement of her death was received with a degree of sorrow which is not often bestowed upon a foreigner, and especially one of a different faith.

"On the 29th of June the bombardment from the French camp was very heavy, shells and grenades falling from every part of the city. In the afternoon of the 30th I received a brief note from Miss Fuller, requesting me to call at her residence. I did so without delay, and found her lying on a sofa, pale and trembling, evidently much exhausted. She informed me that she had sent for me to place in my hands a packet of important papers, which she wished me to keep for the present, and, in the event of her death, to transmit it to her friends in the United States. She then stated that she was married to the Marquis Ossoli, who was in command of a battery on the Pincian Hill. That being the highest and most exposed position in Rome, and directly in the line of the bombs from the French camp, it was not to be expected, she said, that he could escape the dangers of another night such as the last, and therefore it was her intention to remain with him, and share his fate. At the Ave Maria, she added, he would come for her, and they would proceed together to his post. The packet which she placed in my possession, contained, she said, the certificates of her marriage, and of the birth and baptism of her child. After a few words more, I took my departure, the hour she named having nearly arrived. At the porter's lodge I met the Marquis Ossoli, and a few moments afterwards I saw them walking towards the Pincian Hill.

"Happily the cannonading was not renewed that night, and at dawn of day she returned to her apartment, with her husband by her side.

"On the same day the French army entered Rome,

and, the gates being opened, Madame Ossoli, accompa-
nied by the Marquis, immediately proceeded to Rieti, a
village lying at the base of the Abruzzi Mountains,
where she had left her child in the charge of a confidential nurse, formerly in the service of the Ossoli family.
She remained, as you are no doubt aware, some months
at Rieti, whence she removed to Florence, where she
resided until her ill-fated departure for the United
States. During this period I received several letters
from her, all of which, though reluctant to part with
them, I inclose to your address, in compliance with your
request.

"I am, Madam, very respectfully, your obedient servant,   LEWIS CASS, JR." [1]

The circumstances under which Margaret Fuller and her husband first met have been several
times described ; and every account of them must
mainly rest upon the important narrative by Mrs.
William W. Story, the greater part of which was
published long since in the "Memoirs." [2]   In this
letter she not only describes the occasion when
Madame Ossoli confided the secret of the marriage and placed the evidences of it in Mrs.
Story's hands ; but she gives from immediate authority a narrative of the first interviews between
those who were thus strangely brought together.
If I vary somewhat from this account, as heretofore printed, it is because Mrs. Story's original
letter lies before me ; and I have attached impor-

---

[1] Fuller MSS. i. 669. Published also with *Women in the Nineteenth Century*, when reprinted in 1869.

[2] *Memoirs*, ii. 281.

tance to certain passages which were omitted, perhaps for want of space or reasons of literary convenience, in the " Memoirs."

Soon after Margaret Fuller's first coming to Rome, early in 1847, she went, one day, to hear vespers at St. Peter's, and, after the service, proposed to her companions, Mr. and Mrs. Spring, that they should wander separately, at will, among the chapels, and meet at a certain designated point. Failing, however, to find them again, she walked about, in some perplexity, scanning different groups through her eye-glass. Ere long a young man of gentlemanly address came up to her, seeing her evident discomfort, and offered his services as guide. After they had continued their search in vain, for some time, during which the crowd had dispersed, he endeavored to find a carriage for her; and this failing, they walked together to her residence, conversing with some difficulty, as he knew no English and she had not yet learned Italian. At the door they parted, and she told her friends the adventure. A day or two after this, she observed the same young man walking before the house, as if meditating entrance; and they finally met once or twice before she left Rome for the summer. She was absent from June to October, visiting Florence, Bologna, Venice, Milan, the Italian lakes, and Switzerland. In October she established herself again in Rome, having an "apartment" in the Corso, and trying to live for six months on four hundred dollars.

She wrote to her mother that she had not been so well since she was a child, or so happy even then. She had grown accustomed to the climate, which had at first affected her unfavorably; she could study history and antiquities; she had near her some tried friends, such as Mr. and Mrs. Cranch and Mr. and Mrs. Story; and she received her acquaintances, at her rooms, in a simple way, every Monday evening. Among these guests came constantly her new acquaintance, the young Italian, — well known by this time as Giovanni Angelo, Marquis Ossoli. He sympathized in her zeal for what then seemed the promise of Italian liberty, and it is thought by those who best knew them that she did much in strengthening his purpose to throw off the traditions of his family, and pledge himself to the party of the people. Yet through his kindred he still kept up some relations with the other side, and the two attended the meetings held by the different factions; being meanwhile steadily drawn together by the excitement of a common interest.

It happened that the old Marquis Ossoli died of a lingering illness that winter, and, as Angelo was his youngest and only unmarried child, the care of the father came peculiarly upon this son. During this time of anxiety he used to spend a few daily moments with Margaret Fuller, sure of sympathy and strength; and it was immediately after his father's death that he disclosed his love, "telling her," according to Mrs. Story "that he must marry her or be miserable." "She refused to look on him as a lover," continued Mrs. Story, "and insisted that it was not fitting, — that it was best he should marry a younger woman; that she would be his friend but not his wife. In this way it rested for some weeks, during which we saw Ossoli pale, dejected, and unhappy. He was always with her, but in a sort of hopeless, desperate manner, until at length he convinced her of his love, and she married him." [1]

After this followed the siege of Rome, and Margaret Fuller's service in the hospitals, — as already described in Mr. Cass's letter, — while Ossoli was in the army outside the city. One day, after great anxiety, she called Mrs. Story to her, and confided to her the secret of her marriage, showing her the marriage certificate and those relating to the birth of her child. These she confided to Mrs. Story, with a book containing the narrative of her whole acquaintance with her husband. The papers were kept for a time by Mrs. Story, and at length returned to Madame Ossoli; and every trace of them is now lost forever. The conclusion of Mrs. Story's narrative will now be given almost entire, its picture of the married life of the Ossolis being too valuable to be omitted. Like the passages just quoted, this has never before been printed : —

. . . "At once, Ossoli, Margaret, and the child went to Florence. Rome was shut upon them, and they had

[1] MS.

16

some difficulty in getting a permission to remain even in Florence. (Mr. Greenough interested himself to get this for them.) After this we never saw them; some letters I have which tell a tale of deep maternal happiness and satisfaction — of the tenderness of her husband, and of serene days such as her life had known but few. I look back upon those days in Florence as the peacefullest she had ever known; in them she had sweet communion with nature, love, and a tender mother's joy. I believe that she was coming home to richer blessings, and a life if of some struggles, still of sure enjoyment.

"I have heard it suggested by some one that Ossoli had married Margaret under the impression of her having a large fortune. That this is utterly false I can declare, since to my own knowledge he was in the habit, even from their first acquaintance, of making for her what the Italians term little economies, and was in Margaret's unreserved confidence as to the feeble state of her purse.

"Again, I have heard it said that he was a person entirely without education. I can only say that his education was equal to that of most Roman gentlemen, not thorough, but such as suited him for his rank and position. He had from his youth been under the care of a priest, who taught him as a tutor. He knew not much of foreign languages, read French a little, and was a good deal interested in Italian history.

"Many of our countrymen who saw him could discover little in him, but that was rather because he was not quickly interested in others, than that he lacked interesting points. He was always reserved, and, when with Margaret, preferred always to hear her talk, even when she spoke a language he did not know, than to talk himself or hear any one else.

" His manner towards Margaret was devoted and lover-like to a striking degree. He cared not how trivial was the service if he might perform it for her. I remember to have seen him one morning, after they had been married nearly two years, set off on an errand to get the handle of her parasol mended, with as much genuine knightly zeal as if the charge had been a much weightier one. As he took it, he said, ' How sweet it is to do little things for you ; never attend to such yourself, always leave them to me for my pleasure.' When she was ill he nursed and watched over her with the tenderness of woman. When she said to him, ' How have you learned to be so good a nurse,' he said, ' My father was ill, and I tended upon him.' No service was too trivial, no sacrifice too great for him. He never wished her to give up any pleasure because he could not share it, but if she were interested, he would go with her to any house, leave her, and call again to take her home. Such tender, unselfish love I have rarely before seen ; it made green her days, and gave her an expression of peace and serenity which before was a stranger to her. ' No companion in nature was ever so much to me as is Ossoli ; ' does not this show that his soul was deep and full of emotion ; for who that knew Margaret Fuller would believe that any other companion would have been agreeable to her in her communion with nature. What a beautiful picture is that of their return to Rome after a day spent on the Campagna ! " [1]

To this narrative I will add another letter, from Mrs. Story to Mrs. J. R. Lowell, transcribed

[1] MS.

by the latter for Miss Sarah F. Clarke, and giving some additional particulars. It is without a date, but belongs to just this period, and has not before been printed : —

"MY DEAR MISS CLARKE,— I have just received a letter from my friend, Emelyn Story, in which she speaks of a friend of yours, and of her husband, in a way which I thought might be interesting and pleasant to you, so I copy it.

"'As to Margaret Fuller's marriage, I might write you at any length upon that subject, but from lack of room to do so, I shall merely tell you that I have known of the marriage since May, now some six months, during which time I have been under a solemn pledge of secrecy ; now she releases me, I can only say that we knew and liked Mr. Ossoli, or, as his title goes, the Marquis Ossoli, very much; he is much younger than Margaret, being, as I should judge, about William's age (thirty), is good looking, quite handsome, as the Italians go, has a melancholy expression about the eyes — is tall and thin. In character he seems to be remarkably amiable and tender, not intellectual, simple, natural, and good. During the attack of the French on Rome he showed great courage, spirit, and zeal, was conspicuous among the officers for his devotion to his duties. So much we saw ourselves, for we often went to his post and found him exhausted and faint for want of food and rest, but always firm and resolute to remain to the end. He was a captain of the Civic Guard, and in many respects conspicuous for his adherence to Mazzini's views, so that now they cannot remain in Rome, and were obliged to leave at once upon the entrance of the French. His family are distinguished for the same zeal on the other side, that of the Pope, and are in the Papal household, his two brothers being chamberlains to the Pope. His radicalism causes him to be looked upon as the black sheep in the family, and it was on account of family difficulties that the marriage was not sooner made known. If people were not always the best judges for themselves, it would seem better that it should have been made known at first; but I know enough of their affairs to say that they were prevented solely by family matters from declaring it at the time it occurred.

"'Margaret is now living in Florence; their future is rather dark in a pecuniary point of view, as the small fortune he inherited is tied up, in some way, by the change of government and depreciation of property, so that, at least for the present, it is not available, and I doubt if it ever comes to much. All I know is that Margaret will have to exert herself. Now that their little boy is with them, and is well, they are perfectly happy. I wish with all my heart that Margaret might be able to enjoy this happiness without anxiety about meeting the expenses, etc., etc. Ossoli is a devoted lover; he is all kindness and attention to her, and I think she has chosen the better part in marrying him, for his love must be most precious to her. Judging from what he was after a year's marriage, I should say he was more of a lover than before their marriage. He is a gentleman in manners and bearing, as he is by birth. His father is at the head of one [of] the *Rioni* [wards or quarters] in Rome, and his family are of undoubted rank and position there. I believe her child is healthy and strong, although it suffered much from the faithless

ness of its nurse, whose milk failing, [she] fed it upon
wine and bread, and this at the time when Mr. and Mrs.
Ossoli were shut up in Rome, during the siege. When,
at last, she could leave Rome and go into the country to
see him, she found him quite ill, almost, as she feared,
beyond recovery, so that she at once took him to Florence, where he has regained his health.

" ' Mr. Ossoli does not speak English, not even a sentence, that I ever heard, so that he has not been known
to many Americans, not even to some of William's
friends; but he was often at our house, and we knew
him, perhaps, better than any one.'

" You may have seen this before, but not in the same
form, and I thought it might be interesting to you to
hear from a fresh person so pleasant a statement of Mr.
Ossoli's character, pleasanter than those we have sometimes heard here.

" I shall not give up that day you promised me, but
find you soon, and make you fix upon one.

" Yours very truly,
" MARIA LOWELL.
" CAMBRIDGE, ELMWOOD, *Friday morn.*"

It is a curious fact that, throughout this letter,
Mrs. Lowell uniformly spells the name of Margaret Fuller's husband " Ossili," and it illustrates
how vague a knowledge of the whole affair had at
first reached America. Through such statements
as these it came to be better understood; and the
really simple and noble character of Margaret
Fuller's young lover stood out above all distrust.
There lie before me two old-fashioned daguerreo-
types of him, and a lock of his hair, the charac-

teristic blue-black hair of his nation. The pictures represent a thoroughly Italian face and figure : dark, delicate, slender ; by no means the man,
one would say, to marry at thirty an American
woman of thirty-seven, she being poor, intellectual,
and without beauty. Yet it will be very evident,
when we come to read their letters to each other,
that the disinterested and devoted love which
marked this marriage was so far a fulfillment of
Margaret Fuller's early dreams. Mr. Kinney, the
American consul, wrote to Mr. Emerson from
Turin, May 2, 1851 : "It is abundantly evident
that her young husband discharged all the obligations of his relation to her *con amore*. His admiration amounted to veneration, and her yearning
to be loved seemed at least to be satisfied." [1] There
is every reason to believe that this statement was
none too strong.

[1] MS.

XVI.

LETTERS BETWEEN HUSBAND AND WIFE.

By a happy fatality, the only Italian papers of
Margaret Ossoli's that are preserved are the letters that passed between her and her husband,
during their various separations, before and after
the birth of their child. The originals are now,
partially at least, in the possession of Miss Edith
Fuller, in Cambridge; and a translation of the
whole, made by Miss Elizabeth Hoar, is in my possession. I wish that they could all be published,
for more loving and devoted letters never passed
between husband and wife. Fragments of them
appeared in the " Memoirs ; " but I have avoided
making use of any which are there printed, except
in one or two cases where scattered portions alone
have appeared. The preference has been given
to those written about the time of her child's
birth, because there is no period which tests more
deeply the depth and the heroism of conjugal affection than those anxious weeks. At the birth of a
first child, every mother knows, and her husband
knows, that she is to meet much the same sort of
peril with any soldier who marches up to a battery ; except that this danger is to be met alone,

without trumpet-blast or the thrill of companionship in danger, and that it also involves the peril
of a life unborn, and more precious than one's
own. In the case of a mother past her first youth,
the peril is doubled ; and, where she is without
skilled medical attendance or nursing, it is quad-
rupled. All these evils were combined in the
case of Madame Ossoli; and she lived withal
among ignorant and sordid mountaineers, whom
she could not propitiate, for the want of money, in
the only way that could reach them. This was
the situation ; the letters will speak for themselves. I have employed Miss Hoar's translation,
with some modifications.

FROM OSSOLI.

[*Between August 3d and 15th, 1848.*]

"DEAR WIFE, — There is nothing at the banker's but
the journals, which I send you. I fear that it will be
difficult for us to see each other again, because Pio IX.
now wishes the Civic Guard to go to the frontiers and
defend Bologna. I hope that I may at least be able
to come and make a visit, and embrace you yet once
more, but I cannot tell you anything certain. I have
been trying to deliver the letter for the doctor ; but his
coachman assures me that he will be in Rome in September. To-morrow he will find some one to deliver
your letter.

"While I am awaiting good news of yourself, and of
a beautiful and good child, adieu, my love, and believe
me your   G. O."

FROM OSSOLI.

ROME, 17*th August,* 1848.

" MIA CARA, —My state is the most deplorable that
can be; I have had an extraordinary struggle. If your
condition were not such as it is, I could decide more
easily, but in the present moment I cannot leave you;
I cannot remove myself to a distance from you, my dear
love; ah! how cruel is my destiny in this emergency.
It is true that my friends would not advise me to go,
hoping for me always a better fortune. But then must
I always *hope,* and be always in the presence of my
unkind brothers, at a moment when I might remove myself from their hateful sight. The heart, duty, cannot
resolve it.

" In your dear last of the 7th, I understand well how
much you would sacrifice yourself for me. I am deeply
grateful to you for it, but I cannot yet decide."

FROM MADAME OSSOLI.

"RIETI, 18*th August,* 1848.

" I feel, love, a profound sympathy with your tor-
ments, but I am not able to give you a perfectly wise
counsel. Only it seems to me the worst possible moment
to take up arms except in the cause of duty, of honor.
The Pope being so cold, his minister undecided, nothing will be well or successfully done. As the interven-
tion of France and England is hoped for, it is yet uncertain whether the war will continue. If not, you will
leave Rome and the employment with your uncle for
nothing.

" If it is possible to wait two or three weeks, the
public state and mine also will be decided, and you can

make your decision with more tranquillity. Otherwise, it seems to me that I ought to say nothing, but leave it to your own judgment what to do. Only, if you go, come here first. I must see you once more.

"It troubles me much that I can tell you nothing certain of myself, but I am still in the same waiting state. I have passed a very bad night, my head is this morning much disturbed. I have bled a good deal at the nose, and it is hard for me to write.

"Do not ask permission of your uncle, if it is so difficult. We shall know how to arrange things without that. If you do not come I shall expect a letter from you on Sunday; also (if there are any) from the banker's, and also the last of those Milanese papers. Poor friends, shut up there. I wish so much for some certain intelligence of their fate.

"Adieu, dear; our misfortunes are many and unlooked for. Not often does destiny demand a greater price for some happy moments. Never do I repent of our affection, and for you, if not for me, I hope that life has still some good in store. Adieu, may God give you counsel and help, since it is now not in the power of your affectionate ——."

FROM MADAME OSSOLI.

" Sunday, 20th August [1848].

"Mio Caro, — I expected you a little this morning, and had your coffee all ready, but I believe you had reason for delay. If there is nothing to the contrary, come next Saturday evening.

"My nights become more and more disturbed, and this morning I was obliged to be bled again; since then, I find myself relieved, but weak, and unable to say more than that I am always your affectionate ——.

"Inclosed is another order on the banker, in case you come Saturday. I write it now, being uncertain that I can write many days longer. I embrace you!"

FROM OSSOLI.

ROME, 21*st August*, 1848.

MIO BENE, — I have received your dear letter, and am very sorry not to have found myself there to breakfast with you; but I am waiting a message from you to bring me directly to you, and I hope to find myself some day so situated that you will no longer have need of a companion. You tell me that you are not very well able to write, and I am sorry for you; but since it gives you so much fatigue, ask the master of the house to write, if nothing else, a little assurance of your health, since this is a great solace to me, and I wish you would at least put your seal ring upon it, for that is enough for me. Believe me always the same. I embrace you, adieu; thy affectionate   G. A. O."

FROM MADAME OSSOLI.

"RIETI, 22*d August*, 1848.

"I am a little better, dearest; but if I could thus pass a less suffering day! On the contrary, it troubles me that this seems rather an indication that I must wait yet longer. *Wait!* That is always hard. But — if I were sure of doing well — I should wish much to pass through this trial before your arrival; yet when I think that it is possible for me to die alone, without the touch of one dear hand, I wish to wait yet longer. So I hope for your presence on Sunday morning.

"I see by the papers that the Pope suspends the departure of the troops. He acts as I thought he would, and I am now very glad that you did not actually enter the service yet. In a short time our affairs will be more settled, and you can decide more advantageously than now.

"Try if you can hear any particulars from Milan; would it not be possible in the Caffé degli Belli Arti? I am much troubled by the fate of those dear friends; how much they must suffer now.

"I still think so much of you. I hope that you are less tormented. If we were together, it would be a consolation. Now everything goes wrong, but it is impossible it should always be so. Adieu, love; it vexes me that so many days must pass before your coming — so many, so many. I am glad that I have the little picture; I look at it often. God keep you."

FROM MADAME OSSOLI.

"RIETI, *25th August.*

"My LOVE, — I have this morning your letter of Wednesday. You do not say whether you are to come Saturday evening or no, but I hope for it confidently. I cannot wait longer, in any event, if I am not obliged to do it by your affairs. Nothing comes for me yet. I do not know what to think.

"There is a beautiful spot near, where we can go together, if I am able still to go out when you come. I shall expect you on Sunday morning, and will have your coffee ready again. Nothing more now, because writing is really difficult for your affectionate ——."

On September 5, 1848, her child, Angelo Philip Eugene Ossoli, was born. Two days after, she writes, by an amanuensis, only signing the letter herself: —

DICTATED BY MADAME OSSOLI.

" Rieti, *Thursday, 7th September,* 1848.

Dear Husband, — I am well, much better than I hoped. The baby also is well, but cries much yet, and I hope that he will be more quiet when you come. For the rest, I desire that you should be without anxiety about me, and I will send you frequent accounts of myself, writing again very soon. You may send to the post, prepaid, the letter of mine for Paris, which you have.

" All this family with whom I am staying salute you. Giving you an embrace and a kiss, in the person of this dear child whom I have in my arms, I am your affectionate   [in her own hand] Margherita."

FROM MADAME OSSOLI, IN PENCIL. HER OWN WRITING.

Saturday.

" My Love, — I write in bed, a few words only. I have received yours this morning, and hope for another for to-morrow. I have been ill with milk-fever, but am to-day better, and hope to gain strength daily. There is need of it; I am to-day obliged to send away Giuditta to Rome, I can do nothing with her now. I am taking one [a nurse], who also has milk, in case mine is not sufficient. The baby is very beautiful. All say so. I take much delight in watching him. He sends you a kiss, as also your   M." [1]

[1] Of these two brief notes, — the first dictated to a scribe and taken down by him more or less accurately, and the second written in pencil by herself, — I give the Italian originals, kindly copied for me by Miss Edith Fuller, the niece of Madame Ossoli.

" Rieti, 7 *Settembre,* 1848.

" Caro Consorte, — Io sto bene, molto meglio che io sperava Il Bambino anche va bene ma piange molto ancora, e spero che

FROM OSSOLI.

"ROME, 14*th September*, 1848.

"MIA CARA, — This morning I received your dear letter, and am always more comforted in hearing of the good condition of our dear baby, and likewise of yours. I have also great pleasure in hearing that he is so beautiful, our child. How much I wish to see him, the time seems very long to me, which must yet be passed. Meanwhile give him a kiss and a tender embrace from me."

FROM MADAME OSSOLI.

"*Friday*, 15*th September* [1848].

"MIO CARO, — I received this morning your dear letters, and the papers. The news from Milan seems to be too good to be true, but I wait with anxiety to hear more.

"When you do not hear from me do not be anxious;

sarà piu tranquillo quando tu vieni. Per altro voglio che per me sei tranquillo, e ti darò spesso mie nuove, scrivendoti di nuovo ben presto. La mia lettera che hai per Parigi potrai affrancarla alla Posta.

"Tutti di questa famiglia dove io mi trovo ti salutano. Dandoti un abbraccio, ed un bagio in questo caro Pupo che ho nelle braccia sono. Vra affma

"MARGHERITA."

"*Sabato.*

"MIO BÉNE, — Scrivo nel letto alcune parole solamente. Ricevo tuo questa mattina, e spero altro per dománi. Son stata male col febbre di latte ma oggi meglio e spero tutti i giorni stare piu forte. C'e di bisogno; son d' obbligo oggi inviare Giuditta in Roma, lei non può fare niente adesso. Io prendo una che ha anche latte si mio non basta. Il bambino e molto bello, tutti dicon così, io prendo molto piacere riguardarlo. Lui ti da un bacio come anche tua   M."

you know I must necessarily be very weak for some time yet; I am not always able to write, or to rise, and Ser Giovanni is not always here to write for me. It is a miracle that I am as well as I find myself; my circumstances were so difficult. Now that I find myself so content with my nurse, her child becomes ill; and if she is forced to leave me, the struggle begins again — but I hope not. If it is necessary to bear this too, I can only hope counsel from God."

FROM MADAME OSSOLI.

"*Sunday, 17th September* [1848].

"MY LOVE,—This morning I have nothing from you but the journal of Friday. I suppose now I shall have to wait till Tuesday to hear from you, as no post comes to-morrow.

"The nurse's child is better, and I feel relieved. We must have courage, but it is a great care to be alone and ignorant with an infant in these first days of its life. When he is a month old, I shall feel more quiet. Then he will be stronger for the changes he will have to undergo. Now he is well, begins to sleep well, is very pretty for his age, and all the people around, without knowing what name I thought of giving him, call him *Angiolino*, because he is so lovely. He has your mouth, hands, feet. It seems to me that his eyes will be blue. For the rest, he is altogether a rogue (*birbone*), understands well, is very obstinate to have his will.

"I shall have much to say when you come, and also we shall then have much to plan, because it will be too cold in this room for me to stay here late in the au- tumn. The forty days will terminate 15th October and I wish to leave as soon as possible after that — the 20th or 25th, if I can. Adieu, love; always your M."

FROM MADAME OSSOLI.

"RIETI, *Saturday, 23d September* [1848].

"MIO CARO,— I have received this morning the papers and your letter. I feel the truth of what you say, that there ought to be the greatest care in the selection of a nurse. I shall wait to consult with you about everything. Consider only, if the baby is out of Rome, you cannot see him often. Otherwise, the air of the country would be better, without doubt, for his health.

"He is so dear, it seems to me sometimes, among all the difficulties and disasters, that if he lives, if he is well, he will become such a treasure for us two, that it will compensate for everything. I wish very much that you should see him again, but you must have patience with his frequent cry; he is an obstinate fellow. Also, I hope that by the time you come my shoulder will be cured again, and I strong enough to go out a little with you. Now it is fine weather, and I go out on the balcony. Ser Giovanni is good to me, but his sisters are detestable, meddling in everything, and so avaricious, so interested; they would save me money in order that they may get it for themselves. Yet I try to keep the peace with them; there are bad people everywhere, and these, so interested and vulgar, are at least not treacherous like Giuditta. Adieu, love.

"Thy   M."

[It illustrates the kind of people among whom Madame Ossoli was at this time living, that this Ser Giovanni, who was her scribe in illness and

the one person who was " good " to her, was all the
time amusing himself with the effort to seduce
Angelo's nurse, who was, according to another letter, " the loveliest young woman in the village,"
and whose beauty was to Madame Ossoli a source
of constant anxiety, in view of the neighborhood
of Garibaldi's half-brigand troops, and those from
Naples who were worse. It was amid such solicitudes and vexations that an inexperienced and
exhausted mother had to struggle for life in behalf of her baby and herself.]

FROM MADAME OSSOLI.

" RIETI, *Tuesday*, 26*th September*, 1848.

. . . " Now we begin to be really well, my baby and
I. He sleeps all night, and my shoulder, the last night,
has not tormented me, so I have slept also. He is always so charming, how can I ever, ever leave him? I
wake in the night, I look at him, I think, ah! it is impossible to leave him. Adieu, love; it seems that like
me you are impatient for your arrival; then we can
speak and again have a few happy moments more.

Thy   M."

FROM MADAME OSSOLI.

" RIETI, 7*th October*, 1848.

"MIO CARO, — I have received this morning the paper and your letter. I am glad that at least you had
a tranquil night for the journey. Yesterday it began
again to rain here. All that I have said to Ser Giovanni was, that it would be pleasant to have some friend
for a godfather. I am not very competent to give advice in this matter of baptism, which I do not well un-

derstand, but the godfather who would please me for the baby is my friend, the Pole. He knows of the existence of the child, is a devout Catholic, is a distinguished man, who could be an aid to him in his future life ; and I wish for him to have some friend in case of accident to us. You can consider this unless you have some confidential friend whom you wish as a godfather, who could interest himself in the child if you were obliged to leave him.

" It must be considered that your nephew will know this affair at last, by means of Catalane. But I do not know your relatives, nor if you can confide in one of them."

FROM MADAME OSSOLI.

" RIETI, *Thursday, 28th September,* 1848.

. . . "I have seen more bad people this last year than in all my life before, and I fear that I have not yet ended. I think of your letter which came on Sunday morning. How much I wish to see you ! The baby does not grow much, but he is always so lovely — has really delicate little ways, like a dancer. For the rest I can speak so much better than write, that, while awaiting your visit, I will say no more now.

"Your affectionate   M."

FROM OSSOLI.

" ROME, *9th October,* 1848.

"MIA CARA, — I have received this morning your two dear letters, it makes me very happy to continue to hear from you often, and it is a great comfort for me to hear that the baby knows who I am ; dear child, how I long always to press him in my arms. As to what I said of a godfather for our dear one, it would please me also to have the Pole, as he is a distinguished person; but how to find him, the time being so short? Really I do not know what to do, and I requested you to take advice of Ser Giovanni, if you think best; to tell him that the person whom we decided on for a godfather is too far off for us to get him in season, and plan to inform me what can be done. If not, I will try to provide differently; as far as I see, it is a somewhat difficult matter. You say that you are surprised the doctor should leave Rome, but it was necessary, since there are absolutely no foreigners in Rome.

"Saluting you dearly, and giving you, with our dear love, a kiss, I am your   G. A. OSSOLI."

FROM MADAME OSSOLI.

"RIETI, 15*th October*, 1848.

. . . "Think always in seeking a house for me, not to pledge me to stay in Rome. It seems to me often that I cannot stay long without seeing the baby. He is so dear, and life seems to me so uncertain, I do not know how to leave my dear ones. Take the apartment for a short time. It is necessary that I should be in Rome at least a month, to write, and also to be near you, but I wish to be free to return here if I feel too anxious for him, too suffering. O love, how difficult is life! But you, you are good; if it were only possible for me to make you happy!"

FROM OSSOLI.

"ROME, 21*st October*, 1848.

"MIA CARA, — I learn by yours of the 20th that you have received the ten scudi, and it makes me more tranquil. I feel also Mogliani's indolence in not coming to inoculate our child ; but, my love, I pray you not to disturb yourself so much, and not to be sad, hoping that our dear love will be guarded by God, and will be free from all misfortunes. He will keep him for us and give us means to sustain him."

FROM MADAME OSSOLI.

" *Saturday Evening,* 28th *October,* 1848.

. . . "It rains very hard every day, but to-day I have been more quiet, and our darling has been so good, I have taken so much pleasure in being with him. When he smiles in his sleep, how it makes my heart beat ! He has grown fat and very fair, and begins to play and spring. You will have much pleasure in seeing him again. He sends you many kisses. He bends his head toward me when he asks a kiss."

FROM MADAME OSSOLI, AFTER BEING IN ROME.

" RIETI, 22d *December,* 1848.

" MY LOVE, — I made the journey comfortably, and arrived here at half-past four. I find our darling little changed, — much less than I expected. What surprises me is, that he appears fat enough, seems to be perfectly well, but is not much larger than when I left him. He has the same ways, is very graceful, but otherwise he is better than with me, sleeps well at night, rarely cries, and then not so violently. He is diverted in this family, seeing so many persons, and all play with him and seem to wish him well. The house is dreadful, the wind coming in on all sides, but he does not seem to take cold, and I hope that he will be stronger for being exposed so much in his first months. He has had the small-pox terribly ; his head, his body have been covered with spots; it is wholly by the favor of Heaven that he has passed through it so well. The physician, Mogliani, never came to visit him; his family say that I am avaricious. I suppose he thought it not worth the trouble to save our baby. His face is not injured. They have not changed the house yet, and I do not know if they will. They talk, in this house, of receiving ten scudi a month for one room. These Rietines are all alike. If I can do it without injury to my health, I shall remain here. I have received nothing from you this morning, and the family here had not received on Wednesday the letter which was put in the post the Saturday before. My letters never failed so before. I suppose it is the fault of the post. I shall write every post-day.

"The baby salutes you with many kisses. He seemed to recollect me; when I took him, he rested his dear head so long on my shoulder. I took so much pleasure in sleeping with him last night. In the daytime it does not go on so well, it is smoky and cold. Farewell, my beloved, I will write a few lines on Sunday; all the details I will tell you when I come. Always thy M."

FROM MADAME OSSOLI.

"RIETI, 27th March, 1849.

"MIO CARO, — I found our treasure in the best health, and now so good! He goes to sleep all alone in bed, day or night. He is asleep now, sucking his little hand. He is very fat, but strangely small, his hair does not grow at all, and he still wears those horrid black caps.

"At first all talked so loud, he looked at me all surprised, and cried a little. But when he was alone with me, he seemed to recollect me, and leaned and rubbed his forehead as in the first days."

FROM MADAME OSSOLI.

"RIETI, *30th March,* 1849.

. . . "Yesterday the family were at dinner below, and our darling asleep above in bed. I was sitting at his side thinking how dear he was. Since I have bathed him and dressed him well, he has seemed like another child. Suddenly I heard tables and seats falling and the women screaming terribly, 'Help!' I flew down, and there stood Niccolà and Pietro [two brothers] trying to kill one another. I spoke to Niccolà, he did not answer, but looked at me like a wild beast. The women held his arm so that he could not draw his knife; he seized their hair. Pietro, who had no knife, threw wood — a great piece just missed my head. All the neighbors ran in directly. The landlord of Niccolà took away his knife, but if our baby had been below, he would probably have been killed. I am convinced that Niccolà is a drunkard. I cannot tell you particulars in writing, but I want to see you."

FROM THE SAME. — BOTH IN ROME.

"CASA DIES, *Friday,* 4th *May,* 2 P. M.

"MIO CARO, — I am going out at four, and return at six, and shall be here an hour. At half-past seven I go to the hospitals, and hope to return at nine. If you come while I am gone out, wait for me, if possible, if not, come up and leave a word to say when you can come to-morrow morning. Do not fail to see me, I pray; it is terrible to pass so many uncertain hours without meeting. It is said that the Neapolitans do not advance, but all seems so uncertain. Always, always your M——. If ever you have need, send some one immediately, dearest; we can pay for this."

"*Monday, June 5th* [1849].

"MIO CARO, — This morning I went to the garden of the Vatican at half-past eight; they sought you and said when they returned that you had gone out. I returned immediately home; but as you have not been here, I think it was a mistake. This evening I hope to be in the house at eight; if you come first, wait, I beg of you. Thank God that you are yet living. How much I suffered yesterday you can believe. Till we meet again, *caro consorte*, as that wicked Ser Giovanni always wrote. I go out, because I ought to go to the hospitals."

"How hard it was for me, love, to miss you yesterday, and possibly also to-day, if you can come. I am going to Casa Dies; if possible, inquire there, the last floor, if I am still there or have gone to the hospitals. God keep you! How much I have suffered in seeing the wounded, and I cannot know if anything should happen to you — but I must hope. I have received the letter from Rieti; our Nino is perfectly well, thanks for this. It does me good that the Romans have at least done something, if only you can remain. In event of the death of both, I have left a paper with a certificate in regard to Angelino, and some lines praying the Storys to take care of him. If by any accident *I* die, you can revoke this paper if you will, from me, as being your wife. I have wished Nino to go to America, but you will do as seems best to you. We ought to have planned this better, but I hope that it will not be needed. Always, with benedictions, your

"MARGHERITA.

"If you live, and I die, be always most devoted to Nino. If you ever love another, think first for him, I pray, pray, love."

This last imploring caution was never needed.

XVII.

CLOSING SCENES.

ALTHOUGH Mrs. Story once read the certificate of the marriage of her friends, and had it long in her possession, she did not fix the date of it in her memory, and this will probably remain forever unknown. Their child was born September 5, 1848; and the mother was compelled, in order to disarm suspicion and to earn money, to be alternately at Rieti and in Rome. Finally she was unable to leave Rome, because of the siege; and after returning to Rieti, she wrote this letter to Mr. Cass, in which she has made an evident effort to describe what is around her, and not to dwell on her own great anxieties.

"RIETI, 19th July, 1849.

"DEAR MR. CASS, — I seem to have arrived in a different world, since passing the mountains. This little red-brown nest, which those we call the aborigines of Italy made long before Rome was, lies tranquil amid the net-work of vineyards, its casinos and convents gleam pleasantly from the hillsides, the dirt accumulates undisturbed in its streets, and pigs and children wallow in it, while Madonna-veiled, bare-legged women twirl the distaff at every door and window, happy, if so they can

earn five cents a day. We have not been able to find
an apartment, so we have rooms at the rustic *locanda*,
which is on the *piazza*, clean and airy, and where may
be studied all the humors of the place. There is the
fountain where come the girls in their corset, long shift-
sleeves, and colored petticoat, the silver needle in their
fine hair; attractive they look from my window, for the
dirt disappears in distance. Near, it not dismays their
lovers, who help them to adjust the water-vase on their
heads (N. B. no husband does this). All the dandies
of Rieti in all kinds of queer uniforms are congregated
below; at the barber's, the druggist's, the caffé, they sit
and digest the copious slander, chief product of this, as of
every *little* hive of men. The baronesses and countesses,
in the extreme of Italian undress, are peeping through
the blinds; at half-past seven, if the band plays, they
will put on their best dresses (alas! mongrel French
fashions prevail here), and parade, fanning themselves
whether the weather be hot or cold, on foot, for the
Corso of Rieti is nominal. At present the scene is
varied by presence of the Spanish force, who promise
to stay only three days; and I hope they will not, for
they eat everything up like locusts. For the moment,
it pleases to see their foreign features, and hear the
noble sounds of their language. We have performed
our social duties; have called on the handsome doctor's
wife, whom we found ironing in her antechamber; ——,
the Gonfaloniere's sister, who had just had a child, and
received us in her chamber; and on the father, guardian
of the beautifully placed monastery of St. Antonio, who
insisted on making us excellent coffee, which we must
take under the shade of the magnificent cypresses, for
women must not enter, 'only,' said he chuckling, 'Gar-

ibaldi obliged us to let his enter, and I have even seen them braiding their hair.' Maria of the episcopal garden has left her card in the form of a pair of pigeons. I could find much repose for the moment in these simple traits of a limited life, and in this pure air, were it not for the state in which I find my baby. You know, my dear Mr. Cass, I flattered you with the thought you would be happy in having a child; may you never know such a pang as I felt in kissing his poor, pale little hand which he can hardly lift. He is worn to a skeleton, all his sweet childish graces fled; he is so weak it seems to me he can scarcely ever revive to health. If he cannot, I do not wish him to live; life is hard enough for the strong, it is too much for the feeble. Only, if he dies, I hope I shall, too. I was too fatigued before, and this last shipwreck of hopes would be more than I could bear. Adieu, dear Mr. Cass, write when you can ; tell me of the world, of which I hear nothing here, of suffering Rome — always dear, whatever may oppress me — and of yourself. Ever yours,   M. O." [1]

I add one more extract from a letter, without date, but of the same period, from Madame Ossoli to Mrs. Story : —

. . . "You say no secret can be kept in the civilized world, and I suppose not long. But it is very important to me to keep this for the present, if possible, and by and by to have the mode of disclosure at my option. For this I have made the cruelest sacrifices. It will, indeed, be just like the rest, if they are made of none effect.

"After I wrote to you I went to Rieti. The weather

[1] MS.

was mild when I set out, but by the fatality that has attended me throughout, in the night changed to a cold unknown in Italy, and remained so all the time I stayed. There was, as is common in Italy, no fireplace except in the kitchen. I suffered much in my room with its brick floor, and windows through which came the cold wind freely. My darling did not suffer, because he was robed in wool. When I first took him in my arms, he made no sound, but leaned his head against my bosom, and stayed so. He seemed to say, how could you abandon me. They told me that all the day of my departure he could not be comforted, always looking toward the door. He has been a strangely precocious infant. I think it was through sympathy with me; and that in that regard it may be a happiness for him to be with these more plebeian, instinctive joyous natures. I saw that he was more serene, that he was not sensitive as when with me, and slept a great deal more.

"You speak of my being happy. All the solid happiness I have known has been at times when he went to sleep in my arms. You say when ———'s beautiful life had been so wasted, it hardly seemed worth while to begin another. I had all those feelings too; I do not look forward to his career and his manly life, it is *now* I want to be with him, before passion, care, and bafflings begin. If I had a little money I should go with him into strict retirement for a year or two, and live for him alone. This I cannot do; all life that has been or could be natural to me is invariably denied. God knows why, I suppose.

"I receive with profound gratitude your thought of taking him, if anything should happen to us. Should I live, I don't know whether I should wish him to be an

Italian or American citizen. It depends on the course events take here politically." [1]

And now the pen that had so often described the beauties of nature or art or literature is used again and again to portray the charming gambols of a little child. Here, for instance, is a passage only partially printed in the "Memoirs," while I give it in full; or it may be that this is a companion-picture sent to another person at about the same time, and using many of the same words : —

" When our little boy wakes, he always beckons and cries to come into our room. He draws the curtains himself with his little dimpled hand ; he laughs, he crows, he dances in the nurse's arms, he shows his teeth, he blows like the bellows, pretends to snuff candles, and then, having shown off all his accomplishments, calls for his playthings. With these he will amuse himself on the floor while we are dressing, sometimes an hour after. Then he goes to the window to hear the Austrian drums, to which he keeps time, with head and hand. It is soon eleven, and he sleeps again. Then I employ myself. When he wakes, we go out to some church, or picture-gallery or museum, almost always taking him." [2]

This was written in Florence, where they took up their residence after the entrance of the French army into Rome. She busied herself with her history of the Italian struggle, and he with efforts to rescue his share of his father's estate. Another picture of child-life records their very last Christmas Day : —

" Christmas Day I was just up, and Nino all naked on his sofa, when came some beautiful large toys that had been sent him : a bird, a horse, a cat, that could be moved to express different things. It almost made me cry to see the kind of fearful rapture with which he regarded them, — legs and arms extended, fingers and toes quivering, mouth made up to a little round O, eyes dilated; for a long time he did not even wish to touch them; after he began to, he was different with all the three, loving the bird, very wild and shouting with the horse; with the cat, putting her face close to his, staring in her eyes, and then throwing her away. Afterwards I drew him in a lottery, at a child's party given by Mrs. Greenough, a toy of a child asleep on the neck of a tiger ; the tiger is stretching up to look at the child. This he likes best of any of his toys. It is sweet to see him when he gets used to them, and plays by himself, whispering to them, seeming to contrive stories. You would laugh to know how much remorse I feel that I never gave children more toys in the course of my life. I regret all the money I ever spent on myself or in little presents for grown people, hardened sinners. I did not know what pure delight could be bestowed. I am sure if Jesus Christ had given, it would not have been little crosses.

" There is snow all over Florence, in our most beautiful piazza. Santa Maria Novella, with its fair *loggia* and bridal church, is a carpet of snow, and the full moon looking down. I had forgotten how angelical all that is ; how fit to die by. I have only seen snow in mountain patches for so long. Here it is the even holy shroud of a desired power. God bless all good and bad to-night, and save me from despair." [1]

[1] MS.

It is evident from the closing words of this and many other letters that a sense of foreboding was always upon her. In the midst of revolution, war, and death; seeing constantly the separation of families, the ruin of households; her whole soul clung with even more than a mother's usual yearning to the actual presence of her boy. In interpreting the last tragic moment of her life, this must always be borne in mind. She writes to an American friend in Italy: "I have never answered what you said of the loss of Maria L.'s [Lowell's] child. These things make me tremble with selfish sympathy. I could not, I think, survive the loss of my child; I wonder daily how it can be done." How fine and penetrating is that phrase, "selfish sympathy." No other two words ever expressed the precise emotion she describes, and no one ever felt that emotion more absorbingly than she. It is something, that the one danger she dreaded was the one calamity from which she was to be spared.

After the brief vision of a Roman republic had passed away, it seemed best for the Ossolis to leave Italy for America. Apart from the trifle that Ossoli had been able to secure of his own property, their main dependence must be on her pen. Her book on the Roman republic was ready for publication, and she believed that she could make better terms for it, if once in America, than the offers which she had received by mail. She thus writes: —

" I do not think I shall publish till I can be there [in America] in person. I had first meant to [publish] in England ; but you know this new regulation that a foreigner cannot hold copyright there. I think if I publish in the United States I should be there to correct the proofs, see about the form of the work and alterations in MS. ; also I hope on the spot I may make better terms than are offered by letter." [1]

This was soon so plain that nothing stood in the way but the obstacles which she thus reported to her brother : —

"FLORENCE, 24*th February,* 1850.

. . . " I hoped by this time to say decisively when I [shall] come home, but do not yet know, we not being sure yet we can get the money. The voyage, made in the cheapest way we can, must cost us about two hundred and fifty dollars, as, even if we have the length and discomforts of voyage by a merchantman, and go without any help for care of the baby in case of being sick, we must still buy stores, and have a cow or goat to insure him proper food. We may have in this way two months on the ocean. I have always suffered much in my head at sea. However, to go by France would be more than double the expense. Happy the fowls of the air, who don't have to think so much about these things. I hope by hook (we shan't try by crook) to get the means and come somehow." [2]

There were thus some actual difficulties in the way, and there was, besides, an obstacle of foreboding. It is common for those who are undertaking an important step in their lives, especially

[1] MS.   [2] MS.

if it involves a voyage or a long journey, to be
haunted by some vague premonition of coming
evil. If all goes well, they afterwards laugh and
forget the foreboding ; if evil comes, they or their
friends remember it forever. This is, at any rate,
the commonest and easiest explanation of such
emotions, but if ever there was a case where the
solicitude seemed to amount to a prediction, it was
in regard to the voyage of the Ossolis. Italians
are apt to dread the sea, and Ossoli had been cau-
tioned to beware of it by one who had told his fortune when a boy. His wife, on the other hand,
had cherished a superstition that the year 1850,
probably as being the middle of the century,
would be a marked epoch in her life. But there
were more definite omens and warnings, or what
passed for such. On April 6 Madame Ossoli
wrote to her friend, the Marchioness Visconti
Arconati : —

"I am absurdly fearful about this voyage. Various
little omens have combined to give me a dark feeling.
Among others, just now we hear of the wreck of the
Westmoreland bearing Powers' 'Eve.' Perhaps we
shall live to laugh at these. But in case of mishap I
should perish with my husband and child, perhaps to be
transferred to some happier state." [1]

Again she wrote to Madame Arconati (April
21, 1850) : —

"It was an odd combination. I had intended, if I
went by way of France, to take the packet ship Argo

[1] MS.

from Havre; I had just written to Mrs. Story that I should not do so; and at the same time requested her to find Miss Fitton, who had my muff, etc. ; having closed the letter, I took up ' Galignani,' and my eye fell on these words, — ' Died, 4th April, at No. 10 Rue Ville l'Évêque, Miss E. Fitton.' Turning the leaf, I read of the wreck of the Argo returning from America to France. There were also notices of the wreck of the Royal Adelaide, a fine English steamer, and of the John Skiddy, one of the fine American packets. Thus, as it seems, safety is not to be found in the wisest cal- culation. I shall embark more composedly in my mer- chant ship; praying, indeed, fervently, that it may not be my lot to lose my babe at sea, either by un- solaced sickness, or amid the howling waves. Or, that if I should, it may be brief anguish, and Ossoli, he and I go together. Pray with me, dear friend, as yours ever, forever, MARGARET." [1]

It seemed best, finally, to take passage on the Elizabeth, a merchant vessel that was to sail from Leghorn. This was a new vessel, and Madame Ossoli took the precaution of going with her friend, Mrs. Mozier, to see it; they were much pleased with Captain Hasty and his wife, who came to Florence and spent a few days, as visitors, with Mrs. Mozier. Yet at the very last moment the feeling of foreboding recurred, and it was dif- ficult for Madame Ossoli to force herself on board. Still, she went; they sailed May 17, 1850, the only other passengers being Horace Sumner, of Boston, — a younger brother of Charles Sumner,

[1] MS.

— and a young Italian girl, Celeste Paolini. Misfortune soon began ; Captain Hasty sickened and died of malignant small-pox, and was buried beneath the waves in the harbor of Gibraltar. There they were detained a week by adverse winds, setting sail again June 9. Two days after, little Angelo was also attacked with small-pox, and was restored with difficulty. At noon of July 18 they were off the coast of New Jersey ; the weather was thick, the officer in command steered east-north-east, hoping, with the southeast wind that was blowing, to be next morning in a position to take a pilot and run before the wind past Sandy Hook. So sure was he, that they packed their trunks for landing. By nine P. M. there was a gale, by midnight a hurricane ; but the commander kept the vessel close-reefed, on her fatal course, till at four o'clock on the morning of July 19 she struck on that fatal Fire Island beach which has engulfed so many.

The story of that shipwreck has been told again and again ; nor is it possible now to obtain much new material to remould the description. But to one point it is right to call attention ; the too hasty assumption drawn from time to time, in the successive reproductions of the story, that Madame Ossoli sacrificed the lives of the party by her persistent refusal to be separated from husband and child. Had she done so, I know no one who could justly condemn her ; it was within her right and her husband's to elect whether they and their boy should cling together or be separated; and we know that all her prayer before setting sail was that there might be no division of the tie gained so late and so hardly won. But when it comes to actual evidence of such persistent refusal, it not only has no support, but is directly contrary to the final events. The simple fact that the little Angelo was drowned in the arms of the steward is sufficient refutation of the charge that his mother refused to intrust him to anybody; and it remains only a question of judgment whether the attempt to save him should have been made sooner. On that point almost any inexperienced landsman might think that he could have bettered the decision of those on the wreck, just as every civilian sees where he could have won the particular battle that Grant lost; but the more closely even a landsman looks at the actual evidence, the less possible a revision of judgment becomes.

Upon what rests the impression that Madame Ossoli peremptorily refused to risk the fate of her husband or child apart from herself? Mainly on the evidence of the commanding officer; an officer who, having first wrecked his ship, and then saved his own life while leaving all his passengers and four seamen on board, was under the strongest conceivable inducement to throw all the blame possible on some one else. Nothing is more difficult than to obtain a clear account of the circumstances of a shipwreck, even by sifting the testimony of all witnesses; an eminent admiralty lawyer, who has spent his life in attempting to do this in his successive cases, tells me that he has never yet thoroughly accomplished it. It is hard enough to be perfectly sure of the facts in case of a runaway accident which takes place in broad daylight opposite our own windows. It is difficult to this day to get a thoroughly correct account of the most insignificant skirmish during our civil war; and of a wreck that happens at daybreak in a howling storm, on a lee shore, the longest cross-examination of the survivors hardly avails. In this particular case there are now no witnesses to reëxamine ; we only know that the acting captain left his ship long before his passengers, while four seamen remained. Either they remained because they thought they would have personally a better chance by so doing, in which case their judgment may have been as good as his ; or they remained because of a devotion to their passengers which the captain did not share. While they were still on the wreck the case naturally did not seem hopeless to the passengers. There was the shore in sight ; with the life - boat which they might suppose that the captain would get launched if nobody else had ; with its life-saving mortar for throwing a rope, which he at least might employ. There was the chance of a lull in the storm, dur- ing which a raft might be built, on which they might go together. It was not so clear that the only mode of escape was to trust themselves singly on a little plank like that from which Mrs. Hasty,

ere landing, had been twice washed off. So at
least it may well have seemed to those on board.
All we know is that Angelo was in the steward's
arms to be taken on shore, when the deck was
swept away; and that, by Mrs. Hasty's account,
the sailors "had just persuaded her [Madame
Ossoli] to trust herself to a plank, when the final
wave broke over the vessel." [1]

Two of the four sailors reached land alive; and
the still warm bodies of the child and steward
came ashore. This shows that, even at the last,
rescue would not have been impossible, had the
life-boat been launched. The whole case is probably summed up in the remark made by one of
the life-boat men to the Rev. W. H. Channing, —
from whom I have it in writing, — "Oh! if we
had known there were any such persons of importance on board, we should have tried to do our
best." It was natural for the passengers on the
wreck to suppose that the life-boat men were
there to do their best in any case.

Two only of Margaret Ossoli's treasures reached
the land, — the beautiful body of her child, and a
trunk holding the letters that had passed between
herself and her husband. The body of little Angelo was placed in a seaman's chest, while his
rough playmates stood tearfully around, and was
afterwards buried among the sand-hills; to be at
last disinterred and brought to Mount Auburn
Cemetery by the relatives who had never seen

[1] *At Home and Abroad,* Appendix, p. 451.

him in life. Among the papers in the trunk was found one memorial which lies before me now, faded and wave-stained. It is a memorandum that was written long before by Margaret Ossoli, during one of her Italian intervals of separation from her child, and folded round a lock of her husband's hair. The paper is as follows: —

" *4th February* [1849 ?].

" I saw this morning a beautiful child beginning to walk. He had only eight months, yet is large, fair, rosy, has sixteen teeth. His mother has begun to give him food and wants to wet-nurse another child. Lives 55 via St. Basileo. He had already plenty of hair.

" How will Angelino seem when I go to him ? "

Little could she have foreseen under what circumstances of deeper tragedy this mother's reverie would be read by strangers. As we read it, the final question expands to a vaster significance than it first had ; and represents the eternal unanswered longing of the human heart.

XVIII.

LITERARY TRAITS.

LOOKING the other day into a manuscript journal of a visit to London in 1878, I came upon a
description of a London dinner-party with this
remark in regard to Miss Helen Taylor, the
adopted daughter of Stuart Mill: "She is the
only woman I have happened to meet in England who seems to associate with intellectual men
on terms of equality." This same remark might
have been made by a traveler in America, forty
years ago, of Margaret Fuller. And it must be
remembered that, whereas the men who were her
companions had almost all been trained in the regular channels of school, college, and profession, had
been stimulated by the hope of rank, aided by re-
wards, or incited by professional ambition, she accomplished whatever she attained by sheer zeal
for knowledge. She was encouraged, no doubt, by
her father, and helped by residence in a college
town; but she was destitute of most of the advantages which her friends enjoyed. They fulfilled
their career, whatever it was, in the capacity of
men, and with men's facilities; she attained hers,
so far as it was attained, under the disadvantages

of a woman. In spite of all this she associated with them as their equal at least, and was really for a time, as editor of the " Dial," their organizer and their point of union.

Sharing their advantages, she also shared, to some extent, their drawbacks. If they, with all their more regular training, were yet apt to be discursive, unsystematic, with too much reliance on intuition and imagination, — if that in short was the habit of the time, — it was natural that she should share the fault. Her defects were those of Emerson and of Thoreau ; and yet, after her " Tribune " training, she learned to shorten her sword better than either of these; became more capable of precise concentration on a specified point. It is also to be noted that, unlike them, she cannot be judged by her maturest work ; not a page of her history of the Roman republic of 1848 remains; we can only infer what it might have been from the progress already seen.

And sharing also the drawbacks, she also shared inevitably the prejudices that her companions inspired. These prejudices might be divided into two general heads; it was thought that they were unintelligible and it was said — if this was not indeed the same allegation — that they were German. It is now difficult to recall the peculiar suspicion that was attached to any one in America, forty years ago, who manifested much interest in German thought. Immanuel Kant is now claimed as a corner-stone of religion by evangelical divines, but he was then thought to be more dangerous than any French novelist; and good Mrs. Farrar, as I have already indicated, traces the materialism of Miss Martineau's latter years partly to her early studies of this philosopher. " I have since thought," Mrs. Farrar writes, "that her admiration of the philosophy of Kant may have been one of her first steps on that path which has conducted her to a disbelief in all revelation and the immortality of the soul — too melancholy a subject for me to dwell on here." [1]

If this feeling existed about Kant it was still stronger about Goethe. Even the genial Longfellow spoke of " that monstrous book, the ' Elective Affinities,' " although this story was written with a moral purpose, and would be far more leniently judged at the present day. Longfellow's friend Felton translated Menzel's " German Litature," in which Goethe appears as a pretender and quite a secondary person. Yet Margaret Fuller, who has been lately censured by Professor Harris as not admiring the great German poet enough, was held up to censure in her day for admiring him too much. This ardent, slowly-tamed, and gradually-tempered feminine nature, yearning to be, to do, and to suffer, all at the same time, was supposed to model herself after the marble statue, Goethe. The charge was self-contradicting; and is worth naming only as being a part of that misconception which she, like all other would-be reformers, had to endure.

[1] *Recollections of Seventy Years*, p. 262.

In the most important period of her early life she wrote, " As to Goethe . . . I do not go to him as a guide or friend, but as a great thinker who makes me think." [1] At this very time she was planning to write Goethe's biography and preparing to translate Eckermann's conversations with him. In her correspondence, here and there, she doubtless speaks of him as " the master," but the light use of a trivial phrase is not to be set against her distinct disclaimer, as just quoted. She was indeed too omnivorous a reader, too ardent and fertile a thinker, to go through the successive bondages by which many fine minds — especially the minds of women — work their way to freedom. Miss Martineau, for instance, with all her native vigor, was always following with implicit confidence some particular guide or model ; in early life her brother James, then Malthus, then Garrison, then Comte, then even Atkinson ; but in Margaret Fuller's case, though there were many friendships, there was no personal and controlling ruler. Emerson came the nearest to this, and yet we see by her letters how frankly she could criticise even him. Her danger lay in the direction of originality, not of imitation ; of too much divergence, not too much concentration. Coming in contact, as she did, with some of the strongest men of her time ; first the Boston Transcendentalists ; then Horace Greeley in New York; then Mazzini in Italy : she was still her own mistress, still *nul-*

[1] MS. letter : Providence, R. I., July 3, 1837.

lius addicta jurare in verba magistri. This showed
not merely a strong nature — for strength alone
does not secure independence — but a rich and
wise one.

In regard to unintelligibleness, she also shared
the charge with others; and I do not know that
she especially deserved it. She may be confused,
rambling, sometimes high-flown, but she offers no
paradoxes so startling as some of Emerson's, and
is incomparably smoother and clearer than Alcott. Nor is her obscurity ever wanton or whim-
sical, but is rather of that kind which, as Coleridge has said, is a compliment to the reader.
Note also that she is merciful to her public, and
if she has a thought with which she struggles so
that she can hardly get it into every day words, it
is to be found in her letters, not in her publications. Such a statement as this, for instance, she
would hardly have put into print; because it is
not worked out so clearly that he who runs may
read. Yet it is full of suggestion. She is speaking of what she calls " The Third Thought."

"CAMBRIDGE, *October* 27, 1843.

. . . " Your mind has acted with beneficent force on
mine, and roused it now from a repose which it has long
enough enjoyed. Let me try a little to note some results
of my reflections.

" The third thought which is to link together each
conflicting two is of course the secret of the universe.
It is sought alike by the fondest dream of love, the
purest pain of thought; the philosopher exacts, the poet

expects it, the child believes it is already here. It is the beloved Son in whom both God and man will be well pleased. . . .

"Faith and hope are gradually transmuted into knowledge, but very slowly is this mass of matter leavened by the divine wisdom. Yet the third thought is gradually taking possession of us; when we have at last become thoroughly possessed by, we may in turn possess it." [1]

This statement belongs upon the same plane with that made by Emerson in his essay on the "Over-Soul," that "In all conversation between two persons, tacit reference is made to a third party, to a common nature;" but Margaret Fuller's proposition is a somewhat different thing, and is even more suggestive. Scattered through her letters and journals everywhere there are passages of which this is an example; and it is such as these to which Emerson refers when he speaks of her "lyric glimpses." But in her published writings she rarely attempted more than she felt herself able to state clearly; though her standard of clearness was not just that which now prevails.

Even in her printed essays, however, she suffered from an exuberance of mental activity, which she had not yet learned to control. Trained early to be methodical in her use of time, she had neither the leisure nor the health nor perhaps the impulse to be methodical in thought. In that teeming period when she lived, method was not

[1] MS. (W. H. C.)

the strong point, nor did her friend Emerson set
her, in this respect, a controlling example. The
habit of conversation was perhaps bad for her, in
this way, and may have tended, as does all extem-
poraneous speaking, toward a desultory habit of
mind. Journalism, which was her next resource,
leads in the same way; that is, the single editorial demands concentration, but two successive
editorials are rarely linked together, and still
more rarely give room for what she calls "the
third thought." Accordingly her "Tribune" articles had more symmetry than her previous writings, but it was symmetry within the restricted
field of the newspaper column, which often un-
fits the best journalist for a more sustained flight.
How far the maturer experience of Italy may
have remedied this, in her case, we never shall
know, since her book was lost with her; and her
record as a writer remains therefore unfinished.
Still it is something to know that on the whole
she tended more and more to completeness of
form, and to the proper control of her own abundant thoughts.

The evidence of this is not to be found in her
"Woman in the Nineteenth Century," — which,
while full of thoughts and suggestions, is yet discursive and unmethodical, — but in her "Papers
on Literature and Art." The most satisfactory of
these is the essay on Sir James Mackintosh, which
still seems to me, as it has seemed for many years,

one of the very best critical essays yet written in
America. Sir James was a peculiarly good sub·
ject to test her powers, because his temperament
was wholly alien from hers. He stood to her in
a clear light, as the man who by the consent of
all contemporaries was best equipped for great
deeds, yet never accomplished them; who must
be judged by his results as against his promise;
omnium consensu capax imperii, nisi imperásset.
This has often since been pointed out, but no one
stated it so early, or at least so clearly as Margaret Fuller. I know nobody else in American literature who could have handled the theme so
well; Lowell would not have done the work so
simply, or Whipple so profoundly, while Emerson would not have done it at all. If any reader
of this book wishes to be satisfied that Margaret
Fuller had her own place and a very high place
among American prose-writers, they may turn to
that essay.

There were two points in which no one exceeded
her at the time and place in which she lived.
First, she excelled in "lyric glimpses," or the
power of putting a high thought into a sentence.
If few of her sentences have passed into the common repertory of quotation, that is not a final test.
The greatest poet is not necessarily the most
quoted or quotable poet. Pope fills twenty-four
pages in Bartlett's "Dictionary of Quotations,"
Moore eight, Burns but six, Keats but two, and
the Brownings taken together less than half a

page. The test of an author is not to be found merely in the number of his phrases that pass current in the corners of newspapers — else would " Josh Billings " be at the head of literature ; — but in the number of passages that have really taken root in younger minds. Tried by this standard, Margaret Fuller ranks high, and, if I were to judge strictly by my own personal experience, I should say very high indeed. I shall always be grateful to the person who fixed in my memory, during early life, such sentences as these : —

" Yes, O Goethe ! but the ideal is truer than the actual. This changes and that changes not."

" Tragedy is always a mistake ; and the loneliness of the deepest thinker, the widest lover, ceases to be pathetic to us so soon as the sun is high enough above the mountains."

[In reading fiction] " We need to hear the excuses men make to themselves for their worthlessness." [A better criticism never was made on the current villain of the drama and the novel.]

" For precocity some great price is always demanded sooner or later in life."

" Genius will live and thrive without training, but it does not the less reward the watering-pot and pruning-knife."

" A man who means to think and write a great deal must, after six and twenty, learn to read with his fingers."

" Man tells his aspiration in his God ; but in his demon he shows his depth of experience ; and casts light

19

into the cavern through which he worked his cause up to the cheerful day."

Other such passages might easily be added; indeed they are already to be found, here and there, distributed through this memoir. And her critical verdicts are often condensed into passages as compact as the following — as where she says of Coleridge, " Give Coleridge a canvas and he will paint a single mood as if his colors were made of the mind's own atoms; " or of Southey, " In his most brilliant passages there is nothing of inspiration; " or of Shelley, " The rush, the flow, the delicacy of vibration in Shelley's verse can only be paralleled by the waterfall, the rivulet, the notes of the bird and of the insect world ; " or when she speaks of the " balm " applied by Wordsworth to the public heart after the fever of Byron ; or depicts the " strange bleak fidelity " of Crabbe ; or says of Campbell that he did not possess "as much lyric flow as force; "[1] or of literary phases and fashions generally, " There is no getting rid of the epidemic of the season, however amazing and useless it may seem ; you cannot cough down an influenza, it will cough you down; "[2] in all these statements she makes not merely a series of admirable points, but she really gives the condensed essence of criticism.

She seems to me to have been, in the second place, the best literary critic whom America has

---

[1] *Papers, etc.* p. 71, 77, 83, 93, 98.
[2] *Ibid.* p. 87.

yet seen. Her friend Ripley, who succeeded her
in the " Tribune " and held such sway for many
years, was not, in the finer aspects of the art,
to be compared with Margaret Fuller. Passing
from her single phrases and *obiter dicta* to her
continuous criticisms, I should name her second
paper on Goethe in the " Dial ; " [1] as ranking
next to that on Mackintosh ; and should add,
also, her essay on " Modern British Poets " in
" Papers on Literature and Art ; " and the " dialogue " between Aglauron and Laurie in the same
volume. In this last there are criticisms on Wordsworth which go deeper, I venture to think, than
anything Lowell has written on the same subject.
I do not recall any other critic on this poet who
has linked together the poems " A Complaint "
and the sonnet beginning

"There is a change and I am poor,"

and has pointed out that these two give us a
glimpse of a profounder personal emotion and a
deeper possibility of sadness in Wordsworth than
all else that he has written put together. There
are also admirable remarks on Coleridge and on
Shakespeare; and how fine in thought, how simply and admirably stated, is this conclusion : —

" Were I, despite the bright points so numerous in
their history and the admonitions of my own conscience,
inclined to despise my fellow-men, I should have found

---

[1] *Dial*, ii. 1 (July, 1841, reprinted in *Life Without and Life
Within*, p. 23).

abundant argument against it during this late study of Hamlet. In the streets, saloons, and lecture rooms we continually hear comments so stupid, insolent, and shallow on great and beautiful works, that we are tempted to think that there is no public for anything that is good ; that a work of genius can appeal only to the fewest minds in any one age, and that the reputation now awarded to those of former times is never felt, but only traditional. Of Shakespeare, so vaunted a name, little wise or worthy has been written, perhaps nothing so adequate as Coleridge's comparison of him to the pine-apple ; yet on reading Hamlet, his greatest work, we find there is not a pregnant sentence, scarce a word that men have not appreciated, have not used in myriad ways. Had we never read the play, we should find the whole of it from quotation and illustration as familiar to us as air. The exquisite phraseology, so heavy with meaning, wrought out with such admirable minuteness, has become a part of literary diction, the stock of the literary bank ; and what set criticism can tell like this fact how great was the work, and that men were worthy it should be addressed to them ? " [1]

In this conversation, as in all the imaginary conversations which were so in fashion at that period, there are traces of Landor ; but Margaret Fuller achieved, both in " Aglauron and Laurie," and in " The Two Herberts," what Landor rarely accomplished — what Lowell could not achieve in his " Conversations on the Dramatists," or her other fellow-townsman, Story, in his more recent " He and She," — the distinct individualization of

[1] *Papers on Literature and Art,* p. 173.

the two participants. Through the whole dialogue we see two persons, not merely one person
speaking through two mouths. For instance, Laurie asks Aglauron : —

" But have I not seemed heartless to you at times ? "

and Aglauron replies : —

" In the moment, perhaps, but quiet thought always
showed me the difference between heartlessness and the
want of a deep heart."

Here we have not only an admirable glimpse into
the recesses of human character, but we have a
sharp demarkation between the two friends. Here
and elsewhere, the conversation is a real interchange of thoughts and not a disguised monologue.

Margaret Fuller's career as a critic encountered,
at two points, the sincere opposition and even
hostility of many readers, especially in her own
home ; in relation, namely, to her fellow-towns-
men Longfellow and Lowell. It may readily be
admitted at this time that she did less than justice to them both. This admitted, the fact remains that there was not a trace of personal ran-
cor or grievance in either case ; her whole career,
indeed, being singularly free from this lowest of
literary vices. In regard to Longfellow, she in
the first place, as Horace Greeley tells us, wished
to be excused from reviewing him ; and then
stated without disguise why she criticised him so
frankly : because he seemed to her over-praised,
and because she thought him exotic. This she

says in her own words more distinctly than **any** one else can say it for her : —

"We must confess to a coolness towards Mr. Longfellow, in consequence of the exaggerated praises that have been bestowed upon him. When we see a person of moderate powers receive honors which should be reserved for the highest, we feel somewhat like assailing him and taking from him the crown which should be reserved for grander brows. *And yet this is, perhaps, ungenerous.*"

The italics are my own. Then she defends him from the special charge of plagiarism, which Poe was just trying to fasten upon him, and goes on : —

"He has no style of his own, growing out of his own experiences and observations of nature. Nature with him, whether human or external, is always seen through the windows of literature. There are in his poems sweet and tender passages descriptive of his personal feelings, but very few showing him as an observer, at first hand, of the passions within, or the landscape without.

"This want of the free breath of nature, this perpetual borrowing of imagery, this excessive, because superficial, culture which he has derived from an acquaintance with the elegant literature of many nations and men, out of proportion to the experience of life within himself, prevent Mr. Longfellow's verses from ever being a true refreshment to ourselves. . . .

"And now farewell to the handsome book, with its Preciosos and Preciosas, its vikings and knights and cavaliers, its flowers of all climes and wild flowers of none. We have not wished to depreciate these writings below their current value, more than truth absolutely demands. We have not forgotten that, if a man cannot himself sit at the feet of the muse, it is much if he prizes those who may ; it makes him a teacher to the people. Neither have we forgotten that Mr. Longfellow has a genuine respect for his pen, never writes carelessly, nor when he does not wish to, nor for money alone. Nor are we intolerant to those who prize hot-house bouquets beyond all the free beauty of nature ; that helps the gardener and has its uses. But still let us not forget — ' Excelsior ' ! ! " [1]

This is, no doubt, overstated, but who will now deny that there was a certain force in it ? As Longfellow underwent deeper experiences and mellowed into his beautiful old age, this criticism seemed plainly inadequate ; and Margaret Fuller herself, had she lived, would have been the first to recognize the deepening Americanism of his tone — this being what she chiefly demanded of him. The poems that she had singled out for praise in his early volumes were those like " The Village Blacksmith " and " The Driving Cloud," which had a flavor of the soil ; and as he grew older, this quality became unmistakable. But hers was at any rate legitimate literary criticism, and would perhaps have left no sting behind but for the single fact that she compared the weak portrait of him, prefaced to the first illustrated edition of his poems (Philadelphia, 1845), to "a dandy Pindar."

[1] *Papers on Literature and Art*, pp. 330–335.

Any one who will look to-day at that picture will
see that there could hardly be a more felicitous
characterization of it than in these three words;
but it was fancied at the time, most gratuitously,
that she meant it for a hit at Longfellow himself;
and hence followed a very needless irritation, which
fortunately the amiable poet did not greatly share.

In regard to Lowell, the case was a little different, and her tone was blunter, though equally free
from all personal grudge. She had welcomed
very cordially his first volume of poems in the
" Dial ; " and again in 1845, when reviewing his
" Conversations " in the " Tribune," had taken
pains to do him justice while pointing out, as in
the case of Longfellow, that she felt bound to resist a certain tone of exaggeration in his admirers. She wrote of him : —

" He shows great justness of feeling, delicacy of per-
ception, comprehensive views ; and, for this country, an
unusual refinement and extent of culture. We have
been accustomed to hear Mr. Lowell so extravagantly
lauded by the circle of his friends, that we should be
hopeless of escaping the wrath of his admirers, for any
terms in which our expressions of sympathy could be
couched, but for the more modest and dignified tone of
his own preface, which presents ground on which the
world at large can meet him. With his admirers, we
have often been reminded of a fervent Italian who raved
at one of our country-women as ' a heartless girl,' because she would not go to walk with him alone at midnight. But Mr. Lowell himself speaks of his work as
becomes one conversant with those of great and accomplished minds."

Later in the same year (1845), however, in that essay on "American Literature" which appeared for the first time in her "Papers," she wrote the words which created so much indignation, and which simply show that no critic can look forward with infallible judgment to the future development of a poet. She wrote of Lowell, as has already been said, that he was "absolutely wanting in the true spirit and tone of poesy," adding : —

"His interest in the moral questions of the day has supplied the want of vitality in himself; his great facility at versification has enabled him to fill the ear with a copious stream of pleasant sound. But his verse is stereotyped; his thought sounds no depth, and posterity will not remember him." [1]

This last is very nearly what Coleridge said of Scott. He said, "Not twenty lines of Scott's poetry will ever reach posterity; it has relation to nothing." [2] Coleridge erred as to Scott, and Margaret Fuller as to Lowell; but we must remember that Scott's poetry was all published when Coleridge's criticism was made; while Margaret Fuller wrote when Lowell had printed only his "Class Poem" and two early volumes; the "Biglow Papers" and "Sir Launfal," and all the works by which he is now best known being still unwritten. It was simply a mistaken literary estimate, not flavored with the slightest personal sting ; and it

[1] *Papers on Literature and Art*, p. 308.
[2] Alsop's *Letters, Conversations, etc. of Coleridge*, Am. ed. p. 116.

would be hardly possible, in these milder days, for such a criticism to call out the kind of retaliation that is to be found in the "Fable for Critics." But that was a period, as has already been intimated, of great literary truculence; a time when, as Heine says of the Germans, an author, like an African chief, felt bound to moisten the base of his own throne with the blood of his slain foes. Lowell, probably, also thought that, in the case of Margaret Fuller, he was immolating the good-natured Longfellow's literary enemies with his own.

XIX.

PERSONAL TRAITS.

THAT woman of genius, Mrs. Sarah Helen Whitman of Providence, — best known to the world as having been the betrothed of Edgar Poe, — wrote once, in the "Providence Journal," a description of a scene where the brilliant and audacious John Neal gave a parlor lecture on Phrenology, then at its high-tide of prominence; and illustrated it by Margaret Fuller's head. The occasion is thus described : —

"Among the topics of the evening, phrenology was introduced, and Mr. Neal expressed a wish to give what might be termed a topical illustration of his favorite theory. Miss Fuller slowly uncoiled the heavy folds of her light brown hair and submitted her haughty head to his sentient fingers. The masterly analysis which he made of her character, its complexities and contradictions, its heights and its depths, its nobilities and its frailties, was strangely lucid and impressive, and helped one who knew her well to a more tender and sympathetic appreciation of her character and career, a character which only George Eliot could have fully appreciated and portrayed." [1]

[1] *Providence Journal*, July 24, 1876.

Many men, including some of the most gifted in
our American community, have since tried their
hands on Margaret Fuller's head ; and they have
given such varying results as their point of observation might justify.   With ready recognition of
my own inferiority to them as respects personal
knowledge, I find myself, after long and patient
study of her writings, forming conclusions sometimes different from theirs.   I do not think that
Mr. Emerson, with his cool and tranquil temperament, always did quite justice to the ardent nature
that flung itself against him ; and it seems to me
that her other biographers have sometimes been
too much influenced by their own point of contact
with her to see that the self-culture which brought
her to them was by no means the whole of her
aim.   Let me, therefore, consider her character
rather more minutely.

It is to be remembered, in the first place, that
her life was always saddened by the feeling that
she had been defrauded of her childhood by too
forced a precocity and deprived of her rightful
health through mismanagement.   Under this disadvantage she led thenceforward a life of constant checking and restriction, not as to pleasures, for which she rarely sighs in her diaries,
but as to doing her appointed work in the world
and employing the talents given her.   Rising in
the morning, as Emerson says of all of us, " with
an appetite that could eat the solar system like a
cake," she soon finds herself restricted as to food

and wholly wanting in digestion. With the largest views as to the aims and destiny of her nation,
she was obliged to see the timid and the pessi-
mists work on while she was fettered. There are
many who, because they cannot do the great
things, refuse to do the little ones; she was ready
to lavish herself on the smallest; no one ever saw
a more devoted daughter, sister, friend; and only
her diary and a very few intimates knew how
much this cost her or how she yearned for something more. With inexorable frankness she saw
that even her resignation was often a kind of
despair, even the alms she gave were only a miserable substitute for the larger work she longed to
do; and thus much she often expressed, not only
to herself but to others.

She thought that we human beings ought not,
as she wrote to Mr. Emerson (in 1839), "to suppress the worst or select the best of ourselves," but
to be "*altogether* better." Even her own good
deeds thoroughly dissatisfied her, and she often
points out in her diaries that what passes for virtue in her is only the resigned acceptance of what
seems to her subordinate and unsatisfactory. Her
life, so far from being selfish, overflowed with constant acts of private kindness; she was incessantly
bearing burdens for others, but she was haunted,
as many other strong natures have been, by the
spirit of Emerson's couplet, —

> " He who feeds men serveth few,
> He serves all who dares be true."

She demanded to serve all. When ill-health, domestic care, unsatisfied longings after life and action combined to depress her, she found, as so many others have found, that even self-devotion was only a palliative. She writes in her diary: —

"I went to walk with Richard, then sang psalm tunes with Lloyd, then wrote to Aunt Mary. When I have not joyous energy in myself, I can do these little things for others; very many of my attentions are of this spurious sort; they are my consolations; the givers [of gratitude] who thank me are deceived. But what can I do? I cannot always upbear my life all alone. The heart sinks and then I must help it by persuasions that it is better for others I should be here and theirs. It is mere palliative, I know.

"In earliest days how many night-hours have found me thus. I was always so lonely. I used to cheer myself with my piano. I wish I had it now.

> " When no gentle eye-beam charms,
>   No fond hope the bosom warms,
>   Of thinking the lone mind is tired,
>   Nought seems bright to be desired,
>   Music, by thy sails unfurled,
>   Bear me to thy better world;
>   O'er the cold and weltering sea
>   Blow thy breezes warm and free,
>   By sad sighs they ne'er were chilled,
>   By skeptic spell were never stilled." [1]

Again she writes, at the same period, she having then various classes to teach: —

"Did not get home till just before my class came. Was obliged to lie on the bed all the time they were

[1] MS. Diary, 1844.

with me. It was the last time, and they were pleasant. They love me and fancy I am good and wise. Oh that it gave me more pleasure to do *a little* good, and give *a little* happiness. But there is no modesty or moderation in me." [1]

These extracts are quite inconsistent, I think, with the charge most commonly made against Margaret Fuller, — that of vanity and undue self-absorption. It must always be remembered that some previous descriptions of her have been in a manner warped by the fact that they proceeded from the most gifted and intellectual persons whom she knew; all these persons being almost always men whom she met under a certain amount of intellectual excitement, to whom she showed her brightest aspirations, her deepest solicitudes. It was in the very nature of such a description that the every-day aspects should be left out; that we should see chiefly the seeress, the dreamer, the student. She writes reproachfully to a cultivated friend after an interview, " You seemed to consider me as some *tête exaltée*, at the hour when I was making bitter sacrifices to duty." Could a memoir have been made up out of her letters to her mother, full of suggestions about flower bulbs, plans as to the larder, and visions of a renovated silk dress; or could we have before us a long series of the sensible, warm-hearted, motherly letters she wrote every week to her absent younger brothers, the whole effect produced would have been

[1] MS. Diary, 1844.

very different. The complaint is constantly made
that all her attainments and her self-culture did not
bring her happiness. It is asking a great deal of
any single woman to be positively happy in the
presence of tormenting ill-health, poverty, and a
self-sacrificing habit that keeps her always on the
strain. It is even something to ask of a person,
under such circumstances, that she should be habitually cheerful and hopeful. That this last was the
predominant tone of Margaret Fuller's daily life is
proved by all her more familiar letters and by the
general testimony of those who knew her best. No
doubt, in her diaries, there are passages which
record depression and sometimes almost morbid
periods of self-inspection and self-reproach. That
is what diaries are made for; they exist in order
that imaginative and passionate natures may re-
lieve themselves by expressing these moods, and
may then forget them and proceed. The trouble
comes when sympathetic biographers elevate these
heights and depths into too great importance and
find the table-lands of life uninteresting. There
never was a year of Margaret Fuller's life, after
her precocious maturity, when the greater part
of it was not given to daily, practical, common-
sense labor, and this usually for other people.

All periods have their fashions. It does not
mar our impression of the admirable capacity and
self-devotion of Abigail Adams that she signed her
early letters to her husband, John Adams, as
" Portia." It was the fashion of the time ; and

when Margaret Fuller afterwards tried to write out her imaginative and mystical side under the name of " Leila," it belonged to that period also; a period when German romance was just beginning to be translated, and Oriental poetry to be read. These were her dreams, her idealities; but when it was a question how to provide school-books and an overcoat for her little brother, no mother of ten children ever set about the business with less of haziness or indefiniteness of mind. If I have seemed in this book to bring my heroine down from the clouds a little ; it is simply because I have used the materials at my command, and have tried to paint her as she was; a being not fed on nectar and ambrosia, after all, but on human nature's daily food.

It may be asked why, with this daily and noble self-devotion she was not universally beloved. It can be very briefly told : she wanted tact. As some essentially selfish persons go through the world winning all hearts by merely possessing that quality, so others are always underrated for want of it. There is a story told of her, that at a party given expressly for her in Cambridge she took a piece of cake from a plate offered, and then impulsively replaced it with the remark, " I fear there will not be enough to go round," thereby giving more offense than if she had personally appropriated the whole plateful. It was this simple and not always judicious honesty of purpose which accounted for her frequent failure to attract at

20

first sight, while there have been few women — I
at least have never known any woman — who left
behind an affection so deep and strong. It is now
thirty years since her death, and there is scarcely
a friend of hers who does not speak of her with as
warm a devotion as if she had died yesterday.

If Margaret Fuller was strict and unflinching
in her judgments of other people, it was because
she was so, above all, in dealing with herself.
This is seen on every page of her diaries, which
record the very heights and depths of a nature
as yet uncontrolled and passionately aspiring.
Feeling her own powers and capacities, she also
recognized her limitations; but her statements of
these two sides of the question might be wholly
detached, and so gave the appearance of more
moodiness than really existed. At any rate,
moody or not, they were sincere. A lady once
said to me of the Fuller family: "Their only pe-
culiarity was that they said openly about themselves the good and bad things which we commonly suppress about ourselves and express only
about other people." This was true, as has been
said, about the elder Fullers, even in public; it
was true of Margaret Fuller in her diaries. She
was an acute analyst of character, and again and
again in her various diaries we come upon sketches
delineating the traits of each person in the room.
Some of these are printed in the "Dial."[1] She
always includes herself, and is usually more un-

[1] *Dial,* i. 136, etc.

flattering to herself than to anybody else. This may be called self-consciousness, but it certainly does not imply vanity; it quite as often takes the form of an almost excessive humility.

It would be easy to illustrate all this at great length from her unpublished papers. The most presumptuous passage about herself that I have been able to find is this, which bears no date. In speaking of Shelley's "Defense of Poesie," just read, she expresses her joy at finding that he had taken the matter up very much from the point of view she had been presenting in her conversations. "At least," she says, "I have all the great thoughts, and whatever the world may say, I shall be well received in the Elysian fields." [1] Yet this follows close upon a passage expressing her admiration of Shelley's prose style and her utter despair of ever being able to write like him; she can only console herself by thinking that in conversation, at least, she had met him on his own ground. Soon after follow, again and again, passages like these, written at different times: —

"I feel within myself an immense power, but I cannot bring it out. I stand a barren vine-stalk; no grape will swell, though the richest wine is slumbering in its roots."

"I have just about enough talent and knowledge to furnish a dwelling for friendship, but not enough to deck with golden gifts a Delphos for the world."

"As I read Ellery [Channing] my past life seems a

[1] Fuller MSS. i. 588.

poor excuse for not living; my so-called culture a collection of shreds and patches to hide the mind's nakedness. Cannot I begin really to live and think now?"[1]

How many authors, surrounded by a circle of admiring friends, are found to have descended, in their secret diaries, to quite such depths of humility as appear in these extracts?

Another point where I should diverge strongly from the current estimate of Margaret Fuller is in the prevailing assumption that her chief aim at any period of her life was self-culture. The Roman thread in her was too strong, the practical inheritance from her parentage too profound, for her to have ever contented herself with a life of abstraction. The strong training that came from her father, the early influence of Jefferson's letters, all precluded this. What she needed was not books but life, and if she ever expressed doubts of this need, she always came back to it again. "Is it not nobler and truer," she wrote in 1842 to W. H. Channing, "to live than to think?"[2] Here it is that she sometimes chafes under the guidance of Emerson; always longs to work as well as meditate, to deal with the many, not the few, to feel herself in action. This made it the best thing in her Providence life to have attended the Whig caucus, and made her think, on board the French war-vessel, that she would like to command it; this made her delight in studying

[1] Fuller MSS. i. 589, 593, 597.
[2] MS.

Western character; this led her to New York, where the matter-of-fact influence of Horace Greeley simply confirmed what had been so long growing. Like the noble youth in her favorite Jean Paul's "Titan," she longed for an enterprise for her idle valor. She says in her fragment of autobiographical romance: —

"I steadily loved this [Roman] ideal in my childhood, and this is the cause, probably, why I have always felt that man must know how to stand firm on the ground before he can fly. In vain for me are men more, if they are less, than Romans."

Again and again she comes back in her correspondence to this theme, as when she writes to W. H. Channing (March 22, 1840) : —

"I never in life have had the happy feeling of really doing anything. I can only console myself for these semblances of actions by seeing that others seem to be in some degree aided by them. But oh! really to feel the glow of action, without its weariness, what heaven it must be!"[1]

Again she writes to the same friend, contrasting the meditative life of Socrates and the active life of Jesus Christ: —

"CAMBRIDGE, *June* 17, 1842.

"In my quiet retreat I read Xenophon and became more acquainted with his Socrates. I had before known only the Socrates of Plato, one much more to my mind. Socrates took the ground that you approve; he conformed to the Greek Church, and it is evident with a

[1] MS.

sincere reverence, because it was the growth of the national mind.   He thought best to stand on its platform,
and illustrate, though with keen truth, by received
forms : this was his right way, for his influence was
naturally private, for individuals who could, in some degree, respond to the teachings of his ' demon ; ' it made
no difference to him ; he knew the multitude would not
understand him ; but it was the other way that Jesus
took, preaching in the field and plucking ears of corn
on the Sabbath day." [1]

Again, after a day in the woods with Emerson's
"Nature," — reading it through for the first time
to herself, Mr. Emerson himself having originally
read it aloud to her, — she thus writes to him
(April 12, 1840) : —

" The years do not pass in vain.   If they have built
no temple on the earth, they have given a nearer view
of the city of God.   Yet would I rather, were the choice
tendered to me, draw the lot of Pericles than that of
Anaxagoras.   And if such great names do not fit the
occasion, I would delight more in thought-living than in
living thought.   That is not a good way of expressing
it either, but I must correct the press another time." [2]

This feeling led her to criticise more than once,
as we have seen, her friend's half cloistered life at
Concord.   Describing in one of her letters some
speech which called for action, perhaps Kossuth's,
she says : —

" Read these side by side with Waldo's paragraphs
and say, is it not deeper and truer to live than to think?

[1] MS. (W. H. C.)   [2] MS.

. . . Yet is his [Emerson's] a noble speech! I love to reprove myself by it." [1]

As I read her letters and diaries, it seems plain that her yearning desire, during her whole life, was not merely to know but to do. She was urged on by an intense longing, not for a selfish self-culture, nor even for self-culture in its very widest sense, but for usefulness in her day and generation.

"He who alone knoweth," she writes in August, 1843, "will affirm that I have tried to work whole-hearted, from an earnest faith, yet my hand is often languid and my heart is slow; — I must be gone, I feel, but whither? I know not: if I cannot make this plot of ground yield corn and roses, famine must be my lot forever and forever, surely." [2]

In accordance with this thought, she felt that this country must create, as it has now done, its own methods of popular education, especially for the training of girls. She wrote in her "Summer on the Lakes:" —

"Methods copied from the education of some English Lady Augusta are as ill suited to the daughter of an Illinois farmer as satin shoes to climb the Indian mounds. . . . Everywhere the fatal spirit of imitation, of reference to European standards, penetrates and threatens to blight whatever of original growth might adorn the soil." [3]

Had this protest come from an ignorant per-

[1] MS. (W. H. C.) [2] MS. (W. H. C.)
[3] *Summer on the Lakes*, p. 47.

son, it would have simply amounted to turning one's back on all the experience of the elder world. Coming from the most cultivated American woman of her day, it meant that there was something worth more than culture — namely, original thoughts and free action. Whatever else she was, she was an American.

These are the reasons for thinking that neither the charge of vanity nor of undue self-culture can be sustained against Margaret Fuller. And this is said after reading many hundred pages of her letters and journals. They are clearly written, in a hand quite peculiar, not a little formal, and as it were jointed rather than flowing, and not greatly varying throughout her whole life. She is always clear in style where she takes pains to be clear, is even business-like where she aims at that, and knows how to make herself emphatic without the aid of underscoring; indeed she abstains from this to an extent which would quite amaze Mr. Howells. To be sure, she was not at all one of those charming, helpless, inconsequent creatures whom he so exquisitely depicts; she demanded a great deal from life, but generally knew what she wanted, stated it effectively, and at last obtained it. It was indeed fortunate for her younger brothers and sisters that she was of this constitution. She lived at a time when life in America was hard for all literary people, from the absence of remuneration, the small supply of books, the habit of jealousy among authors, and the lingering prevalence of the colonial spirit, which she battled stoutly to banish. It was especially hard for women in that profession because there were few of them, their early education was won at great disadvantage, and much was conceded reluctantly that now comes as a matter of course. Were she living to-day her life would be far smoother; she would find plenty of remunerative work, fair recognition, and kindly sympathy. On the other hand, she would have to adapt herself to a somewhat different world, for she would not be surrounded by that ardent and effusive social atmosphere which prevailed throughout the limited world of Transcendentalism. It was a fresh, glowing, youthful, hopeful, courageous period, and those who were its children must always rejoice that they were born before it faded away.

My friend Mr. O. B. Frothingham, the only direct historian of the Transcendental period, has failed, in my judgment, to give more than the husk and outside of it, although for this his book is valuable. The trouble was that he was neither a part of that great impulse nor immediately its child; in the day of Transcendentalism he was looking in a different direction and had no sympathy for its aims; and yet he was not quite far enough away to view it in perspective. To its immediate offspring, even if of a younger race, it bequeathed a glow and a joy that have been of life-long permanence. I have noticed that most of those who were nurtured under that influence have had the good fortune to grow old slowly; their world is still poetic; the material achievements, the utilitarian philosophy of later years may come or go, leaving their ideal, their confidence, their immortal hope unchanged. And now that much which Transcendentalism sought is fulfilled, and that which was ecstasy has — as Emerson predicted — become daily bread, its reminiscences mingle with all youth's enchantments, and belong to a period when we too "toiled, feasted, despaired, were happy."

And as for Margaret Ossoli, her life seems to me, on the whole, a triumphant rather than a sad one, in spite of the prolonged struggle with illness, with poverty, with the shortcomings of others and with her own. In later years she had the fulfillment of her dreams; she had what Elizabeth Barrett, writing at the time of her marriage to Robert Browning, named as the three great desiderata of existence, "life and love and Italy." She shared in great deeds, she was the counselor of great men, she had a husband who was a lover, and she had a child. They loved each other in their lives, and in their death they were not divided. Was not that enough?

BIBLIOGRAPHICAL APPENDIX.

———◆———

WORKS OF MARGARET FULLER OSSOLI.

BOOKS.

1. Correspondence with Goethe in the Last Years of his Life. Translated from the German of Eckermann. Boston, 1839.
2. Correspondence of Fräulein Günderode and Bettine von Arnim. Boston, 1842. [Reprinted, with additions, by Mrs. Minna Wesselhoeft. Boston, 1861.]
3. Summer on the Lakes. Boston, 1843.
4. Woman in the Nineteenth Century. New York, 1844.
5. Papers on Literature and Art. New York, 1846.
6. Collected Works, edited by Arthur B. Fuller, with an introduction by Horace Greeley. New York, 1855.
   I. Woman in the Nineteenth Century, and Kindred Papers, relating to the Sphere, Condition, and Duties of Woman.
   II. At Home and Abroad. [Including Summer on the Lakes; Tribune Letters from Europe; Letters to Friends from Europe; Accounts of the Homeward Voyage; and Memorials.]
   III. Art, Literature, and the Drama. [Including Papers on Literature and Art, reprinted; and a translation of Goethe's Tasso.]
   IV. Life Without and Life Within. [Including essays, reviews, and poems, nearly all hitherto unpublished in book form.]

CONTRIBUTIONS TO PERIODICALS.

Boston Daily Advertiser. Defense of Brutus. November 27, 1834.

Western Messenger. Review of Lives of Crabbe and More. i. 20.

Western Messenger.   Review of Bulwer's Works.   i. 101.

Western Messenger.   Review of Philip van Artevelde.   i. 398.

Western Messenger.   Review of Körner.   i. 306, 369.

Western Messenger.   Review of Letters from Palmyra.   v. 24.

Dial. Vol. I. No. 1. Essay on Critics ; Allston Exhibition;
Richter (poem) ; A Sketch (poem) ; A Sketch (poem) [?].
No. 2. Record of the Months (part). No. 3. Klopstock and
Meta ; The Magnolia of Lake Pontchartrain ; Menzel's View
of Goethe; Record of the Months. No. 4. Leila; A Dia-
logue.

Dial. Vol. II. No. 1. Goethe ; Need of a Diver ; Notices of
Recent Publications. No. 2. Lives of the Great Composers;
Festus. No. 3. Yucca Filamentosa; Bettine Brentano and
her Friend Günderode ; Epilogue to the Tragedy of Essex ; Notices of Monaldi and Wilde's Tasso (including part of her
translation of Goethe's Tasso).

Dial. Vol. III. No. 1. Entertainments of the Past Winter.
Notices of Hawthorne. No. 2. Romaic and Rhine Ballads ;
Tennyson's Poems, in Record of the Months. No. 4. Canova ;
Record of the Months (part).

Dial. Vol. IV. No. 1. The Great Lawsuit ; Man *vs.* Men,
Woman *vs.* Women. No. 3. The Modern Drama. No. 4.
Dialogue.

New York Tribune, 1844–46. Too numerous to be here catalogued.
They are usually designated by an asterisk (*) in the Tribune,
and many are reprinted in the volume " Life Without and
Life Within," mentioned above.

Liberty Bell (Anti-Slavery annual, 1846). The Liberty Bell
(prose essay).

PUBLICATIONS CONCERNING HER.

BIOGRAPHIES.

1. Memoirs of Margaret Fuller Ossoli, by R. W. Emerson, W.
H. Channing, and J. F. Clarke, 2 vols. Boston, 1852. [Edited
mainly by W. H. Channing. Reprinted at New York, 1869 ;
at Boston, 1884.]

2. Margaret Fuller (Marchesa Ossoli), by Julia Ward Howe.
[" Eminent Women " series.] Boston, 1883.

3. Margaret Fuller Ossoli, by Thomas Wentworth Higginson.
[" American Men of Letters " series.] Boston, 1884.

BRIEFER MEMOIRS AND SKETCHES.

Crosland, Mrs. N.   In "Memorable Women."   London, 1854.

Dall, Mrs. C. H.   In "Historical Pictures Retouched."   Boston, 1850.

Frothingham, O. B.   In "Transcendentalism in New England."   Boston, 1876.

Griswold, R. W.   In "Prose Writers of America."   Philadelphia, 1846.

Griswold, R. W.   In "Female Poets of America."   Philadelphia, 1849.

Hale, Mrs. S. J.   In "Woman's Record."   New York, 1853.

Higginson, T. W.   In "Eminent Women of the Age."   Hartford, Conn., 1868.

Powell, T.   In "Living Authors of America."   New York, 1866.

Russell, W.   In "Extraordinary Men and Women."   London, 1860.

Russell, W.   In "Eccentric Personages."   New York, 1866.

Smiles, T.   In "Brief Biographies."   Boston, 1861.

REVIEWS, ETC., IN PERIODICALS.

[Prepared from Poole's Index, by the editor's permission, a few references being added.]

1. Margaret Fuller and the Reformers.   Brownson's Quarterly, ii. 249.

2. "At Home and Abroad" (F. H. Hedge), N. A. Review, lxxxiii. 261 ; London Athenæum (1856), 489.

3. Character and Works (C. H. Dall), N. A. Review, xci. 119.

4. Life and Works.   Democratic Review, xxx. 513.

5. "Memoirs."   New Quarterly Review, i. 168; Prospective Review, viii. 199 ; Southern Literary Messenger, xx. 129; Living Age, xxxiii. 28, 289 ; Eclectic Review, xcv. 678 ; London Athenæum (1852), 159 ; Emile Montégut, Revue des deux Mondes, xiv. 37.

6. "Papers on Literature and Art."   Democratic Review, xix. 198, 316.

7. Place in Literature.   Potter's American Monthly, x. 74.

8. "Woman in the Nineteenth Century."   Christian Examiner, xxxviii. 416.   Southern Quarterly, x. 148.   (A. P. Peabody), N. A. Review, lxxxi. 557.

9. Miscellaneous Notices. British Quarterly, xvi. 221. (S. Waddington), Tinsley's Magazine, xvi. 172. (A. L. Johnson), Galaxy, vi. 121. (M. R. Whittlesey), Radical, vi. 1. (A. C. Brackett), Radical, ix. 354. Chambers's Journal, xvii. 322. Dublin University Magazine, xcii. 542, 686. Household Words, v. 121. Sharpe's Magazine, xv. 201. Same article in Eclectic Magazine, xxvi. 171. National Magazine, i. 314, 409, 529. Canadian Monthly, xiii. 289. International Monthly, i. 162.

POEMS.

Ames, Mary C. At Home and Abroad, p. 458.

Cranch, C. P. Atlantic Monthly, xxvi. 231.

Cranch, C. P. At Home and Abroad, p. 456.

James, G. P. R. At Home and Abroad, p. 463. Also in International Monthly, i. 165.

Landor, Walter Savage. At Home and Abroad, p. 464.

Smith, E. Oakes. At Home and Abroad, p. 460.

Anonymous. At Home and Abroad, p. 461.

BOOKS ON THE FULLER FAMILY.

Fuller, R. F. Chaplain Fuller, a Memoir. Boston, 1863.

Higginson, T. W. Memoir of Arthur B. Fuller (in Harvard Memorial Biographies). Cambridge, 1866.

INDEX.

ADAMS, Abigail, 304.
Adams, John Quincy, 12, 27, 29.
Alcott, A. B., diary quoted, 75, 143, 144, 146–148, 180, 191; other references, 77–80, 95, 130, 140, 142, 148, 155, 159–162, 165, 175, 181, 285.
Alfieri, Victor, 45.
Allston, Washington, 95.
"American Literature," essay on, 203, 297.
Americanism in literature, 137.
Anaxagoras, 5.
Arconati, Marchioness Visconti, letter to, 274; other references, 231.
Arnim, Bettina (Brentano) von, 18, 190–192.
Atkinson, H. G., 224.
Austin, Sarah, 189.
Autobiographical romance, 21, 22, 309.

BACHI, Pietro, 33.
Bacon, Lord, 45.
Baillie, Joanna, 229.
Ballou, Adin, 180.
Bancroft, G., 33, 47, 48, 50, 103, 144.
Barker. See Ward.
Barlow, D. H., 39.
Barlow, Mrs. D. H., letters to, 39, 54, 62, 94, 154.
Barlow, F. C., 39.
Barrett, Miss. See Browning.
Bartlett, Robert, 138, 144, 146.
Bartol, C. A., 142, 144.
Beck, Charles, 33.
Belgiojoso, Princess, 236.
Béranger, J. P. de, 230.
Birthplace of Madame Ossoli, 20.
Bolivar, Simon, 15.
Bonaparte, Napoleon, 13, 15.
Bracebridge, Mr. and Mrs., 224.
Bradford, George P., 144.
Brentano, Bettina. See Arnim
Briggs, Miss, 225.
Brook Farm, 173.
Brown, Charles Brockden, 132.
Brown, Samuel, 226.
Brown's "Philosophy" studied, 24.

Browne, M. A., 39.
Browning, Elizabeth (Barrett), 220, 314.
Browning, Robert, 19, 69, 220, 229.
Brownson, O. A., 142–144, 147, 148.
Brutus, defense of, 47–50.
Bryant, William Cullen, 131.
Buckingham, J. T., 77.
Bull, Ole, 211.
Burges, Tristam, 87.
Burleigh, Charles, 176.
Burns, Robert, 226.

CABOT, J. E., 159.
Cambridge, Mass., between 1810 and 1830, 32.
Campbell, Thomas, 290.
"Carlyle-Emerson Correspondence," 4, 135, 145, 151, 164, 170.
Carlyle, Thomas, 45, 69, 102, 135, 145, 164, 175, 190, 220, 222, 229.
Cass, Lewis, Jr., 241; letter to, 266; letter from, 234.
Chalmers, Thomas, 229.
Chambers, Robert, 226.
Channing, Edward T., 33.
Channing, W. E. (Boston), 53, 86, 106, 122, 144, 171.
Channing, W. Ellery (Concord), 30, 100, 156, 164, 307.
Channing, Ellen (Fuller), 30, 31, 52, 55, 92, 234.
Channing, W. H., letters to, 91, 110, 111, 120, 148, 151, 161, 180, 183, 191, 201, 207, 308, 309; other references, 3, 34, 206, 212, 279.
Channing. See Eustis.
Chapman, M. W., 125.
Chappell, H. L., letter to, 64.
Cheney, E. D., 128.
Child, L. M., 114, 115, 128, 132, 203, 206, 211.
Cicero, Marcus Tullius, 50.
Clarke, James Freeman, 84, 85, 122, 142, 144, 146, 155, 162, 164, 168, 169, 193, 199.
Clarke, Sarah F., 193, 199, 200; letter

from, 117; illustrations for "Summer on the Lakes," 200.
Clarke, William H., 193.
Club, a literary, 142.
Coleridge, Hartley, 223.
Coleridge, S. T., 69, 134, 135, 223, 290-292, 297.
Combe, Andrew, 229.
Cooper, J. F., 131, 132.
Cousin, V., 135.
Crabbe, G., 290.
Cranch, C. P., 155, 162, 164, 211, 240.
Cranch, Mrs. C. P., 211.
Crane, Peter, 17.
Crane, Mrs., description of, 17.
Crowe, Mrs., 226.

Dana, Chief Justice, 27.
Dana, R. H., 95.
Dana, R. H., Jr., 24
Dante degli Alighieri, 86.
Davis, George T., 3, 34.
Davis, J. C., 3.
Davis, W. T., 52.
Degerando, Baron. 69.
De Quincey, Thomas, 226, 229.
Derby, Mrs., 223.
Dewey, O., 62.
"Dial," origin and history of, 130; prospectus of, 152.
Dwight, J. S., 146, 149, 162, 164.

Eastman, Mrs. S. C., 3.
Eckermann, J. P., 91, 189, 284.
Edgeworth, Maria, 132.
Eichhorn, J. G., 45.
Emerson, Ellen, 67.
Emerson, R. W., letters to, about "Dial," 151, 154, 157, 166, 168, 169, 171; about Brook Farm, 181, 182; from Chicago, 193, 196; on sailing for Europe, 220; other letters to, 67, 68, 70, 80, 86, 89, 94, 199, 301, 310. Description of, in diary, 66; passages from unpublished poems of, 66; letters concerning, 62, 63; criticisms on, by M. F. O., 66, 70, 72, 121, 157, 166, 167, 284, 310; extracts from his "Dial" papers, 137, 176; his inadequate estimate of M. F. O., 300; his defense of Alcott, 77; other references, 3, 45, 53, 64, 65, 69, 71, 75, 77, 88, 101, 103, 104, 116, 121, 130, 135, 138, 140, 142, 144, 146, 148-150, 156-160, 162, 164, 165, 172, 175, 177, 179, 180, 191, 205, 216, 221, 226, 247, 284-286, 308, 311.
Emerson, Mrs. R. W., 67, 69, 128.
Emerson, Waldo, 67.
Erckmann-Chatrian, 17.
Eustis, Dr., 96.
Eustis, Mary (Channing), 128.
Everett, Edward, 33.

Farrar, John, 41, 45, 52, 53, 182.
Farrar, Mrs. John, 35, 36, 41, 45, 51, 52, 62, 63, 283.
Fitton, Miss E., 275.
Flowers, Mrs. Fuller's love of, 18.
Follen, Charles, 33.
Francis, Convers, 142, 144, 146.
Friendship, letter on, 72.
Frothingham, O. B., 313.
Fuller, Abraham, 11, 54.
Fuller, Arthur B., letters to, 59, 83; other references, 3, 22, 58, 105, 203.
Fuller Edith, 248.
Fuller, Ellen. See Channing.
Fuller, Eugene, letters to, 202, 208; other references, 51, 52.
Fuller, Hiram, 79, 80, 87.
Fuller, Hon. Timothy, 12, 14, 16, 20, 22, 26, 28, 32, 48; addresses of, 13, 16; oration of, 15; letter to, 51.
Fuller, Margaret (Crane), 17, 20.
Fuller, Rev. Timothy, 9, 10.
Fuller, Richard F., letters to, 59, 105, 106, 273; other references, 17, 21, 220.
Fuller, Thomas, poem by, 8.

Garrison, W. L., 129.
Gibbon, E., 45, 50.
Giovanni, Ser, 256-258, 260, 264.
Goethe, J. W. von, 45, 47, 63, 68, 69, 91, 101, 135, 158, 188-191, 283, 284.
Gould, B. A., 134.
Graham, S., 175.
Gräter, Friedrich, 33.
Greeley, Horace. Recollections quoted, 80, 213; Life by Parton quoted, 213, 218; other references, 3, 80, 201, 206, 207, 209-214, 284, 293, 309.
Greeley, Mrs. Horace, 207
Greene, A. G., 3, 163.
Greene, W. B., 163.
Greenough, Harriet (Fay), 36.
Gregory, O., 223.
Greys, The, 225.
Günderode, Caroline von, 18, 190-192.

Hahn Hahn, Countess, 225.
Harring, Harro, 219.
Hasty, Captain, 275, 276.
Hasty, Mrs., 275, 278, 279.
Hawthorne, Nathaniel, extract from "Note-Books," 103; other references, 173, 174, 178, 179.
Hedge, F. H., letters to, 43, 44, 48, 63, 141, 149, 150; other references, 3, 22, 34, 44, 45, 62, 141-144, 146, 162, 188.
Heine, Heinrich, 17, 45, 298.
Heraud, John A., 145-147, 160, 161, 229; his magazine, 140, 145, 160.
Herschel, F. W., 45.
Higginsons, The, 52.

Hoar, Elizabeth, letters from, 64, 119; other references, 3, 248, 249.
Holmes, John, 24.
Holmes, O. W., 24, 25, 30, 34, 36.
Hooper, Ellen (Sturgis), 154, 156.
Houghton, Lord (R. M. Milnes), 69.
Howe, Julia (Ward), 2.
Howitts, the, 229.
Hudson, H. N., 211.
Hunt, Leigh, 145.
Hutchinson Family, the, 176.

INDIANS, study of the, 195.
Ireland, Mr., 221.
Irish, defense of the, 214.
Irving, Washington, 131, 132.

JACOBS, Sarah S., 80, 84.
Jahn, F. L., 45.
James, Henry, 134.
Jameson, Anna, 195.
Jefferson, Thomas, 4, 16, 45, 308.
Jonson, Ben, 69, 134.

KANT, Immanuel, 45, 282, 283.
Kinney, Mr., letter from, 247.
Kittredge, Rev. Mr., 53.
Knapp, J. J., 39.
Kneeland, Abner, 77.

LAFARGE, John, 134.
Lafayette, Marquis de, 15.
La Mennais, H. F. R. de, 230.
Lane, Charles, 160, 166.
Leonidas, 47.
Lewes, G. H., 229.
Longfellow, H. W., criticisms on, 138, 204, 218, 293; other references, 131, 283, 293–295, 298.
Loring, Mr. and Mrs. E. G., 122, 128.
Lowell, J. R., criticisms on, 217, 296; retaliation by, 5, 298; other references, 128, 164, 176, 203, 216, 217, 293, 296–298.
Lowell, Maria (White), 128, 272 ; letter from, 244.
" Lyric Glimpses," 286, 288.

McDOWELL, Mrs., 211.
Mackie, J. M., 163.
Mackintosh, Sir James, 187, 287, 288.
Mann, Horace, 11, 12.
Mariana, story of, 23.
Marston, J. Westland, 146, 160.
Martineau, Harriet, 36, 45, 53, 122–129, 222, 223, 283, 284.
Martineau, James, 221.
Mary Queen of Scots, 226.
Mazzini, Joseph, 5, 229, 231, 236, 244, 284.
Middleton, Conyers, 50.
Mill, John Stuart, 145.
Milman, H. H., 223.

Milnes, R. M. See Houghton.
Milton, John, 69.
Morris, G. P., 80.
Mozier, Mrs., 275.

NEAL, John, 299.
Newton, Stuart, 32.
Novalis (F. von Hardenburg), 45, 145.
Nuttall, Thomas, 33.

OSSOLI, A. P. E., birth of, 253 ; descriptions of, 259, 268, 270, 271; death of, 279.
Ossoli, G. A., descriptions of, 243, 244, 247 ; letters from, 249.
Ossoli, Sarah Margaret (Fuller), personal relations of author with, 2; manuscript letters and journals of, 3 ; demanded something beyond self-culture, 4, 6, 87, 88, 111, 213, 308, 309, 311 ; reading Jefferson's correspondence, 4, 45, 87, 308 ; criticism on her " Memoirs," 5, 203, 300 ; criticisms of Lowell on, 5, 298 ; ancestry, 7 ; birthplace, 20 ; autobiographical romance, 22, 188, 309 ; division of her hours, 24, 81 ; appearance at school, 24; appearance in company, 29 ; mode of education, 21, 28 ; early companions, 34, 36 ; women who influenced her, 35 ; early verses, 38 ; letters from, 17, 21, 39, 43, 44, 48, 51, 54, 56, 59, 62, 63, 70, 72, 78, 81, 83, 86, 87, 89, 91, 94, 95, 97–99, 101, 105, 106, 110–112, 120, 123, 124, 141, 149–151, 154, 157, 162, 165, 166, 168, 169, 171, 180–183, 191–193, 196, 198, 200–202, 207–209, 212, 220, 250, 266, 268, 270, 271, 273, 274, 309–311 ; passages from diaries, 22, 28, 31, 37, 41, 66, 100, 104, 106, 114, 122, 167, 187, 188, 195, 221–228, 232, 302 ; removal to Groton, 43 ; early composition, 46 ; first publication, 47 ; first journey, 53 ; care of family, 54, 58, 301, 303 ; friendship with Emerson, 62 ; love of children, 67, 82, 107, 210 ; reading, 68 ; verses, 38, 70, 102, 185, 302 ; criticisms on Emerson, 71, 72, 157, 310 ; teaching in Boston, 75 ; in Providence, 79 ; description of party in Boston, 86 ; self-esteem and humility, 88, 303, 306–308, 312 ; life at Jamaica Plain, 94 ; flower-pieces, 96 ; description of nature, 98 ; " ryebread days," 104 ; conversations, 109 ; interest in mythology, 114 ; relations with Miss Martineau, 123 ; women who took part in her conversations, 128 ; criticisms on contributors to " Dial," 165 ; not a resident at Brook Farm, 173; books pub-

lished, 187; Western journey, 193; removal to New York, 205; investigations of poverty and crime, 206, 211; religious feeling, 206; criticisms on Longfellow, 138, 204, 218, 293; on Lowell, 217, 296; departure for Europe, 220; her European notebook, 220; stay in London, 229; arrival in Rome, 230; the Italian revolution, 231; marriage and motherhood, 231, 253; early feeling about them, 232; early attachment, 233; service in hospitals, 236; first meeting with Marquis Ossoli, 239; life at Rieti, 238, 250, 266; removal to Florence, 241, 245; correspondence with husband, 248, 279; description of child, 268, 270, 271; her book on Roman republic, 272, 282; voyage to America, 272; forebodings, 273; shipwreck, 276; literary traits, 281; not a disciple of any one, 284; examples of her power of statement, 289; personal traits, 299; phrenological examination, 299; her life on the whole successful, 314.

PALMER, Edward, 175.
"Papers on Literature and Art," 203.
Park, Dr., 23.
Parker, Theodore, letter from, 162; other references, 3, 86, 130, 132, 140, 142, 144, 160, 165, 169, 181.
Parker, Mrs. Theodore, 128.
Parton, James, 213.
Paterculus, Velleius, 49, 50.
Peabody, Miss Elizabeth P., 75, 114, 142, 168, 178, 192; letter to, 81.
Pericles, 5.
Perkins, Mr., 24.
Petrarch, F., 136.
Plutarch, 49, 50, 69.
Poe, Edgar Allan, 156, 216, 217.
Prescott, Misses, 23.
Putnam, George, 142.

QUINCY, Mrs. Josiah, 131.

RADZIVILL, Princess, 231.
Randall, Elizabeth, 39.
Récamier, Madame, 37.
Reformers in New England (1840–1850), 175.
Richter, Jean Paul, 28, 45.
Ripley, George, 91, 142, 144, 146, 147, 149, 154, 157, 179–181, 188, 189, 291.
Ripley, Mrs. G., 163, 180, 183; letter to, 112.
Robbins, S. D., 181.
Robinson, Rev. Mr., 53, 68.
Rosa, Salvator, 95.
Roscoe, William, 221.
Rotch, Mary, letter to, 212.

Russell, Le Baron, 144.
"Rye-bread days," 104.

SAND, George, 173, 230.
Saxton, Rufus, 163.
Schiller, J. C. F. von, 45.
Scott, David, 225, 226.
Scott, Sir Walter, 228, 297.
Scougal, Henry, 69.
Ségur, Comte de, 109.
Shakespeare, William, 291, 292.
Shelley, P. B., 42, 134, 290, 307.
Shepard, Mr., 9.
Sismondi, J. C. L. S. de, 24.
Slavery, American, 10, 12, 14, 126.
Smith, Southwood, 229.
Socrates, 309.
Southey, Robert, 45, 290.
Spring, Edward, 223.
Spring, Marcus and Rebecca, 219, 220, 228, 229.
Spurzheim, J. G., 49.
Staël, Madame de, 30, 37, 45, 109
Stetson, Caleb, 142, 144.
Stone, T. T., 163.
Storer, Mrs. R. B., 3.
Storrow, Miss Ann G., 35.
Storrow, Samuel, 51, 52.
Story, Joseph, 33.
Story, William W., 240.
Story, Mrs. William W., 238, 240, 241, 266, 275; narrative of, 241; letter from, 244; letter to, 268.
"Summer on the Lakes," 194.
Sumner, Horace, 275.

TAPPAN, Caroline (Sturgis), 87, 111, 154, 156, 199, 200, 211.
"Tasso," by Goethe, translated, 47, 63, 188.
Taylor, Helen, 281.
Tennyson, Alfred, 69, 220.
"The Great Lawsuit" (essay in "Dial"), 200.
"The Third Thought," 285.
Thoreau, H. D., 130, 134, 144, 154, 155, 164, 282.
Thorndike, Mrs., 86.
Ticknor, George, 33.
Tieck, Louis, 45.
Tocqueville, A. de, 126.
"Transcendental" movement, the, 133, 314.
"Tribune," New York, papers in, 213.
Trimmer, Mrs., 132.
Tuckerman, J. F., 163.

UHLAND, J. L. 45.

VAUGHAN, Mr., 149.
Very, Jones, 144, 146.
Visconti, Marchesa, 231.

WARD, Anna (Barker), 36, 68.
Ward, Samuel G., letter to, 56.
Wayland, Francis, 90.
Webster, Daniel, 86.
Webster, Mrs. J. W., 35.
Weiss, John, 3.
Wesselhoeft, Mrs. Minna, 192, 193.
Whitman, Sarah Helen, 299.
Whittier, John G., 131.

Williams, Abraham, 10.
Willis, N. P., 80, 229.
Wilson, William D., 144, 163.
"Woman in the Nineteenth Century," 202, 287.
Woodward, E., 41.
Wordsworth, William, 45, 134, 223-225, 229, 290, 291.
Wordsworth, Mrs. William, 224.

American Men of Letters.

Edited by Charles Dudley Warner.

WASHINGTON IRVING. By Charles Dudley Warner, author of "In the Levant," etc.

NOAH WEBSTER. By Horace E. Scudder, author of "Stories and Romances," "A History of the United States of America," etc.

HENRY D. THOREAU. By Frank B. Sanborn.

GEORGE RIPLEY. By Octavius Brooks Frothingham, author of "Transcendentalism in New England."

JAMES FENIMORE COOPER. By Thomas R. Lounsbury, Professor of English in the Scientific School of Yale College.

MARGARET FULLER OSSOLI. By Thomas Wentworth Higginson, author of "Malbone," "Oldport Days," etc.

RALPH WALDO EMERSON. By Oliver Wendell Holmes, author of "The Autocrat of the Breakfast-Table," etc.

EDGAR ALLAN POE. By George E. Woodberry, author of "Studies in Life and Letters," etc.

NATHANIEL PARKER WILLIS. By Henry A. Beers, Professor of English Literature in Yale College.

BENJAMIN FRANKLIN. By John Bach McMaster, author of "History of the People of the United States."

WILLIAM CULLEN BRYANT. By John Bigelow, author of "Molinos the Quietist," etc.

WILLIAM GILMORE SIMMS. By William P. Trent, Professor of English Literature in the University of the South, Sewanee, Tenn.

GEORGE WILLIAM CURTIS. By Edward Cary.

Other volumes to be announced hereafter. Each volume, with Portrait, 16mo, gilt top, $1.25; half morocco, $2.50.

HOUGHTON, MIFFLIN AND COMPANY,

4 Park St., Boston; 11 East 17th St., New York.

"WASHINGTON IRVING."

Mr. Warner has not only written with sympathy, minute knowledge of his subject, fine literary taste, and that easy, fascinating style which always puts him on such good terms with his readers, but he has shown a tact, critical sagacity, and sense of proportion full of promise for the rest of the series which is to pass under his supervision. — *New York Tribune.*

It is a very charming piece of literary work, and presents the reader with an excellent picture of Irving as a man and of his methods as an author, together with an accurate and discriminating characterization of his works. — *Boston Journal.*

It would hardly be possible to produce a fairer or more candid book of its kind. — *Literary World* (London).

"NOAH WEBSTER."

Mr. Scudder's biography of Webster is alike honorable to himself and its subject. Finely discriminating in all that relates to personal and intellectual character, scholarly and just in its literary criticisms, analyses, and estimates, it is besides so kindly and manly in its tone, its narrative is so spirited and enthralling, its descriptions are so quaintly graphic, so varied and cheerful in their coloring, and its pictures so teem with the bustle, the movement, and the activities of the real life of a by-gone but most interesting age, that the attention of the reader is never tempted to wander, and he lays down the book with a sigh of regret for its brevity. — *Harper's Monthly Magazine.*

It fills completely its place in the purpose of this series of volumes. — *The Critic* (New York).

"HENRY D. THOREAU."

Mr. Sanborn's book is thoroughly American and truly fascinating. Its literary skill is exceptionally good, and there is a racy flavor in its pages and an amount of exact knowledge of interesting people that one seldom meets with in current literature. Mr. Sanborn has done Thoreau's genius an imperishable service. — *American Church Review* (New York).

Mr. Sanborn has written a careful book about a curious man, whom he has studied as impartially as possible; whom he admires warmly but with discretion; and the story of whose life he has told with commendable frankness and simplicity. — *New York Mail and Express.*

It is undoubtedly the best life of Thoreau extant. — *Christian Advocate* (New York).

"GEORGE RIPLEY."

He has fulfilled his responsible task with admirable fidelity, frank earnestness, justice, fine feeling, balanced moderation, delicate taste, and finished literary skill. It is a beautiful tribute to the high-bred scholar and generous-hearted man, whose friend he has so worthily portrayed. — *Rev. William H. Channing* (London).

"JAMES FENIMORE COOPER."

We have here a model biography. The book is charmingly written, with a felicity and vigor of diction that are notable, and with a humor sparkling, racy, and never obtrusive. The story of the life will have something of the fascination of one of the author's own romances. — *New York Tribune.*

Prof. Lounsbury's book is an admirable specimen of literary biography. . . . We can recall no recent addition to American biography in any department which is superior to it. It gives the reader not merely a full account of Cooper's literary career, but there is mingled with this a sufficient account of the man himself apart from his books, and of the period in which he lived, to keep alive the interest from the first word to the last. — *New York Evening Post.*

"MARGARET FULLER OSSOLI."

Here at last we have a biography of one of the noblest and the most intellectual of American women, which does full justice to its subject. The author has had ample material for his work, — all the material now available, perhaps, — and has shown the skill of a master in his use of it. . . . It is a fresh view of the subject, and adds important information to that already given to the public. — REV. DR. F. H. HEDGE, in *Boston Advertiser.*

"RALPH WALDO EMERSON."

Dr. Holmes has written one of the most delightful biographies that has ever appeared. Every page sparkles with genius. His criticisms are trenchant, his analysis clear, his sense of proportion delicate, and his sympathies broad and deep. — *Philadelphia Press.*

"EDGAR ALLAN POE."

Mr. Woodberry has contrived with vast labor to construct what must hereafter be called the authoritative biography of Poe, a biography which corrects all others, supplements all others, and supersedes all others. — *The Critic* (New York).

"NATHANIEL PARKER WILLIS."

Prof. Beers has done his work sympathetically yet candidly and fairly and in a philosophic manner, indicating the status occupied by Willis in the republic of letters, and sketching graphically his literary environment and the main springs of his success. It is one of the best books of an excellent series. — *Buffalo Times*.

"BENJAMIN FRANKLIN."

One of the most interesting and instructive volumes of the series. . . . The pictures which are given of the momentous period in which he lived are full of vigor, and betray an astonishing amount of research in many directions. — *Boston Gazette*.

We have had many lives of Franklin, but none so absolutely impartial as this, and although it is short it omits no important fact that can help to reveal the man. . . . Mr. McMaster tells his story with extreme charm of narration. — *Hartford Courant*.

"WILLIAM CULLEN BRYANT."

There were many aspects in which Mr. Bryant presented himself as a subject for biography. He was a chief in the department of American journalism. He was a controlling power in American politics. He was also a man of letters in the pure and simple sense of the term. One might have known him well in either of these relations and yet had no thought of the others. Mr. Bigelow has, it seems to us, done justice to all. — *The Churchman* (New York).

"WILLIAM GILMORE SIMMS."

As a biography it will rank with the best in the series. It is clear in style, full in statement of fact, impartial, discriminating and critical, and at the same time generous and sympathetic. Professor Trent has performed a difficult task with rare discretion and good taste. — *Christian Union* (New York).

⁎⁎ *For sale by all Booksellers. Sent, post-paid, on receipt of price by the Publishers,*

HOUGHTON, MIFFLIN AND COMPANY,
BOSTON AND NEW YORK.